THE POLICY
PREDICAMENT

THE POLICY PREDICAMENT

Making and Implementing Public Policy

GEORGE C. EDWARDS III
Tulane University

IRA SHARKANSKY
*The Hebrew University of Jerusalem
and The University of Wisconsin, Madison*

W. H. Freeman and Company
San Francisco

Library of Congress Cataloging in Publication Data

Edwards, George C
   The policy predicament.

   Includes bibliographical references and index.
   1. Policy sciences. 2. Public administration—
Decision making. I. Sharkansky, Ira, joint author.
II. Title.
H61.E33   300'.1   77-28212
ISBN 0-7167-0019-0

Printed in the United States of America

9 8 7 6 5 4 3 2 1

TO WENDY AND INA

Contents

Preface

Politics attracts people for a variety of reasons. For observers and for citizens who participate only as voters, politics offers an opportunity to watch the struggle of groups with different interests or beliefs and to see how a society deals with conflicts that are potentially explosive. For participants it offers the thrill of competition, the chance for fame, and the sense of being at the center of an historic process. For many of the people actively engaged in politics, however, its main attraction is that it leads to the control of public policy.

Public policy is the subject matter of this book. Policymaking is what officeholders do with their power. Insofar as policies reflect major governmental decisions that seek to shape the lives of citizens, they become the focus of demands for what government should or should not do. Whether your ideology is left, right, or centrist, extreme or moderate, whether you are an active participant or an observer of politics, because you care what politicians do once in office, you are interested in public policy.

The Policy Predicament, as the title suggests, concentrates on the problems that hinder the smooth translation of public needs through policy into benefits. In the book we take a skeptical look at the influence of public opinion on policymaking and at the capacity of officials to make policy on the basis of a rational selection of the best options. We consider economic and political constraints on policymakers, describe decisionmaking under existing conditions, and show how the same problems that impinge on the formulation of policy also leave their mark on the ways that policies are implemented, that is, delivered to the people who are supposed to benefit from them.

The title of the book does not refer to a single, easily definable predicament of policymaking. It refers to the general inability of policymakers to respond in a clear and productive manner to the many signs of unmet needs. Our principal message for anyone trying to understand public policy is that the complexities of the problems faced by policymakers and the procedural complications of policymaking per se hinder any simple and successful attack on most of the world's problems.

Consistent with this message, we propose that there is no simple solution to the policy predicament. Accordingly, we feature the problems of policymaking rather than solutions. It is the reader's task to go beyond this book to find overall solutions that appear suitable, or to accept the occasional small solutions that most governments devise in response to their big problems. We do believe, however, that understanding the dilemmas faced by policymakers is a prerequisite to fashioning useful solutions.

The authors of a work on public policy encounter some of the same problems as policymakers do. Edwards wrote most of the first draft and Sharkansky revised it. Although we agree on the major points of our presentation, we have had to compromise on numerous points of detail. Each of us feels uncomfortable with some of the choices of language and interpretation. So be it. We agree to share whatever praise is received and to assign to the other's stubbornness any problems that remain.

We would also like to point out our obligations to other writers. We have acquired more assistance than it is possible to acknowledge in detail; much of it is apparent in the notes that cite the large and rich literature on public policy. More directly, we owe great thanks to David Caputo, Kenneth Dolbeare, Robert Eyestone, and Harrell Rodgers for reading our first draft and helping us to sharpen the presentation. Douglas Rose and Michael Smith made useful comments on individual chapters. We also wish to thank Ruth Veres for her outstanding job in editing the entire manuscript, and Norma Reed and Nancy Wirth for their aid in typing parts of the manuscript.

November 1977   George C. Edwards III, New Orleans
                       Ira Sharkansky, Jerusalem

THE POLICY
PREDICAMENT

Introduction

1

Public policy is big business. Government spending in the United States approximates 40 percent of the gross national product, and government payrolls include some 16 percent of the workforce. In addition, an inestimable number of people work for business firms and nonprofit institutions that serve as extensions of government by contributing to the formulation and implementation of policy on a contract basis. All citizens receive the benefits and pay the costs of public policy. The costs, however, often outweigh the benefits for they include not only the direct burden of taxation, but also the disappointments, frustrations, and losses of life or property resulting from policies that are poorly conceived or improperly implemented. None of us can claim to know much about politics or public affairs without an understanding of policy. How is policy made? Why do so many problems remain despite the vast resources spent on policy? These are the crucial questions confronting all analysts of public policy—whether they be beginning students, sophisticated observers, or public officials.

WHAT IS PUBLIC POLICY?

There is no single definition of public policy. It is what governments[1] say and do, or do not do. It is the goals or purposes of government programs, for example, the elimination of ignorance and poverty. Policy is also the important ingredients of programs, like the requirement that all elementary school teachers be college graduates, or the compulsory division of funds earmarked for education between vocational and liberal arts programs. Policy further includes the implementation of intentions and rules.

Policy may either be stated explicitly—in laws or in the speeches of leading officials, or implied in programs and actions. Implicit policy may be apparent only to those who are intimately familiar with the details of programs and able to discern patterns in the sum total of what is being done. Indeed, some policies consist in a lack of action and may be especially hard to discern if officials wish to conceal their real purposes; the decision by local authorities to evade a high court ruling mandating racial integration constitutes such a policy-through-inaction. A change in policy may be proposed and debated in public with the full participation of interest groups and the mass media, or policy may change covertly, as when a chief executive decides to embark on a new venture under a cloak of secrecy or with a contrived explanation designed to mislead the public.

THE SCOPE OF PUBLIC POLICY

The range of public policy is immense. The United States, like most other countries of the world, is witnessing an expansion of the activities of government into many areas that were once private. As citizens demand public control over activities they find to be incomplete or threatening when left in private hands, government regulations and services become more pervasive. Protecting the health and safety of workers and consumers; reducing pollution from automobiles, sewage, and industrial and agricultural wastes; delivering medical care; developing housing and recreational facilities; preserving land prized for its esthetic or ecological value; and eliminating the inequality of women and members of minority groups: each of these is a relatively new area for aggressive government action in the United States. They join the numerous areas of more traditional government activity which have also felt the impact of the expanding scope of governmental functions: in recent years major efforts to enlarge or alter policies have left their mark on education, transportation, income security, police protection and criminal justice, and foreign policy.

The expanding sphere of public policy is reflected in government budgets. In 1950 all governments in the United States (i.e., local, state, national) spent $70 billion, or 25 percent of the Gross National Product, and public employees accounted for 10 percent of the workforce. In 1974 the figures were $556 billion, 40 percent of the Gross National Product, and 16 percent of the workforce. The increasing role of government has an effect on the daily activities of most citizens, determining more and more the answer to both simple questions such as Where will I find a job? and more complex questions like Who and what generates the policies that influence my income, housing, health, longevity, and self-contentment? Whether we work for government, a private firm, or ourselves, the answer to these questions is likely to be "the government."

The political preferences of Americans who participate or take an interest in politics shape policies whose consequences may flow around the world. Although the United States is not the unique colossus it was at the end of World War II, when it was the only country in possession of an undamaged industrial base and atomic weapons, it remains the richest country and the most militarily powerful government of all times. Its global influence stems from the economic transactions of its government and private firms; international prominence in science, technology, and the popular arts; the magnitude of its military establishment; and the government's demonstrated willingness to provide military hardware, technical assistance, and manpower to allies in far-flung regions. When Americans debate international affairs, it is not a question of noisy but impotent discussion; others listen to the words of U.S. candidates and officeholders with the uncomfortable realization that United States policy has an impact worldwide.

OUR APPROACH TO THE ANALYSIS
OF PUBLIC POLICYMAKING

Public policy is a complex field that lends itself to numerous analytic approaches. Some studies examine the details of individual policies, showing what officials intend to accomplish and what actually is accomplished (and sometimes what ought to be accomplished).[2] Others seek to extrapolate society's needs into the future in an effort to identify emerging problems that require the attention of policymakers.[3] Still other research is in the form of case studies that focus on policymaking in substantive fields like education, income security, transportation, or foreign affairs; such research identifies the key people responsible for formulating and implementing policies in those fields and shows how officials receive demands and make their choices amidst political conflict.[4] Analyses of policy can also compare policies across jurisdictions, attempting to assess the relative importance of various factors (e.g., economic development and political party competition) in the formulation of public policy.[5]

For this book we have chosen an approach that differs from, yet complements, each of the above.

We do not utilize the case-study approach in our analysis of how public policy is made because we are concerned more with general principle than with specific application. For example, we are more interested in examining the problems policymakers at the national and state levels face as they attempt to predict and analyze the consequences of policies, than we are in analyzing the decisions that precede, or the consequences that follow from, any given policy per se. Nevertheless, we provide specific illustrations for our more general points, always cognizant of the importance of concrete examples in political science, especially in a discussion of public policy.

Neither do we describe policymaking as the result of impersonal social or economic forces. Although such factors do influence policy (as we show below), we believe it is better to tie their influence into the decisionmaking process and show how they are translated into public policy rather than to simply demonstrate, for example, that wealthy states tend to spend more on education than poor states.

Nor do we analyze policymaking from the perspective of models that highlight the general influence of a particular factor, such as personality or bureaucratic politics, on policymaking.[6] Our approach is more eclectic. We focus on the actual *making* of policy rather than on the factors that influence it because the number of factors that make themselves felt in policymaking is almost limitless, and most models either omit many of these factors or obscure the fact that those factors they do emphasize are more influential in some aspects of policymaking than in others.

We examine policymaking from the perspective of the decisionmakers, scrutinizing the intellectual tasks facing those who must both make policy decisions and see that they are implemented. On what are they to base their decisions? What criteria can they use to choose between alternatives? If there is no cut-and-dried basis for decisions, then how *are* decisions made? And once decisions are made, are they implemented as the decisionmakers intended? By examining policymaking from this standpoint, we are in a position to learn whether policy is made as we might expect and why or why not.

POTENTIAL CRITERIA FOR POLICY DECISIONS

Public Opinion

One potential criterion decisionmakers can use in determining policy is public opinion. To utilize this gauge, they need only consult and evaluate public opinion and make their decisions in line with the public's wishes. Reliance on public opinion as the basis for decisionmaking conforms with a prominent view of the way decisions *ought* to be made in a democracy. Indeed, much of democratic theory assumes that the public generates policy. The constitutions of the nation and the states allow the public to express its will through the ballot box and thus assign crucial roles in determining policy to elected officials. Other forms of citizen participation such as petitioning, speaking, writing, and campaigning also receive constitutional protection.

Yet, the expression of the public's will is not a simple matter. Elections, public opinion polls, and even personal contacts are blunt instruments for the expression of political views; they seldom pinpoint just what policy the public wants from the government. Moreover, most of the people most of the time express no policy preferences at all. Interest groups press their own demands on officials, often claiming to speak for broad segments of the population (sometimes for "all the people"), but it is unlikely that such groups are accurate in their claims. Likewise, newspapers and political candidates claim to speak for the masses, but it is difficult to separate their personal interests from their allegations about representing the public interest.

Even when public preferences seem clear, there are no assurances that elected officials will implement them. Because the utility of the constitutionally elaborated devices for assuring citizen participation in government is limited, public control of policymakers is restricted. Moreover, government institutions play an independent role in the shaping of policy and can serve to isolate the officials who actually make decisions from their constituents. In addition, there is so much overt and covert *effort by government officials to influence the public* that it is difficult to say who is influencing whom.

Rationality

A second possible criterion decisionmakers can rely on in formulating policy is rational analysis. Using this criterion they would follow a well-known format:

1. *Identify a problem.* Is there a problem? If so, what has caused it?
2. *Clarify and rank goals.* What should be done about the problem? What is the priority of this goal in relation to other goals (i.e., in relation to solutions for other problems)?
3. Collect all relevant *options* for meeting the goal and all available *information* on them.
4. *Predict the consequences* of each alternative and *assess* them according to standards such as *efficiency* and *equity.*
5. *Select the alternative* that comes closest to achieving the goal, perhaps for the least cost and with the greatest equity.

Unfortunately, it is not possible to follow such a formula in decisionmaking. Instead, policymaking is an ambiguous, complex, and conflictual process which cannot be broken down into neat categories. Questions about policy arise from technical and political conflicts that are often inter-mixed. Technical analysts with more-or-less similar preferences do not always agree about existing conditions or about the benefits promised by various remedies. Politicians in opposing parties or factions seem inclined by reason of ideology or partisan advantage to take one position or another. In many prominent controversies, there is such a variety of technical and political issues that it is impossible to ascribe clear positions to the protagonists. Do they take their stands for technical or political reasons? Often the answer is "both," with technical arguments setting people who share ideology or party membership against one another and political considerations causing disputes among experts. The difficulty in choosing among alternatives that pit economic growth against the conservation of the environment illustrates the problems faced by decisionmakers who would like to make rationality the basis of policy.

Ecologists clash with economists on the technical and political aspects of issues ranging from local controversy over the construction of a new power plant to foreign policy disputes (with global consequences) over the promotion of population control and economic development in the poor countries. (Of course, even the local power plant issue may depend on some global considerations, like the future availability and price of low-sulfur petroleum.) On the worldwide issues of population growth and economic development the opposing factions develop competing scenarios: the ecologists emphasize the depletion of irreplaceable resources and suffocating pollution whereas the economists stress the prospect of a greatly improved standard of living. The pessimism of the Club of Rome—whose *Limits to Growth* projects "exponential growth of population and capital, followed by collapse"—offsets the Hudson Institute's prediction for "a world of 15–20 billion people with an average per capita income of $20,000 (the current figures are just under 4 billion and $1,200)." Both of these projections come out of the sophisticated computers of prestigious institutions. The fact that their statements of the future and their implications for current policy are diametrically opposed reflects technical differences in the information fed into those computers and the methods employed in extrapolating from the present to the future.[7] Thus, there is neither technical nor political agreement on whether or not the environmental problems resulting from too much population and economic growth are serious enough to warrant government control.

The issues of economic growth and conservation also show up frequently in contemporary domestic policy disputes, often attached to proposals for new power plants, dams, highways, or projects for industry, recreation, or housing. The process of resolving these issues includes much of the complexity and turmoil associated with most policymaking. Differences in goals and priorities are related to who will benefit from different policies: business executives want investment opportunities and profits; union leaders seek to provide jobs and increase wages; sportsmen and women want a place to pursue their interests; and conservation groups desire to preserve natural resources and wildlife.

Professional economists and ecologists employed by government agencies or by interested parties outside of government bolster one side or the other with technical arguments: the economist codifies the flow of goods, services, wages, and capital that are likely to result from certain investments and asks "How much is it worth?" to leave a particular marsh, river valley, or other attractive site undeveloped; the ecologist documents relationships between various components in the natural system and predicts the effect of the proposed development on the surrounding plants, animals, and humans.

The technical analyses are complicated by the need to make estimates about the future and the lack of certainty that lies just beneath the surface of those estimates. Calculations of economic costs and benefits depend on projections of population growth, potential markets, demand for electrical power, the cost of fuel, and the cost of capital (i.e., interest rates). Each of these items depends on a host of other factors including explorations for new sources of petroleum and natural gas, political disputes that determine the price of fuel, and new developments in the technology of energy production. Each point of uncertainty may be the source of a dispute between technical experts who have different perspectives.

The ecological "facts" are likewise subject to debate. Experts extrapolate the adaptability of various fauna and flora to changes in their environment from records and experiments that don't reproduce exactly the projected conditions, which are themselves uncertain.

In addition to basing decisions on estimated "facts," policymakers are forced to compare "apples and oranges" in an attempt to resolve conflicts originating at the political interface of economic and ecological interests. How do you decide how many jobs are equivalent in value to the preservation of certain rare natural entities?

And remember, political conflicts often foster technical ambiguities. A calloused observer of past battles knows that each side has its experts, who may be employing a particular bias when approaching the points in the analysis where the lack of hard information requires estimates. Competing studies of benefits and costs find overstatements of benefits and understatements of costs (and vice versa) that substantially affect the conclusions. In sum, each side in a dispute employs its own analysts, who produce results markedly at odds with those of their opponents.

Amidst all this conflict and confusion, policymakers do not have the resources, time, or energy to examine all the possible alternatives that might achieve a goal or all the information on these alternatives. Moreover, policymakers, bureaucratic units, and interest groups each have their own interests to protect, which inevitably influences the options and information top decisionmakers ultimately receive. The flow of information up a multistepped bureaucratic hierarchy and its collection through routine procedures both distort the final picture.

POLITICAL AND ECONOMIC CONSTRAINTS ON POLICYMAKING

Policymakers are constrained not only by the complexities of using public opinion or rationality as guides to policymaking, but also by the actions of politicians, the legacy of the past, the nature of government organization, and economic considerations.

One of the shocks to newcomers in politics is discovering the limited range of discretion available to contemporary policymakers. No matter how rational their decisionmaking, their options are severely restricted. Policymakers need each other to make policy and can rarely act unilaterally. Because they must bargain and negotiate to reach decisions, *political feasibility* is an essential element of policymaking.

Each new generation of decisionmakers does not tackle policymaking with a fresh slate, able to write at will. Even assuming a relatively affluent economy, permissive public opinion, and cooperative colleagues, there are a limited number of options open to policymakers. *The past* is a major constraint. Former commitments cannot be nullified without upsetting the clients of the annulled program as well as the private contractors and suppliers and the government employees who anticipate that their benefits and jobs will continue. In addition, judges and administrators consider themselves bound by the precedents of past cases and actions. These historical restraints are reenforced by habitual modes of behavior inherent in human nature and a constitutionally based governmental structure and political party system that make marked departures from the past difficult and unlikely.

Governmental fragmentation imposes yet another restraint on policymakers by denying them the ability to attack problems comprehensively. Policymakers must adopt alternatives piecemeal and they frequently duplicate or even formulate contradictory policies. Thus, the United States Department of Agriculture encourages the growing of tobacco while the United States Public Health Service warns that it is dangerous to smoke.

The *economy* supplies the money, skilled personnel, and infrastructures that make certain policies possible. At the same time, the relative scarcity of these resources in a jurisdiction acts as a constraint against the adoption of yet other policies. Economic development also influences public policies by serving as their target. Many policies are aimed at raising the level of economic development of a jurisdiction. Finally, the various interests within the economy make conflicting demands on public officials: rich citizens differ in their demands from the poor, farmers from factory workers and bankers, city-dwellers from suburbanites.

HOW POLICYMAKERS COPE

To simplify the complex task of policymaking, policymakers do not simply follow public opinion nor do they act strictly according to the rational model. Often they neither specify nor agree with each other on the nature of problems, nor do they explicitly state goals and establish priorities among them. Moreover, they usually consider only a few alternatives and only a limited amount of information on them, and they seldom rigorously analyze the projected consequences of alternatives. Instead of making public opinion and rationality the basis of policy, they rely on *decision rules,* rules of thumb or standard operating procedures that make policymaking manageable and keep decisions within the bounds of political and economic feasibility. Some rules are simple: rely on precedent; or give interests whatever they want. Others are more complicated and specify whose alternatives carry the most weight and the type of action to take in various situations.

Despite the numerous constraints on policymakers, occasionally they do break from established policy and engage in *innovation.* Any of a number of factors can cause a departure from convention, including aggressive leadership, professionally oriented bureaucracies, sharp public demands, the development of new technologies, or the successful introduction of an innovative policy in another governmental jurisdiction—or some combination of these influences.

THE EFFECT OF IMPLEMENTATION ON POLICY

Politics does not end with the formulation of policy. Many of the same problems that hinder rational decisionmaking (e.g., inadequate communication, ineffectual bureaucratic routines, and lack of resources) also limit the effective *implementation* of policy. Moreover, for some participants the most important part of policymaking begins after the formulation of policy. Interests that are not satisfied with the formal decisions of the legislative, executive, or judicial branches work to shape a policy to satisfy their own desires by maneuvering to control its implementation or administration. At times, this means trying to block any implementation!

Some of the most prominent political issues in recent United States history have focused not so much on the initial statement of government policy as on its implementation. For years after the 1954 Supreme Court decision on school integration, numerous battles were fought between those who would delay or curtail the achievement of genuine integration and those who would promote it. More than 20 years later, the country is still wrestling with the spin-off of that classic decision, whose implementation now focuses on policies for busing. Various interests and governmental authorities have also resisted other Court decisions as the spotty record of compliance with, among others, the ruling to ban prayers in the public schools and decisions to assure the civil and human rights of persons charged with criminal offenses indicates.

Once a decision has been made, the President as well as the Court can be frustrated to find it ignored or distorted. An aide to John F. Kennedy wrote:

> The President was discouraged with the State Department almost as soon as he took office. He felt that it too often seemed to have a built-in inertia. . . . It spoke with too many voices and too little vigor. It was never clear to the President . . . who was in charge, who was clearly delegated to do what, and why his own policy line seemed consistently to be altered or evaded.[8]

Richard Nixon had his own problems with the bureaucracy, including one Air Force General who conducted his own bombing campaign in Southeast Asia at a time when it was official policy to avoid offensives in order to facilitate peace negotiations.

PLAN OF THE BOOK

We have organized the parts and chapters of our book according to the outline of this introductory chapter. Part I deals with the role of public opinion in policymaking: Chapter 2 describes the opportunities and the success of the public in shaping policy; Chapter 3 questions the sovereignty of the public by looking at the inclination of government officials to shape public opinion. Part II explains the shortcomings of rational policymaking: Chapter 4 considers the identification of problems from among the symptoms that indicate something is wrong, and deals with the problem of setting the policy agenda and clarifying goals; Chapter 5 explores the kind of options and information decisionmakers encounter; and Chapter 6 examines how decisionmakers assess policy alternatives and their likely consequences. Part III looks beyond public opinion and rational procedures to other constraints on policymakers: Chapter 7 describes economic constraints; and Chapter 8 political constraints. Part IV analyzes the consequences of these constraints and the other problems of policymaking discussed earlier; Chapter 9 describes some important properties of decisionmaking; and Chapter 10 shows that problems of policymaking do not end with the formulation of a policy but continue to affect its implementation.

Throughout the book, we show that the world of policymaking is complex and difficult. It is not possible to sum up in a few words the nature of the policymaker's predicament, or to suggest a simple solution. That there is a predicament, however, should be clear to anyone who follows our discussion of the problems that impede the work of policymakers and impinge on the citizens who are concerned about their actions.

NOTES

1. Mark V. Nadel has made an excellent argument for including many of the actions of private organizations such as corporations within the boundaries of "public policy." We do not dispute his view but have simply chosen to limit our focus to governmental actions. See "The Hidden Dimension of Public Policy: Private Governments and the Policy-Making Process," *Journal of Politics* 37 (February 1975).

2. See James W. Davis, Jr. and Kenneth M. Dolbeare, *Little Groups of Neighbors: The Selective Service System* (Chicago: Markham, 1968); Gilbert Steiner, *Social Insecurity* (Chicago: Rand McNally, 1960); James S. Coleman et al., *Equality of Educational Opportunity* (Washington, D.C.: United States Government Printing Office, 1966); Francis Fox Piven and Richard Cloward, *Regulating the Poor: The Functions of Public Welfare* (New York: Pantheon, 1971); and Kenneth M. Dol-

beare and Phillip E. Hammond, *The School Prayer Decisions* (Chicago: University of Chicago Press, 1971).

3. See Donella H. Meadows, Dennis L. Meadows, Jørgen Randers, and William W. Behrens III, *The Limits of Growth* (New York: Universe, 1972); H. S. D. Cole, Christopher Freeman, Marie Jahoda, and K. L. R. Pavitt, eds., *Models of Doom: A Critique of the Limits of Growth* (New York: Universe, 1973); and Bruce Briggs, "Against the Neo-Malthusians," *Commentary* 58 (July 1974).

4. See Stephen K. Bailey, *Congress Makes a Law* (New York: Columbia University Press, 1950); Raymond A. Bauer, Ithiel de Sola Pool, and Lewis Anthony Dexter, *American Business and Public Policy*, 2nd ed. (New York: Aldine-Atherton, 1972); A. Lee Fritschler, *Smoking and Politics,* 2nd ed. (Englewood Cliffs, New Jersey: Prentice-Hall, 1975); Aaron Wildavsky, *The Politics of the Budgetary Process*, 2nd ed. (Boston: Little, Brown, 1974); and Jack W. Peltason, *Federal Courts in the Political Process* (New York: Random House, 1955).

5. See Thomas R. Dye, *Politics, Economics, and the Public* (Chicago: Rand McNally, 1966); Ira Sharkansky and Richard I. Hofferbert, "Dimensions of State Politics, Economics, and Public Policy," *American Political Science Review* 63 (September 1969); and Arnold J. Heidenheimer, Hugh Heclo, and Carolyn Teich Adams, *Comparative Public Policy* (New York: St. Martin's, 1975).

6. The most notable use of models is in Graham T. Allison, *Essence of Decision: Explaining the Cuban Missile Crisis* (Boston: Little, Brown, 1971).

7. Meadows et al., *Limits to Growth* ; Cole et al., *Models of Doom;* Briggs, "Against the Neo-Malthusians."

8. Theodore C. Sorenson, *Kennedy* (New York: Harper & Row, 1965), p. 322.

PUBLIC OPINION AS A BASIS FOR POLICY

I

Perhaps the most straightforward, democratic manner of making public policy would be for policymakers to follow public opinion. On each issue they would base their decisions on the preferences of the majority. This would require that the public actually have policy preferences and that its preferences be discernable to policymakers; it would also require that policymakers be willing to follow public opinion and that the views held by the public not be molded by policymakers. In Chapters 2 and 3 we examine the questions inherent in these assumptions to assess the utility of public opinion as a criterion for policymaking.

The Public
and Public Policy

2

Following public opinion may seem like a clear-cut criterion for policymaking, yet things are not as simple as they appear. The public may not have policy preferences, or if it has them, it may not communicate them clearly to policymakers. Moreover, policymakers may choose not to follow public opinion.

A comparison of some of the policy preferences expressed by the public with the corresponding policies actually adopted by policymakers reveals that the two are often incongruent. To clarify the relation between public opinion and policymaking we examine how the public defines and expresses its views, analyzing the effectiveness of various modes of communication between the public and policymakers on two counts: Do those channels of communication accurately transmit the public's views? and Do the channels effectively hold policymakers accountable to their constituents?

CONGRUENCE OF PUBLIC OPINION AND PUBLIC POLICY

Many important public policies exist contrary to the sentiments of the general public. At the time of the 1974 congressional elections the Gallup Poll questioned a representative sample of the American public about fourteen issues of national policy. On only six of the issues did a majority of public opinion match public policy. And the service of legalized abortion proposed by one of these policies was not actually available in numerous localities. Table 2.1 shows the

Table 2.1   Correlation Between Public Support for Fourteen National Policies and the Actual Policies Adopted by the Government (1974)

Policy	Percentage of respondents supporting policy	Majority opinion congruent with existing policy?
Decreased defense spending	56	No
Wage and price controls	62	No
Busing schoolchildren for racial integration	32	No
Gun registration	71	No
Aid to parochial schools	52	No
Establishment of diplomatic relations with Cuba	63	No
Unconditional amnesty	41	Yes
Legalization of marijuana	26	Yes
Equal Rights Amendment	79	Yes*
Federal financing of congressional elections	72	No
Death penalty	63	No
5 percent income surtax	46	Yes
Decreased spending for social programs	34	Yes
Legalized abortions	52	Yes

*Congress passed the amendment although it has not yet been ratified by the requisite thirty-eight states.

Source: Compiled from Gallup Poll reported in "Election Mandates Economic Actions," *New Orleans Times-Picayune,* November 4, 1974, Section 1, p. 12.

results of the survey and indicates that two majorities over 70 percent and three more over 60 percent existed in the face of contrary policy.

Because of the lack of systematic state-by-state surveys on policy issues, there is no similar data analyzing the public's views on state policies. Yet it is possible to estimate public opinion by means of computer simulations. Table 2.2 shows the results of one such simulation designed to extrapolate the correlation between public opinion and public policy on 116 issues for each of the fifty states between 1954 and 1967.[1]

The states with the greatest conformity between opinion and policy, Idaho and New York, show 68 percent of policies matching majority opinion, while the lowest ranking state, Maryland, scored only 50 percent. In the aggregate, the congruence between public opinion and state policy is more impressive than that between public opinion and national policy (Table 2.1). However, the aggregate scores of Table 2.2 conceal many variations in the scores of individual policies. Public opinion and policy matched in 35 states on aid to parochial schools but in only 8 states on firearms control.

THE PUBLIC'S INFLUENCE ON PUBLIC POLICY

To understand why public opinion and public policy are frequently incongruous, it is necessary to probe the various mechanisms by which the public participates in politics. These include voting, responding to public opinion polls, and various modes of direct, personal contact with public officials. The following examination discloses many of the reasons why public opinion often does not serve as the determining criterion for policy decisions.

Voting

The most prominent means of popular political participation is voting. An election not only provides the electorate with an opportunity to express its opinion but also ties key of-

Table 2.2   Percentage of 116 Policies That Matched
Majority Public Opinion in Each of the Fifty States
Between 1954 and 1967 (in order of decreasing percentages)

Idaho	68	West Virginia	60
New York	68	Hawaii	60
		Missouri	60
Michigan	66		
Nevada	66	Alaska	59
New Jersey	66	Arkansas	59
		Connecticut	59
Tennessee	65		
Washington	65	California	58
		Rhode Island	58
Massachusetts	64		
		Kentucky	57
Alabama	63	Louisiana	57
Florida	63	Nebraska	57
Indiana	63		
Texas	63	Delaware	55
		Illinois	55
Georgia	62	Minnesota	55
Mississippi	62	North Carolina	55
North Dakota	62		
Oklahoma	62	South Dakota	54
Oregon	62		
Utah	62	Kansas	53
		Ohio	53
Arizona	61	Virginia	53
Colorado	61		
New Hampshire	61	Maine	52
Wyoming	61	New Mexico	52
		Wisconsin	52
Iowa	60		
Montana	60	Vermont	51
Pennsylvania	60		
South Carolina	60	Maryland	50

Source: Adapted from Frank Munger, "Opinions, Elections, Parties, and
Policies: A Cross-State Analysis," paper presented at the Annual Meeting of
the American Political Science Association, New York, September 1969, p.
18.

ficeholders directly to their constituents. The threat of re-
moval from office can function as a powerful control over
policy. Before we accept voting as an effective means of
translating public opinion into public policy, however, we
must scrutinize the process.

If the votes of a majority of the electorate are to determine the policy decisions of elected officials, the following
conditions must be met:

1. Voters must have opinions on policies.
2. Voters must know candidates' stands on the issues.
3. At least one candidate must support the alternatives
   desired by a majority of the voters.
4. Voters must vote.
5. Voters must vote on the basis of issues.
6. A majority of voters must agree on the issues, en-
   abling politicians to define what we will call a *majority
   opinion* on each issue.
7. Winning candidates must receive the votes of a majority of the electorate.
8. The electoral majority within a constituency must not
   have its vote diluted through gerrymandering or
   other means.
9. Winning candidates must be able to relate their victories to the policy views of their supporters.
10. Winning candidates must carry out their pre-election
    promises.

Opinions on Policy.   If people are to employ their votes in a
deliberate way to control policies, they first must have opinions on the policies themselves. When pollsters ask Americans about their views on matters ranging from arms control
to medical care, they find that most Americans express
opinions.[2] However, these results can be misleading. Many
people respond to questions without giving extensive consideration to the issue raised or without identifying the implications of their answers for other matters, such as future tax
increases. Responses to a poll can also reflect peculiarities in
the wording of the questions or unusual characteristics of
the interviewer.[3]

Some of the policy opinions held by people are weak and
subject to change over a short period. One study found that
about one-half the American population changed its views
on Vietnam between November 1968 and March 1969.[4] Vot-

ers may adapt their views on an issue to conform with electoral choices made for reasons of party affiliation or candidate image. Thus, voters sometimes change their stands on issues to bring them into line with those of their favored candidate.[5]

Most voters do, however, care about public policy. They are, as a rule, interested in economic considerations or matters of social status that touch them directly, such as jobs or civil rights. But policies as distant and complex as nuclear strategy, the federal deficit, bureaucratic reorganization, and the regulation of specific business practices hold little interest for most citizens. The fact is that policymaking is a very complex enterprise, and most voters do not have the time, expertise, or inclination to think extensively about most issues. A 1971 Gallup Poll found that only 19 percent of the people questioned knew what the term "no fault" insurance meant (correct answers had risen to only 31 percent by 1977); a 1969 Gallup Poll revealed that only 41 percent of the adult population had an opinion about the Antiballistic Missile System (ABM), which was a subject of heated controversy in Washington at the time; and a 1975 Gallup Poll found that only 59 percent of the respondents had heard about the disengagement pact between Egypt and Israel, which called for sending 200 American radar technicians to the Sinai Peninsula.

Knowledge About Candidates' Stands. If votes are to be instrumental in influencing public policy, voters must know where candidates stand on issues, but surveys show that public knowledge of even the most rudimentary aspects of politics is not extensive. A 1973 study commissioned by Congress found that although most Americans could name the governor of their state and the most prominent of their United States senators, most of the respondents did not know the names or party affiliations of either their other United States senator or their congressional representative. Only 62 percent knew that Congress is composed of the House and the Senate[6] (see Table 2.3). Most citizens have even less knowl-

Table 2.3 Public's Knowledge of Basic Political Facts (1973)

Information elicited	Percentage of correct answers
Name of state's Governor	89
Governor's party affiliation	77
Name of one U.S. senator	59
Senator's party affiliation	53
Name of second U.S. senator	39
Second senator's party affiliation	36
Name of congressperson	46
Representative's party affiliation	41
Composition of Congress	62

Source: Compiled from Harris Poll reported in U.S. Senate Committee on Government Operations, *Confidence and Concern: Citizens View American Government* (Washington, D.C.: United States Government Printing Office, December 3, 1973), pp. 242–250.

edge about members of the state legislature, elected heads of state departments, and members of the state judiciary.[7]

Similarly, the public is knowledgeable of candidates' positions only on key issues debated during the most widely publicized campaigns. Polls indicate that the public had a fairly accurate idea of the major policy disputes separating Richard Nixon and George McGovern in 1972, Hubert Humphrey and George Wallace in 1968, and Lyndon Johnson and Barry Goldwater in 1964;[8] but a study of ten congressional districts found that fewer than one out of seven adults could identify their congressperson's position on federal subsidies for the Supersonic Transport, a highly visible issue at the time of the survey. Only two out of seven even tried to answer the question, and of those only about one-half were correct.[9] We do not know how many of these merely guessed correctly. The public is probably even less aware of officials' stands on state policy.

Alternatives Offered. The potential influence of voters with opinions on policy and knowledge of where candidates stand on the issues is undermined if no candidate espouses their preferred policy alternatives. The most commonly accepted means of encouraging the offering of preferred alternatives is for there to be an opposition candidate. Without competitive opposition the same set of policy preferences (in the form of elected policymakers) will prevail no matter what the voter does. Although most officials elected to national and state offices do face opposition, it is frequently token opposition. Most legislative districts are won so handily as to be considered "safe" for the dominant party.

There are mixed reports on whether opposing candidates take contrary stands on policy issues. A study of the 1966 elections for the United States House of Representatives concluded that voters had a choice between opposing views on foreign affairs, civil rights, and domestic welfare.[10] However, a study of the 1968 presidential election found that many voters with strong opinions on a key issue (the war in Vietnam) could not differentiate between Richard Nixon and Hubert Humphrey on that issue.[11] (Nixon claimed he had a plan to end the war, but the vague nature of the promise made it difficult to assess.) Finally, a study of party platforms written at presidential conventions shows that roughly one-fourth of the statements are policy pledges. However, the parties take opposing stands on only 10 percent of these pledges; in other words, only 3 percent of the total statements of major party platforms offer policy choices to the voters.[12]

The record of bland or sporadic competition does not spread evenly across the map. Candidates competing in more heterogeneous constituencies are likely to adopt opposing stands on issues of policy because of the greater support for competing policy alternatives among their constituents. By contrast, small-state electoral units are usually fairly homogeneous and the candidate who does not adopt the policy views (to the extent they are defined) of the large majority of voters has little hope of winning. This is an indirect control of voters over elected officials.

Even when voters do have a well-defined choice between policy alternatives, the choice may not be on the policies that have attracted voter interest. Although politicians tend to support policies that have been strongly endorsed by a majority of their constituents, such clear-cut endorsement rarely occurs, and most candidates are intentionally obscure on most issues to minimize the possibility of challenging voters' opinions. In fact, many issues are never raised at all in campaigns. In addition, because only two candidates normally compete in an electoral contest, voter choice is restricted to two sets of policy options. As a result, the available candidates usually offer voters nothing more than approximations of their preferences.

State and local referenda provide citizens with an opportunity to vote directly on issues. Prominent issues raised in referenda in the past have included the use of beach property (California); support for the Winter Olympics (Colorado); and the legalization of casino gambling (New Jersey); plus state, municipal, and school district bond issues. The impact of referenda on policy is diminished by the uneven quality of the public's information, low voter turnout, and the limited range of options offered by "yes" or "no" choices.

Voter Turnout.   The public's views and the options offered by candidates will have little impact on policy if people fail to act, as most eligible voters do in any particular election. In November 1974 less than 40 percent of eligible voters went to the polls, and less than 54 percent voted in the 1976 presidential election. Table 2.4 presents the record of voter turnout in national elections since 1950. Voting in state elections is usually even lighter than in congressional elections, especially when state balloting takes place in the odd-numbered years. Furthermore, only about 70 percent of those 18 and over are registered to vote, and the recent trend is toward a decrease in electoral participation.

While overall voter turnout is low, it is not equally low for all groups. By the simple act of exercising their right to vote, certain kinds of citizens, particularly white, middle-aged members of the middle and upper income groups, wield more power at the polls than others. Citizens who lack political resources such as wealth, information, and prestige make

Table 2.4 Percentage of Eligible Voters Who Voted
in National Elections Between 1950 and 1976

Year	Percentage of eligible voters who voted
1976	53
1974	39
1972	56
1970	45
1968	60
1966	42
1964	65
1962	42
1960	65
1958	46
1956	60
1954	42
1952	63
1950	42

the least use of one of their remaining sources of influence: numbers. The discrepancy is even more pronounced in primary elections where voting is usually lighter than in general elections: those socioeconomic groups that are underrepresented in general elections are underrepresented to an even greater degree in primary elections.[13]

Voting on the Basis of Issues.   Having policy opinions, knowing candidates' stands on the issues, and going to the polls can be instrumental in affecting policy only if voters mark their ballot on the basis of their policy views. Yet many voters base their choices on party affiliation or a candidate's image rather than on the candidate's position on issues.[14] Although there is some evidence that the importance of issues as a basis for choice in presidential elections has increased since 1964, policy views still do not dominate voters' decisions.[15] "Issue-voting" is less important in races for other offices because of the lack of public knowledge and opinion about policy debates affected by congressional, state, and local elections.[16] A 1970 CBS news poll found that only 22 percent of the people asked could name an issue that motivated their voting choice in their local congressional race.

When voters do make electoral decisions on the basis of issues, they vote on issues that are significant to them. These may not be the issues stressed in the campaign; or they may be phony issues raised to distract voter attention. One such phony issue was the "missile gap" which John Kennedy decried in his 1960 presidential campaign. After taking office the gap "disappeared" without any shift in defense policy.

It therefore appears that citizens vote without extensive evaluation of candidates' future contributions to public policymaking. However, *retrospective* evaluation, (i.e., the evaluation of candidates on the basis of their past performance) may be an important means of voter control over policymakers. When the economy or foreign affairs seem to be in good shape, key officials running for re-election do well at the voting booth. When there are major problems, however, many voters hold the incumbents responsible and set out to "punish" them by voting for the opposition.[17]

Needless to say, "retrospective voting" is effective only if an incumbent runs for another term. Although most members of Congress repeatedly seek reelection, many state legislators do not. Moreover, presidents and governors in most states face limits on the number of consecutive terms they may serve; there can be no retrospective voting in response to their final terms.

Members of Congress, and undoubtedly other elected officials, recognize the possibility of retrospective evaluation and try to anticipate voter reactions. They may strive to represent their own conception of their constituents' wishes, even when the policy preferences of the voters are ambiguous and pose little real threat to re-election.[18] Legislators may attempt to predict and respond to public opinion because they accept representational norms that prescribe this activity.[19] Or they may follow public attitudes because they desire to win future elections and overestimate their own visibility and the electorate's concern for issues.[20]

Sometimes policymakers support policies so that their lack of support for those programs will not be used against them in future elections. President Kennedy stressed civil defense in 1961 so he could not be accused of lack of support for it in 1964.[21] Likewise, President Johnson supported the ABM so he would not face charges of being soft on defense in his planned bid for reelection in 1968.[22]

Concern for retrospective voting forces policymakers not only to take certain stands but also to avoid others. Paul Samuelson writes that President Kennedy could not support a tax cut in 1961 because he had just finished a successful presidential campaign in which he had asked people for sacrifices.[23] Kennedy also planned to avoid possible public wrath (for abandoning an anticommunist ally) by waiting until the 1964 election to demand political reform in South Vietnam (on the threat of withdrawal of American support).[24] A similar effort to avoid upsetting the public can be seen in representatives' use of tax concessions. Because provisions of the tax code are less visible to the public than direct subsidies, decisionmakers find tax cuts easier to support than increased expenditures.

One problem with retrospective voting is that a policy-oriented vote *against* a candidate differs from a policy-based vote *for* a candidate. Voters often blindly support a challenger, reasoning that "things could not be worse," which is not the same as voting for a candidate because of agreement with his or her stands on the issues. A second problem with retrospective voting is that congressional representatives are prone to respond to the electoral coalitions that back them and not to their entire constituencies.[25] Outright opponents of elected officials are usually excluded from effective representation because their reactions to policy are not anticipated.

Majority Opinion. If a majority of voters does not share an opinion on an issue, it is impossible for the majority of the electorate to determine the decision of elected officials on that issue. Because many people do not hold an opinion on many issues, and because the views of those who do hold opinions may be split among several alternatives, there is frequently no "majority opinion" on an issue. As a consequence, the opinion of a minority prevails on most issues; for no matter which alternative a decisionmaker ultimately selects, only a minority of his constituents will have supported it.

Majority Vote.   For the votes of a majority of citizens to determine the policy decisions of elected officials, winning candidates must receive a majority of the votes of their electorate. Since voter turnout is usually low, it rarely happens that a majority of eligible voters support one candidate. Moreover, most elections in the United States can be won by a plurality, making it possible for candidates to gain office without receiving a majority of even the votes cast. However, because only two candidates compete in many electoral races, it is common for the winners to receive a majority of the vote. When three or more candidates do run for the same office, the two whose views are closest on the most salient issues of the campaign may split the vote that either running alone would receive; this split enables the third candidate to win a plurality and gain office even though he is the candidate least favored by a majority of the voters.

Dilution of Votes.   The composition of legislative districts also affects the influence of voting on policy. In larger districts where constituents elect several legislators-at-large, minority groups cannot be as influential (through voting coalitions) as in smaller districts where one minority group or another might pre-dominate. Consolidating several small districts into one large one can therefore undermine the electoral influence of minority groups. Conversely, district boundaries can be drawn so as to disperse a physically concentrated group among several districts and thereby minimize its influence. Or boundaries can be drawn to concentrate the influence of certain groups within one or a few districts instead of giving them at least some leverage in several districts.[26] All of these techniques have been used to dilute the vote of black voters.

Studies of congressional elections have found that the ratio of the number of seats a party wins in the House to the number of votes it receives nationally has decreased since the 1950s. Thus, even if we assume that voters mark their ballots on the basis of their policy preferences, we can conclude that the electoral system is not responding consistently to changes in the aggregate preference of voters.[27] The reason for this drop in the swing ratio is not clear and is currently the topic of debate among political scientists.

Interpreting Election Results. If voting is to influence policy, electoral results must provide clear signals about the balance of opinion on issues. However, it is often difficult to discern the relationship between the voters' policy preferences and a candidate's victory at the polls. Many issues are debated in most campaigns and issue-oriented voters may be concerned with several of them. Citizens may support one candidate's positions on two issues yet vote for another because of his or her position on an issue of greater importance to the voters. In practice, voters signal only their choice of candidate and not their choice of that candidate's policies.

Postelection Candidate Behavior. For voting to influence policy, winners must deliver on their promises. There is some evidence that politicians conscientiously work to carry out their campaign pledges. One study found that congressional representatives consistently vote according to their pre-election positions on policy,[28] and another concluded that elected national officials of each party attempt to enact party platforms.[29] However, many issues arise after an election is over, and officials must deal with them without reference to elections. The 1973–1974 Arab oil embargo and the 1971 Indian-Pakistani War are examples of postelectoral events to which U.S. policymakers had to respond. Also, conditions may change dramatically and make the earlier positions of candidates untenable. Such was the explanation offered by President Johnson for his reversal of a 1964 campaign pledge not to get Americans involved in a war in Southeast Asia and by President Nixon for his switch from a 1968 campaign stand against wage and price controls.

Nonelected Officials. In addition to the other limitations on the power of votes to determine public policy, there is the large number of important officials who are not elected. All federal judges, regulatory commissioners, and bureaucrats gain their positions through presidential appointment or civil service recruitment. Federal judges have life tenure and members of regulatory bodies have lengthy terms, designed to insulate them from public opinion as well as from the pressures of special interests. Many of the state judges, regulatory commissioners, and top executive officials, who *are* elected, also have long terms designed to protect them from public pressure.

Public Opinion Polls

Public opinion polls offer voters opportunities to communicate their views on policy to public officials in ways not possible via the ballot alone. Polls, more than elections, enable respondents to express opinions on the specific content of policy. However, polls seldom mesh perfectly with the options considered by policymakers, who rarely consider issues in the "yes" or "no" terms presented by most polls. Evidence of widespread support for a program does not indicate how the public stands on most of the specific provisions under consideration. An understanding of the pros and cons of many of these points requires a specialization of knowledge and judgment well beyond the daily concerns of most Americans. Matters such as economic controls on certain categories of wages, profits, and prices, coupled with precise descriptions of administrative procedures may determine a policy's success or failure in the legislature or its success in meeting its goals. But such details do not lend themselves to mass polling.

Another problem with polling is that responses may reflect the particular wording of the choices presented, especially if respondents do not have crystallized opinions. People asked simply if they favor federal aid to education invariably reply in the affirmative. However, questions about increased federal intervention in education or increased taxes to pay for the aid do not provoke uniformly favorable replies. On policies that are very controversial, like intervention in the war in Vietnam, it may be impossible to ascertain public attitudes without some "contamination" by the use of "loaded" symbols in the questions.

> The specific words that go into a question asked by a pollster may be positive or negative symbols to an individual. If a question is asked in which negative symbols are associated with withdrawal from the war, people sound quite "hawkish" in their responses. Thus people reject "defeat," "Communist take-overs," and "the loss of American credibility." On the other hand, if negative symbols are associated with a pro-war position, the American public will sound "dovish." They reject "killings," "continuing the war," and "domestic costs." Turning the matter upside down, we see the same thing. If positive symbols are associated with the war, the American public sounds "hawkish." They support "American prestige," "defense of democracy," and "support for our soldiers in Vietnam." On the other hand, if positive symbols are associated with "dovish" positions, the people sound "dovish." They come out in support of "peace," "worrying about our own problems before we worry about the problems of other people," and "saving American lives."[30]

Other "cues" in polls can bias the results. If the position of the political party with which the respondent identifies is given in the question, he is more likely to gravitate toward that position in his response. Respondents also appear biased toward existing policy and toward a policy the President supports (especially in foreign affairs). Before the United States' invasion of Cambodia in 1970 only 7 percent of the public favored such a move, but the number rose to 50 percent after the President ordered the invasion; support for a bombing halt in Vietnam went from 40 percent before it was announced in 1968 to 64 percent afterwards; public attitudes toward China "softened considerably" after the President began making overtures toward establishing relations with the People's Republic; and public support for the passage of the 1964 Civil Rights Act was 49 percent in June 1963 but rose to 61 percent in January 1964 after President Johnson had made strong pleas for its passage.[31]

Most high quality polls are national in their coverage and can inform only the President of his constituency's views on an issue. Relatively few states have regularly conducted polls based on state samples, and there are almost no polls that classify samples according to substate regions like congressional districts. Some policymakers have attempted to get around this problem by taking their own surveys. However, few officials can afford a high quality poll, and fewer still poll on a continuing basis, which is the only way to identify changes in opinion. The mail questionnaires United States senators and congressional representatives send out free under their franking privileges have all the problems of interview polls plus a low and unrepresentative response rate (one study puts it at about 14 percent and most from constituents in higher socioeconomic brackets).[32] In addition, these polls sometimes contained "loaded" questions that predetermine answers consistent with the legislator's own attitudes.

Finally, because polls do not reflect intensity of view and are never initiated by the public, they greatly restrict the responses that citizens are able to make. The position of the majority as tabulated in survey results may reflect the attitudes of people for whom the issue is incidental whereas the position of the minority may emerge from intense belief. Further, polls and the specific questions they contain come not at the convenience of the citizen but at the convenience of whoever is paying for them. Thus, the public cannot rely upon polls to transmit its views when it wants them to.

Additional Avenues for Public Influence on Public Policy

Elections and opinion surveys are not the only means by which members of the public may influence public policy. Working in election campaigns, signing petitions, and writing or speaking to officeholders are other ways in which voters can make their views known or work on behalf of sympathetic officials. However, there is limited public participation in many of these political activities. Table 2.5 shows the incidence of various activities as revealed by a 1973 Harris Poll; for the purposes of the survey, people were considered active if they said they had participated in an activity even once in their *entire lifetime*. Since people tend to exaggerate their activity to pollsters, the figures in Table 2.5 probably indicate more public participation in political activity than actually exists.

The activities engaged in by the greatest number of people surveyed are petition-signing and political discussion. About two-thirds of the American adults questioned claim to have signed a petition. About one-half say they have defended the actions of a public official in a *private* conversation, and almost the same number maintain they have attended a speech or rally for a political candidate. For the other activities included in the survey, no more than one-third (and usually considerably *less*) even claim to have participated even once. For each of these activities participation is greatest for white, well-educated citizens with high incomes. Table 2.5 illustrates the differences in political participation between whites and blacks. Although the level of activity among whites is low, that among blacks is much lower. Only 12 percent of those blacks surveyed have written to their congressperson compared to 36 percent of whites, and only 4 percent of blacks have written to a senator, compared to 28 percent of whites.

Despite the relative scarcity of personal political activity among the population as a whole, such activity can be prominent and effective in shaping policy. Officials keep track of phone calls, mail, and telegrams, recording the percentage of those for and against particular issues. Legislators may even quote especially strong or well-phrased arguments in their own remarks to public gatherings or to legislative committee sessions. Because few people participate in personal communications with officials, those who do may have unusual impact. Citizens having direct contacts with officials

Table 2.5   Political Actions People Have Taken in Their Lifetime

Political action	Percentage of all respondents who had taken this action at least once	Percentage of white respondents who had taken this action	Percentage of black respondents who had taken this action
Signed a petition	69	73	39
Actively defended the action of an elected official in private discussion	56	60	29
Attended a speech or rally for a political candidate	50	53	33
Written a letter to your congressional representative	33	36	12
Contributed financially to a political campaign	33	36	15
Written a letter to your U.S. senator	25	28	4
Visited or talked in person with your congressional representative	22	24	6
Written a letter to a local government official	19	21	6
Campaigned or worked actively for a candidate for Congress	14	14	9
Visited a state legislator in the state capitol	14	15	8
Campaigned or worked actively for a candidate for President	14	15	7
Visited or talked in person with your U.S. senator	13	15	5
Campaigned or worked actively for a candidate for the U.S. Senate	11	12	6

Source: Compiled from Harris Poll reported in U.S. Senate Committee on Government Operations, *Confidence and Concern,* p. 256.

often can select the problems to be raised with their representatives. (This is not true in electoral campaigns where the calendar and the candidates set the timetable and the policy agenda.) A rash of complaints, for example, over problems with the Veterans Administration, may appear in the mail and/or conversations, encouraging officials to dig into the matter in greater depth. Much depends, however, on a policymaker's own inclinations. It is doubtful that even the best-written letter will sway an official who is committed to an opposing viewpoint. Yet a well-written message may strengthen the resolve of an official who is predisposed in that direction. And a flood of messages may cause even a contrary-minded recipient to reconsider his or her position.

One form of direct contact is personal conversation. Despite the potential utility of conversation for influencing public policy, only a small fraction of constituents ever converse directly with officials, partly because there are limits on the time and energy a policymaker can devote to such contacts. Those citizens who do engage policymakers in direct conversation are atypical of the population-at-large; they are generally of the highest socioeconomic status.[33] An additional limitation on direct contact with officials exists for judges: conversations on matters before their courts are inappropriate and can force a judge to step down from a case.

Mail is another form of direct contact with policymakers. Yet although a considerable volume of mail reaches legislators, this form of personal political activity also has severe limitations. Most people do not write public officials at all (see Table 2.5). A disproportionate amount of the mail officials do receive is from upper-class citizens, making the opinions expressed unrepresentative of those of the population as a whole. Moreover, most of the mail is either obscure or does not focus on issues at all. Letters typically deal with the personal problems constituents are having with government agencies. Letters related to issues usually come too late to influence the actions of officials who have often already decided their position before the issue ever becomes visible to the writer. Moreover, most issue-related mail is couched in general terms and does not deal with the specifics that policymakers must consider.[34]

By remaining invisible to those they serve, policymakers do little to foster greater communication between themselves and their constituents. This is especially true for judges, bureaucrats, and state legislators. However, direct contacts, despite their limitations, do benefit officials who wish to base their actions on a correct assessment of public opinion. The contacts reflect the intensity of people's attitudes, because only those who feel strongly about an issue are likely to communicate their views. Direct contacts also enable policy-makers to identify the source of the communication more easily than public opinion polls or voting statistics.

In addition to attempting to influence policymakers di-rectly, individuals can try to influence public policy indirectly through efforts to mold public opinion. Table 2.5 shows that more than half the people surveyed had actively defended the action of an elected official in private discussion. Letters-to-the-editor are another means by which citizens may indirectly influence public opinion. However, the read-ership of such letters is limited, and the letters themselves are a poor guide to public opinion. One study found that letters-to-the-editor in 1964 greatly overrepresented the ac-tual support for Barry Goldwater within the Republican party as well as in the country as a whole.[35]

Civil disorders and riots are radical means for expressing dissatisfaction with government policy, but they do not con-stitute an efficient medium of communication. Seldom are there designated spokesmen for the rioters, and the behav-ior itself gives only clues to underlying feelings. Moreover, the radical and destructive aspects of rioting alienate many people. Although analysts try to discern the message of pro-testers, officials often take their cues from the nonrioting segments of the public and pass legislation that punishes rioters instead of precluding the causes of the riots. Whereas most blacks saw the riots of the 1960s as political acts to protest discriminatory unemployment, poor housing, and segregated education, whites were more likely to see them as criminal activity. The rioters therefore provoked a strong "law and order" reaction, making it possible for the Presi-dent and Congress to ignore many of the recommendations of the Commission on Civil Disorders for more jobs, hous-ing, and educational programs in the ghettos.[36] What Con-gress did pass overwhelmingly was a "safe streets" act. And

local governments in cities where riots occurred increased
their expenditures for control and punishment of rioters
more than other municipalities. At the same time, increases
in government expenditures on social policies of apparent
concern to rioters didn't keep pace with the increasing outlay
for riot control.[37]

Reception of Public Opinion

The reception of messages transmitted by the public is a
critical link in the communication between constituents and
policymakers. Several factors work to blur or distort the public's views as they are received by policymakers.

First, there is a general tendency to screen communications. All people distort meanings somewhat by noticing
most those aspects of a communication that are favorable to
their existing views and screening out those that are contrary
to their views. Even a President, at the center of a highly
developed communications system, can be surprised at public reaction to his actions. Richard Nixon, for example, was
unprepared for the public censure he incurred when he ordered the invasion of Cambodia in 1970 or the dismissal of
Archibald Cox as Special Prosecutor in the Watergate scan-
dal in 1973.

Second, policymakers at the national and state levels are
generally of higher socioeconomic status than the majority of
citizens. As a result, they may be insensitive to the views or
experiences of persons of lower status, which contrast markedly with their own. In 1967 middle-class members of Congress publicly made fun of the urban rat problem and voted
down a bill for rat control. Public outrage forced the legislators to reconsider and pass the bill. Spiro Agnew's comment "When you've seen one slum, you've seen them all,"
and the initial disbelief of many in Congress that there was
hunger in America also typify the inability of some officials
to understand the problems of their constituencies.

Another class-related problem concerns the use of language. Many citizens with lower income and less education

do not "speak the same language" as their elected represen-tatives. They rarely rely on analytic (as opposed to descrip-tive or prescriptive) statements, and don't like to deal with abstractions that transcend their particular situation; nor are they in the habit of using general classifications, or seeing their situation from alternative perspectives, or considering long-term solutions. Since these are patterns of thought and speech familiar to many officials with middle- and upper-middle-class backgrounds, citizens and officials may simply talk past one another.[38]

The generation gap as well as differences in modes of communication helped account for the discrepancy between public opposition to the Vietnam war and official support for it. Many of the vocal opponents were young. Older policymakers, with memories of World War I, World War II, and Korea found it hard to consider seriously the views of citizens opposed to a war in which the country was actively engaged. Many policymakers regarded opponents of the war as traitors or cowards and not as citizens with legitimate grievances. David Halberstam and other anti-war journalists were frequently greeted by high military officials in Vietnam with "Whose side are you on?"[39] The peaceful but confronta-tional methods (e.g., demonstrations and civil disobedience) used by people in the anti-war movement to communicate their views also alienated policymakers who were accus-tomed to conventional verbal modes of communication.

The isolation of policymakers is another barrier to the communication of public opinion. It is a major problem for the President, who is shielded from public opinion partly by the aura of respect that surrounds his office. Not only does he hold the political position of head of the executive branch of government, but he also holds the nonpolitical position of chief of state, which is a royal post in some countries. In the United States presidents generally receive great deference. Certain presidents, including Lyndon Johnson and Richard Nixon, have further insulated themselves from the electorate by their own choice. They have restricted their advisors to men who generally agree with their own views, and they have expected these advisers to shield them from the full force of public opinion. Richard Nixon went so far as to avoid the free perusal of the news media. He limited his news reading to a summary prepared by staff sensitive to his tastes.

Problems of communication are less severe when the public shows persistent and strong interest in an issue. A noted study of members of Congress found that they had considerably more accurate views of their constituents' preferences on civil rights than on social welfare issues, and more accurate views about preferences on social welfare policies than on foreign affairs.[40] This ordering matched the priorities voters gave to those issues.

When there is widespread, intense, and stable agreement on a public issue, it is easy to identify citizen preferences. Social security or federally insured savings accounts enjoy such widespread popularity that their repeal is not a live option. Likewise, strong opposition to a policy, such as a large tax increase or the imposition of wage controls, can make its enactment unfeasible. Normally, however, the public shows neither consensus, strong commitment, nor consistency in its views on issues policymakers are actively considering. Decisionmakers can therefore take an active role in defining the public's wishes.

ORGANIZED CITIZENS

Public opinion as the expression of a collection of citizens acting individually generally does not serve as the basis for policy decisions. Lacking expertise in the subject matter at hand and in the procedures of policymaking, most citizens do not know which kind of message to send to which official in order to have the greatest impact. Many citizens who write about policy issues do so in the most general terms and address their messages to the most prominent officeholders. Unless large numbers of other citizens are similarly moved to communicate in similar terms, the chances are that the message will produce only a form letter of acknowledgement and will not be used as the basis for a change in policy.

Given the problems individual citizens face in dealing with policymaking and the barriers policymakers must overcome in dealing with public opinion, we must examine the impact of organizations on the development of public policy. Organizations can aid citizens in communicating their desires to public officials by offering expertise in both subject matter and the procedures of policymaking. They can also represent the interests of enough people to make politicians sit up and take notice. Prominent among the organizations that serve as links between citizens and policymakers are interest groups and political parties.

Interest Groups

Interest groups serve as intermediaries between citizens and policymakers. Such groups offer something to each party and receive something in return. To citizens, interest groups offer the attraction of numbers, financial resources, and personnel with information about substantive matters and the procedures of policymaking. To policymakers, the groups offer expertise, money, and political support as well as interpretations of the views of purportedly large numbers of citizens with a common interest. In exchange, the groups may obtain influence over both citizens and policymakers. Their influence over citizens originates in their ability to formulate the positions that come to be identified with their members. And their influence over policy comes from their role in supplying details of the policies that are formulated in their members' behalf.

Group Resources. Perhaps the most important resource groups have is expertise and information. Legislators find the information provided by interest groups attractive because of limitations in their own personal and committee staffs and their disinclination to accept without question recommendations from the executive branch. Interest groups can provide legislators with speeches, analyses of reports, and key questions to ask witnesses testifying at hearings.

This ammunition can make the legislators more effective in the parliamentary struggle. Some interest groups, particularly those active in state politics, provide sympathetic legislators with entire bills for submission to their chambers. Executive branch personnel also look to interest groups for information and expert evaluation on both policy questions (such as the magnitude of our oil reserves and the consequences of strip mining) and political questions (such as what position do group members support on an issue).

Courts also feel the impact of interest groups which hire attorneys to represent their members, or prepare "friend of the court" briefs supplying information and legal arguments. The Legal Defense Fund of the National Association for the Advancement of Colored People has been a major actor on behalf of black plaintiffs seeking an expansion of their civil rights.

Unlike individual citizens, interest groups are likely to enter the policymaking process in its early and often critical stages. Many interest groups hire lobbyists who, among other things, watch for proposed policies that might affect the group's members. Lobbyists do everything from attempting to persuade legislators and helping parliamentary leaders anticipate votes, to planning strategy and arousing constituents to communicate with their representatives. Some organizations, like the National Rifle Association, can stimulate mass communications from their members to legislators, which encourages policymakers to pay more attention to the policy views supported by those organizations.

Money is another resource interest groups can muster. In the 1974 congressional electoral campaigns maritime unions (principally the Marine Engineers Beneficial Association, Seafarers International Union, and the Masters, Mates, and Pilots Union) gave hundreds of thousands of dollars to help re-elect members of Congress who had supported them on a hotly disputed bill.[41] The American Medical Association plus state and local medical associations contributed heavily to the campaigns of members of the House Ways and Means Committee, which handles proposals for national health insurance. In 1976 maritime unions and medical associations donated about $1 million and $1.8 million, respectively, to congressional candidates.[42]

Interest groups also offer political support to officials whose positions often prevent them from speaking candidly for themselves. Groups can support agency administrators in their requests for funds or help administrators resist directives from an executive or legislative superior without jeopardizing their jobs. Because it has strong support from many private interests, the Army Corps of Engineers is regularly able to ignore the desires of higher officials seeking to limit its pork-barrel projects.[43]

Interest groups can also protect the jobs of sympathetic bureaucrats who may be annoying to their superiors. J. Edgar Hoover, the longtime director of the FBI, is an example of such a bureaucrat. Several presidents were inclined to replace Hoover but feared the political repercussions of firing him. He had the active support of the Association of the FBI, the associations of local police departments (many of whose members the FBI trained and/or aided), and public opinion (influenced by commercial radio and television programs produced in cooperation with the FBI).

Governmental agencies that depend on support from interest groups run the risk of succumbing to narrow private control. Francis Rourke tells how a group might offer political support in exchange for control of a program. Certain farm groups have won control of agricultural educational programs in state universities because, according to Rourke, some universities are willing to lose control of a program in order to gain the support of farm groups for the total university budget.[44]

The extent of official reliance on support from interest groups is reflected in attempts to create interest groups where none exist, as in the efforts to shore up the Office of Economic Opportunity when it came under attack from Congress and the President.

Representativeness of Interest Groups. The claims that lobbyists make on behalf of an interest group are not always representative of the full membership. The leaders of a group are usually of higher socioeconomic status than most of its members, and are likely to place a higher priority on the stated political goals of the group. Moreover, the leaders have to worry about maintaining the organization in addition to pursuing the substantive goals of their followers. These differences in characteristics and responsibilities mean that leaders and followers often view things differently.

Many people join an organization for reasons other than the accomplishment of political goals. Most members of labor unions have no choice: they must join in order to work. Lawyers generally must belong to a state or local bar association to practice law, and many physicians must join local affiliates of the American Medical Association to practice in certain hospitals. Many scholars, lawyers, and physicians join their professional organizations to receive the journals published by these groups, farmers may join organizations to benefit from special insurance policies or social activities, and businessmen join trade associations to make contacts, learn new business techniques, or keep up on new products. Although the leaders of such groups claim to speak for all the members on issues of public policy, officials should view such claims with skepticism.

The representativeness of interest groups is also weakened by the facts that many people belong to no interest group and not all interests have groups to represent them. Only a minority of the population belongs to politically active groups, and this minority is disproportionately middle and upper class. Unions, for example, tend to represent the most well-to-do workers. Most lawyers do not belong to the American Bar Association, and most blue collar workers do not belong to labor unions.

Some interests are difficult to organize. The best example is consumers. They constitute a very large group (covering the entire population), but lack face-to-face contacts among themselves as well as facilities for communicating with producers, suppliers, and each other; do not view themselves primarily in their roles as consumers; are unwilling to invest much in organizing because the benefits of an organized consumer interest appear uncertain, and if they existed would be available to all regardless of organizational membership; and are divided by other interests affecting policy preferences, like political party and social class. The efforts of Ralph Nader have proved more useful in describing the problems of consumers than in creating powerful consumer lobbies.

A study of appointments to the Federal Communications Commission and the Federal Trade Commission found that consumer groups were shut out of the nomination process from 1953 to 1974 and usually were not allowed to comment on people under consideration until their nominations had been formally announced. On the other hand, the White House actively solicited industry's reaction to proposed candidates before committing itself publicly.[45]

The poor are another group which traditionally has been organized only weakly if at all. (One of the purposes of the Community Action Programs of the War on Poverty was to articulate the demands of those who had problems but were unable to have them seriously considered.) Suffering, need, or discontent do not necessarily lead to political organization. People shaped by these circumstances are often at a disadvantage in politics because they lack solidarity, skills of communication, bargaining power and organization, and self-assertiveness. Almost everyone *but* the poor was consulted when War on Poverty legislation was being drawn up.[46] For the most part, the interests of those who are economically and socially disadvantaged are represented by surrogates. Poor people usually have a chance to influence policymaking directly only in the last stages of adopting a program when numbers alone seem important. They are often unable to capitalize on opportunities to participate earlier in the policymaking process even if those opportunities are offered by sympathetic public officials.[47]

In contrast to the underrepresentation of the poor, the makeup and activities of some groups give them the edge in their attempts to influence policymakers. Prestige (church leader, college professor, attorney), strategic location (physicians must be placated if any national health insurance program is to work), legitimacy in involvement, control over jobs in which policymakers may be interested in the future (regulators frequently go to work for those they formerly regulated), the inclusion of policymakers as organizational members who support the goals of their interest group (lawyers, farmers, insurance and real estate agents, bankers), and the development of the right "type" of membership (antiwar groups were more successful when persons other than students joined them) give groups a political advantage. The unequal distribution of resources and influence is thus one more factor determining that the demands policymakers hear are not representative of the views of the population as a whole.

In sum, although interest groups can in theory communicate more effectively than individuals with officials, thereby increasing the possibility that policymakers will base their decisions on public opinion, the interest group system does not accurately reflect public opinion. Another means of enhancing the effect of public opinion is political parties.

Political Parties

Political parties have long been considered agents for establishing popular control over government and policies. Through membership in a political party citizens are no longer simply communicating with policymakers but are organizing to take control of the government. However, to generate this kind of political power and bear responsibility for the actions of elected officials, parties must meet the following conditions:

1. Parties must have programs.
2. Each party's candidates must be committed to its programs.
3. Parties must present their programs to the public.
4. Opposing parties must present alternative programs.
5. There must be only two major parties.
6. People must vote for programs and not individuals.
7. The party that receives a majority of the vote must take control of the government.

8. The party that wins the election must have the internal cohesion and discipline to carry out its programs.
9. The party that wins the election must implement its programs.
10. The governing party must accept responsibility for the performance of the government.
11. The opposition party must be ready to take control of the government.

A two-party system operating under these conditions would simplify the alternatives presented to voters, allow constituents to effectively express their attitudes toward policy, activate public participation in politics, make majority rule effective, and establish popular control over government. Because policymakers would have control of the government and their party, they would be collectively (rather than individually) responsible for their actions. Unchallenged control and the assumption of collective responsibility would further simplify the choices of voters while also giving policymakers the power to carry out the public's wishes.

American political parties do not approach the conditions for "responsible parties."[48] They are too decentralized to take a single national position and then enforce it. Most candidates are self-selected, gaining their party's nomination by their own efforts and not the party's. Because virtually anyone can vote in party primaries, parties do not have control over those who run under their labels. Moreover, candidates are largely responsible for providing the money and organization for their own election, which precludes party control over another aspect of electoral politics.

Further, as we have already seen, there is no guarantee that candidates presenting alternative programs will compete in elections; and many voters are not issue-oriented enough to view politics and electoral choices in terms of programs instead of personalities.

Party responsibility also suffers after elections. The separation of power, including the different terms for officials in the executive, legislative, and judicial branches, makes it difficult for an election to hand control of government to one party. Moreover, the fact that there is no mechanism whereby party leaders can control the actions of elected officials and the fact that the executive branch can remain controlled by a president who lacks legislative support (which cannot happen in parliamentary systems) weaken the party's ability to enforce discipline and cohesion in policymaking. Finally, the opposition party is usually disorganized and therefore incapable of presenting alternative policies to the voters.

Despite the absence of responsible parties in the United States, there is some correlation between the party affiliation of officials and the policies they support. Democratic members of Congress are likely to be more liberal than Republicans on agricultural assistance, civil rights, government intervention in the economy, and social welfare (welfare, antipoverty programs, aid to education, urban development).[49] The same can be said about presidents and their appointees, as well as elected officials in most state governments. If they are not too demanding, voters can influence policy by their choice of one or another party's candidates.[50]

THE CONSTITUTION, THE COURTS, AND THE PUBLIC

Like other aspects of the political system, the fundamental "law of the land" limits the public's influence on policymaking. The United States Constitution prescribes many restrictions on the ability of policymakers to respond to a popular majority, including: the electoral college, which gives states with small populations a disproportionately large voice and denies voters a direct choice in the election of the President; procedures for amending the Constitution that call for a two-thirds vote in the House and Senate plus ratification by three-fourths of the states (here again small states have disproportionate power); the equal apportionment of the Senate's membership to each state, no matter what its population; the privilege given to the Senate and not the House to vote on treaties and presidential appointments; the two-thirds vote needed in the Senate to ratify treaties and convict a president who has been impeached by the House, and in both houses to override a presidential veto; the requirements of age, residency, and citizenship for elected federal offices and the limit on the President's tenure in office, all of which restrict the people's right to choose their representatives; the appointments of federal judges to life terms and the privilege granted these judges to declare acts of the elective branches void. In addition, because the Constitution calls for the separation of powers, it takes a majority in each branch of government, and in each house of Congress, to exert definitive control over policy. But the officeholders in each branch have a different constituency, which means that any official who desires change must be able to put together extraordinary majorities of public opinion and not merely simple ones.

There are also substantive limits on majority rule written into the Constitution to guarantee certain rights of individuals and minorities. Such guarantees necessarily limit the power of the majority. For instance, the Constitution bans *ex post facto* laws (which would make an act a crime or increase the penalties for the crime after the act has been committed); it also outlaws *bills of attainder* (legislative acts that inflict punishment without trial), and proscribes the suspension of the *writ of habeas corpus* in the absence of a rebellion or invasion. The Constitution further states that there can be no infringement by simple legislative enactment of various freedoms (e.g., the freedoms of speech, press, religion, and the freedom from slavery), and no legislation can violate "due process of law" in criminal proceedings, or limit property rights or voting rights. Moreover, according to the Fourteenth Amendment, state governments must also protect these rights and freedoms. Segregated schools, prayers in public schools, failure to explain procedural rights to alleged criminals, and the unequal apportionment of state legislatures between urban and rural districts have all been declared unconstitutional by the courts.

A reexamination of Table 2.1 will show that the courts serve as an important restraint on majority rule. Although a majority of the citizens interviewed opposed "busing" and favored both the death penalty and government aid to parochial schools, various federal and state courts have ordered opposite policies. By contrast, the courts have protected a woman's right to have an abortion, in line with a narrow majority of public opinion.

Many people are concerned that the Supreme Court can declare unconstitutional an act of the elective branches. Until the 1930s, however, the Court resorted only infrequently to judicial review. Moreover, most instances of judicial review have involved laws passed many years earlier. Decisions voiding recently passed laws have customarily been reversed by constitutional amendments or future decisions of the Court itself.[51] Since the 1950s, the exercise of judicial review has become more common.[52] Nevertheless, the theoretical reconciliation of judicial review with majority rule remains difficult. The justification for judicial review in the context of the American system of government rests on conceptions of the democratic process that stress the importance of minority rights as well as majority rule.[53]

SUMMARY

If the opinion of a majority of the electorate were able to determine policy, most citizens would consider policymaking a democratic process. In the United States public opinion is usually not a dominant criterion of decisionmakers. Opinions and policy are frequently incongruent. Many people do not have strong opinions on issues, and fail to express those they have or express them through crude means of communication like voting and public opinion polls. Problems at the receiving end of communications also weaken the influence of public opinion on policy. Policymakers may not "hear" the messages that are sent in their direction. Although both interest groups and parties have the potential to increase the role of public opinion in policymaking, U.S. interest groups tend to be unrepresentative and American parties are too weak to put theory into practice. In addition, as we point out in the next chapter, policymakers themselves have an influence on public opinion and are often able to reverse the constituency-to-officeholder flow of influence.

NOTES

1. Frank J. Munger, "Opinion, Elections, Parties, and Policies: A Cross-State Analysis" (paper presented at the Annual Meeting of the American Political Science Association, New York, September 2–6, 1969), p. 108. For background on the development of this table see Ronald E. Weber, *Public Policy Preferences in the States* (Bloomington, Indiana: Institute of Public Administration, Indiana University, 1971). For an interesting study which finds high correlations between state public opinion on the volatile issues of capital punishment, child labor, and female jurors and state policy in the 1930s, see Robert S. Erikson, "The Relationship between Public Opinion and State Policy: A New Look Based on Some Forgotten Data," *American Journal of Political Science* 20 (February 1976).

2. For example, see William Watts and Lloyd A. Free, eds., *State of the Nation* (New York: Universe Books, 1973).

3. Robert S. Erikson and Norman R. Luttbeg, *American Public Opinion: Its Origins, Contents and Impact* (New York: Wiley, 1973), pp. 29–40.

4. *Ibid.*, pp. 29–33.

5. *Ibid.*, pp. 38–39.

6. U.S. Congress-Senate Subcommittee on Intergovernmental Relations, Committee on Government Operations, *Confidence and Concern: Citizens View American Government,* Committee Print, Part 1 (Washington, D.C.: Government Printing Office, 1973).

7. For a discussion of voter interest in state politics, see M. Kent Jennings and Harmon Zeigler, "The Salience of American State Politics," *American Political Science Review* 64 (June 1970).

8. Robert D. McClure and Thomas E. Patterson, "Television News and Voter Behavior in the 1972 Presidential Election" (paper presented at the Annual Meeting of the Ameri-

can Political Science Association, September 4, 1973), p. 8; Erikson and Luttberg, *American Public Opinion,* pp. 230, 232.

9. Erikson and Luttberg, *American Public Opinion,* pp. 280–281. See also Barbara Hinckley, "Issues, Information Costs, and Congressional Elections," *American Politics Quarterly* 4 (April 1976), pp. 138–139.

10. John L. Sullivan and Robert E. O'Connor, "Electoral Choice and Popular Control of Public Policy: The Case of the 1966 House Elections," *American Political Science Review* 66 (December 1972).

11. Benjamin I. Page and Richard A. Brody, "Policy Voting and the Electoral Process: The Vietnam War Issue," *American Political Science Review* 66 (September 1972).

12. Gerald M. Pomper, *Elections in America: Control and Influence in Democratic Politics* (New York: Dodd, Mead, 1973), Chapter 7.

13. See Austin Ranney, "Turnout and Representation in Presidential Primary Elections," *American Political Science Review* 66 (March 1972); Austin Ranney, "The Representativeness of Primary Electorates," *Midwest Journal of Political Science* 12 (May 1968); Austin Ranney and Leon D. Epstein, "The Two Electorates: Voters and Non-Voters in a Wisconsin Primary," *Journal of Politics* 28 (August 1966).

14. The classic works which support this point are Angus Campbell, Philip E. Converse, Warren E. Miller, and Donald E. Stokes, *The American Voter* (New York: Wiley, 1960); and Angus Campbell, Philip E. Converse, Warren E. Miller, and Donald E. Stokes, *Elections and the Political Order* (New York: Wiley, 1966).

15. On this question see Michael Margolis, "From Confusion to Confusion: Issues and the American Voter (1965–1972)," *American Political Science Review* 71 (March 1977); Arthur H. Miller, Warren E. Miller, Alden S. Raine, and Thad A. Brown, "A Majority Party in Disarray: Policy Polarization in the 1972 Election," *American Political Science Review* 70

(September 1976); Samuel Popkin, John W. Gorman, Charles Phillips, and Jeffrey A. Smith, "Comment: What Have You Done for Me Lately? Toward an Investment Theory of Voting," *American Political Science Review* 70 (September 1976); David E. Repass, "Comment: Political Methodologies in Disarray: Some Alternative Interpretations of the 1972 Election," *American Political Science Review* 70 (September 1976); Arthur H. Miller and Warren E. Miller, "Ideology in the 1972 Election: Myth or Reality—A Rejoinder," *American Political Science Review* 70 (September 1976); Gerald M. Pomper, "From Confusion to Clarity: Issues and American Voters, 1956–1968," *American Political Science Review* 66 (June 1972); David E. Repass, "Issues Salience and Party Choice," *American Political Science Review* 65 (June 1971); James A. Stimson, "Belief Systems: Constraint, Complexity, and the 1972 Election," *American Political Science Review* 19 (August 1975); Richard A. Brody and Benjamin I. Page, "Comment: The Assessment of Policy Voting," *American Political Science Review* 66 (June 1972).

16. See Hinckley, "Issues, Information Costs, and Congressional Elections"; and Barbara Hinckley, Richard Hofstetter, and John Kessel, "Information and the Vote: A Comparative Election Study," *American Politics Quarterly* 2 (April 1974). For exceptions to this view see Robert S. Erikson, "The Electoral Impact of Congressional Roll-Call Voting," *American Political Science Review* 65 (December 1971); and Barbara Sinclair Deckard, "Electoral Marginality and Party Loyalty in House Roll-Call Voting," *American Journal of Political Science* 20 (August 1976).

17. See Richard A. Brody, "How Vietnam May Affect the Elections," *Trans-Action* 5 (October 1968), p. 19.

18. See Donald E. Stokes and Warren E. Miller, "Party Government and the Saliency of Congress," *Public Opinion Quarterly* 26 (Winter 1962); Warren E. Miller and Donald E. Stokes, "Constituency Influence on Congress," *American Political Science Review* 75 (March 1963); Charles F. Cnudde and Donald J. McCrone, "Linkage between Constituency Atti-

tudes and Congressional Voting Behavior: A Causal Model," *American Political Science Review* 60 (March 1966); and Erikson and Luttbeg, *American Public Opinion*, pp. 283–284.

19. See Roger H. Davidson, *The Role of the Congressman* (New York: Pegasus, 1969). For an examination of the norms of state legislators see John C. Wahlke, Heinz Eulau, William Buchanan, and Leroy Ferguson, *The Legislative System* (New York: Wiley, 1962). For a more generalized analysis of representative norms, see V. O. Key, Jr., *Public Opinion and American Democracy* (New York: Knopf, 1961), p. 538.

20. See John W. Kingdon, *Candidates for Office* (New York: Random House, 1968), p. 145; and John W. Kingdon, *Congressmen's Voting Decisions* (New York: Harper & Row, 1973), pp. 59–61.

21. Theodore C. Sorensen, *Kennedy* (New York: Bantam, 1966), p. 692. John Kennedy's brother Robert wrote that the President felt he would have been impeached if he had not forced the Soviet Union to remove its missiles from Cuba in 1962. See Robert F. Kennedy, *Thirteen Days: A Memoir of the Cuban Missile Crisis* (New York: Norton, 1969), p. 67.

22. Morton H. Halperin, *Bureaucratic Politics and Foreign Policy* (Washington, D.C.: Brookings Institution, 1974), p. 68.

23. Paul Samuelson, "Economic Policy for 1962," *Review of Economics and Statistics* 41 (February 1962), p. 3.

24. Halperin, *Bureaucratic Politics*, pp. 69–70.

25. See Kingdon, *Congressmen's Voting Decisions*, p. 34; George C. Edwards III, "Presidential Influence in the House: Presidential Prestige as a Source of Presidential Power," *American Political Science Review* 70 (March 1976); George C. Edwards III, "Presidential Influence in the Senate: Presidential Prestige as a Source of Presidential Power," *American Politics Quarterly* 5 (October 1977); Duncan MacRae, *Dimensions of Congressional Voting* (Berkeley, Calif.: University of California Press, 1958), p. 264; Miller and Stokes, "Constituency Influence on Congress," pp. 49–50; Aage R. Clausen, *How Congressmen Decide: A Policy Focus* (New York: St. Mar-

tin's, 1973), pp. 126, 127, 182, 188; and Lewis A. Dexter, "The Representative and His District," in *New Perspectives on the House of Representatives* (2nd ed.), ed. by Robert L. Peabody and Nelson W. Polsby (Chicago: Rand McNally, 1969). On the Senate see Gregory Markus, "Electoral Coalitions and Senate Roll-Call Behavior: An Ecological Analysis," *American Journal of Political Science* 18 (August 1974).

26. For an interesting study of how different electoral rules affect the outcomes of presidential primaries, see James L. Lengle and Byron Shafer, "Primary Rules, Political Power, and Social Change," *American Political Science* 70 (March 1976).

27. Edward R. Tufte, "Determinants of the Outcomes of Midterm Congressional Elections," *American Political Science Review* 68 (September 1975), pp. 822–824; Edward R. Tufte, "The Relationship between Seats and Votes in Two-Party Systems," *American Political Science Review* 67 (June 1973), pp. 547–554. See also Walter Dean Burnham, "Insulation and Responsiveness in Congressional Elections," *Political Science Quarterly* 90 (Fall 1975), pp. 412–413.

28. Sullivan and O'Connor, "Electoral Choice and Popular Control of Public Policy."

29. Pomper, *Elections in America,* Chapter 8.

30. Milton J. Rosenberg, Sidney Verba, and Philip E. Converse, *Vietnam and the Silent Majority* (New York: Harper & Row, 1970), pp. 24–25.

31. Erikson and Luttbeg, *American Public Opinion,* pp. 38–40, 53–54, 155, and sources cited therein.

32. Donald D. Tacheron and Morris K. Udall, *The Job of the Congressman* (New York: Bobbs-Merrill, 1966), p. 288. See also Donald R. Matthews and James A. Stimson, *Yeas and Nays: Normal Decision-Making in the U.S. House of Representatives* (New York: Wiley, 1975), p. 38, note 9.

33. See G. R. Boynton, Samuel C. Patterson, and Donald D. Hedlund, "The Missing Links in Legislative Politics: Attentive Constituents," *Journal of Politics* 31 (August 1969).

34. See Lewis A. Dexter, "What Do Congressmen Hear? The Mail," *Public Opinion Quarterly* 20 (Spring 1956); Sidney Verba and Richard Brody, "Participation, Policy Preferences, and the War in Vietnam," *Public Opinion Quarterly* 34 (Fall 1970); Sidney Verba and Norman H. Nie, *Participation in America: Political Democracy and Social Equality* (New York: Harper & Row, 1972), pp. 278–284; Tacheron and Udall, *The Job of a Congressman,* 282–283; Kingdon, *Congressmen's Voting,* pp. 56–57; Raymond A. Bauer, Ithiel de Sola Pool, Lewis A. Dexter, *American Business and Public Policy* (New York: Atherton, 1963), pp. 419–420; and Dexter, "The Representative and His District."

35. Philip E. Converse, Aage R. Clausen, and Warren E. Miller, "Electoral Myth and Reality: The 1964 Election," *American Political Science Review* 59 (June 1965).

36. For a short discussion of this point see Thomas R. Dye, *Understanding Public Policy,* 2nd ed. (Englewood Cliffs, N.J.: Prentice-Hall, 1975), pp. 75–78.

37. Susan Welch, "The Impact of Urban Riots on Urban Expenditures," *American Journal of Political Science* 19 (November 1975). See also Michael Betz, "Riots and Welfare: Are They Related?" *Social Problems* 21, No. 3 (1974). For an argument that the rise in the welfare rolls in the 1960s reflected the efforts of Democrats in the national government to appeal to black voters, see Francie Fox Piven and Richard A. Cloward, *Regulating the Poor: The Functions of Public Welfare* (New York: Vintage, 1971).

38. See Claus Mueller, *The Politics of Communication* (New York: Oxford University Press, 1973), pp. 52–55.

39. Bernard Brodie, *War and Politics* (New York: Macmillan, 1973), p. 211. See also Doris Kearns, *Lyndon Johnson and the American Dream* (New York: Harper & Row, 1976), pp. 327–328 for a discussion of the difficulty President Johnson had in understanding opponents of the war.

40. Miller and Stokes, "Constituency Influence on Congress." Similar results were found in studies of two state

legislatures. See Ronald D. Hedlund and H. Paul Friesma, "Representatives' Perceptions of Constituency Opinion," *Journal of Politics* 34 (August 1972); and Erikson and Luttbeg, *American Public Opinion,* p. 278.

41. "Seamen Donate Fortune for Shipping Bill Support," *New Orleans Times-Picayune,* September 1974, Section A., p. 3.

42. "AMA Donates $25,000 to Help Reelect 10 on Key House Panel," *New York Times,* September 15, 1974, Section 1, p. 50; "Interest Group Gifts to 1976 Congressional Campaigns," *Congressional Quarterly Weekly Report,* April 16, 1977, p. 710.

43. The classic article on this point is Arthur A. Maass, "Congress and Water Resources," *American Political Science Review* 44 (September 1950).

44. Francis E. Rourke, *Bureaucracy, Politics, and Public Policy,* 2nd ed. (Boston: Little, Brown, 1976), p. 54.

45. Kay Mills, "Public Dislike for Regulatory Agencies Cited by Symposium," *New Orleans Times-Picayune,* November 9, 1975, Section 1, p. 24.

46. John C. Donovan, *The Politics of Poverty,* 2nd ed. (Indianapolis: Bobbs-Merrill, 1973), pp. 31–32. Also see Daniel P. Moynihan, *The Politics of a Guaranteed Income* (New York: Vintage, 1973), p. 326; and Harry McPherson, *A Political Education* (Boston: Little, Brown, 1972), p. 342 for a discussion of poor people's lack of political activity on behalf of their own interests.

47. See for example, Norman C. Thomas, *Education in National Politics* (New York: McKay, 1975), pp. 223–224.

48. For a thorough treatment of the concept of "responsible parties" see Austin Ranney, *The Doctrine of Responsible Party Government* (Urbana: University of Illinois Press, 1954).

49. See Clausen, *How Congressmen Decide*; David Mayhew, *Party Loyalty Among Congressmen* (Cambridge, Mass.: Harvard University Press, 1966); and John J. Havick, "The Determi-

nants of State Revenue Sharing Expenditures," *Journal of Politics* 37 (May 1975).

50. For an interesting discussion of this point see Benjamin Ginsberg, "Elections and Public Policy," *American Political Science Review* 70 (March 1976).

51. Robert A. Dahl, "Decision-Making in a Democracy: The Supreme Court as a National Policy-Maker," *Journal of Public Law* 6 (Fall 1957).

52. Jonathan D. Casper, "The Supreme Court and National Policy-Making," *American Political Science Review* 70 (March 1976).

53. For several viewpoints on this question see Leonard W. Levy, *Judicial Review and the Supreme Court* (New York: Harper & Row, 1967).

The Influence
of Policymakers
on Public Opinion

3

Policymakers initiate as well as receive public opinion. Sometimes what appears to be a public demand for a policy is actually the result of work by policymakers who want it to seem as though they are responding to popular demand.

The public depends on government officials for information about public policy. Reports from scientific laboratories operated by the government, the testimony of officials before Congress, and interviews with officeholders make major news stories. When the topic is a military or diplomatic crisis, government spokesmen often have a virtual monopoly over information.

Some government activities are designed to receive widespread attention and thereby leave an imprint on public opinion. The months-long inquiry of Senator Sam Ervin's committee dealing with the Watergate break-in and cover-up unearthed vital information and set the stage for the resignation of President Nixon. Earlier, extensive hearings by Senator William Fulbright's Committee on Foreign Relations helped to turn increasing numbers of Americans against the war in Vietnam.

Presidents frequently attempt to influence public opinion through speeches over television or radio, written presen-

tations, or press conferences. Presidents are particularly effective in molding public opinion on foreign policy, about
which the public has little independent knowledge. Studies
have shown public opinion following the President's lead on
issues ranging from bans on nuclear testing to the 1970 invasion of Cambodia.[1]

The major decisions of courts, especially the United States
Supreme Court, are announced in an elaborate ritual devised to impress the media and the public. In handing down
particularly controversial rulings, like the 1954 decision ordering the desegregation of public schools, justices have
bolstered their opinions with extensive sociological and
psychological as well as legal reasonings in an obvious effort
to persuade the doubtful.

Policymakers, then, are not passive recipients of stimuli.
Rather than simply attempting to respond to the inputs that
come to them, they seek to shape public opinion and sometimes go to extreme lengths to obtain political support for
their positions. This aggressive action by policymakers reduces the already limited role of public opinion in influencing decisions of policy.

CONTROL OF INFORMATION

Perhaps the large volume of negative commentary about
United States government efforts at influencing public opinion reflects a popular assumption of public control over government. One topic of concern to most citizens is governmental control of information, which usually refers to the
government's efforts to withhold vital information and disseminate false or misleading information.

Withholding Information

Communications about the war in Vietnam provide many
examples of the government withholding significant information from the public. In 1962 the State Department told

the United States commander in Vietnam to keep reporters away from military personnel who might reveal that Americans were directing combat missions.[2] In mid-1962 the Pentagon for the first time revealed that there were several thousand American troops in South Vietnam, but it was not until early 1963 that the public learned there were actually 11,000 U.S. soldiers in Vietnam six months earlier.[3] The government revealed all of this information *after* the fact, precluding any chance for public debate before the soldiers were sent.

In 1964 there was no official report that American personnel were participating in South Vietnamese raids on North Vietnam, including one that took place the day before the "incident" which led to the Gulf of Tonkin resolution. During the 1964 presidential campaign, President Johnson also failed to tell the public he was planning bombing raids on North Vietnam while he was publicly advocating American restraint. When he decided to commit a significantly greater number of troops to South Vietnam, he ordered officials to keep the decision secret and play down the apparent change in policy. As a result, there was no announcement that American troops had combat roles in addition to their advisory functions.[4]

President Nixon joined Presidents Kennedy and Johnson in withholding information on the Vietnam war. He failed to tell the public that the United States was bombing Cambodia in 1969 and 1970. He also ordered the unsuccessful attempt to prevent the publication of *The Pentagon Papers,* the secret study of decision-making about the war in Vietnam.

When the *USS Pueblo,* a spy ship, was captured by North Korea in 1968, the United States argued that it was captured in international waters but failed to mention that it had previously been in North Korean waters. From 1962 until at least 1972 the CIA financed Laotian tribesmen to fight the Pathet Lao, but the American public was never notified of this fact.

Domestically, President Nixon favored federal subsidies for the Supersonic Transport and withheld a negative assessment of the airplane by his advisers.[5] He also failed to make public a $7 million government study projecting the nation's recreational needs and presenting a detailed program to meet them.[6] In the Johnson administration attempts were made to keep secret the results of the Coleman report on educational opportunity as well as an evaluation of Head Start programs.[7] Each of these reports was eventually released, but not until members of Congress or the media had discovered them and applied pressure for their publication. The public only received some of the information after it was no longer relevant to the formulation of policy.

The classification of information under the rubric of "national security" frequently serves to withhold information that may aid the public in evaluating policy. Most people would support the need for secrecy in handling national security affairs; the question is whether too much information is classified. In 1972 President Nixon complained about excessive secrecy and pointed out that even the menus of official dinners for visiting heads of state came to the White House marked "top secret."[8] The previous year a former Pentagon security officer testified that only one-half of one per cent of all classified Defense Department material contained genuine secrets that should be kept from the public.[9]

The classification system is set up by executive order of the President and is implemented by many thousands of bureaucrats. In 1972, after a major campaign to reduce the number of official classifiers of secrets, there were still 1,647 persons in the State Department alone who could classify material.[10] Many thousands more exercise similar authority in the Defense Department, CIA, FBI, and other federal agencies. The discretion bureaucrats have in classifying information, no matter what the guidelines might say, was dramatically demonstrated in Daniel Ellsberg's trial for releasing the *Pentagon Papers*. Leslie Gleb, the director of the study and the man responsible for its classification, testified that he was unaware of official classification guidelines and made the decision to classify it "top secret" very quickly, without regard for the government's own rules and regulations for the protection of national defense.[11]

The classification system does more than simply deny information to foreign adversaries and the American public, as the following excerpt from congressional testimony by Rear Admiral (ret.) Gene La Rocque illustrates.

> Classification is made for a variety of reasons. First, to prevent it from falling into the hands of a potential enemy; this . . . accounts for only a small portion of the material classified. Other reasons for classifying material are: to keep it from the other military services; from civilians in their own service; from civilians in the Defense Department; from the State Department; and, of course, from the Congress. Sometimes, information is classified to withhold it for later release to maximize the effect on the public or the Congress.
>
> Frequently, information is classified so that only portions of it can be released selectively to the press to influence the public or the Congress. These time-released capsules have a lasting effect.[12]

"Executive privilege," whereby presidential aides are shielded from testifying before Congress, is yet another means by which the President controls the public's access to information. Although Cabinet members regularly testify before Congress, Henry Kissinger, who functioned as the most important foreign policy figure besides the President in Richard Nixon's first term, refused to testify because of this doctrine. At one point Attorney General Richard Kleindienst claimed executive privilege for the entire executive branch.[13] Although this extreme opinion was later rescinded, it points up the problems of this extraconstitutional doctrine which has no clearly delineated boundaries.[14]

De-emphasis

With much less commotion government officials can simply de-emphasize certain facts. During an economic downturn in 1971, for example, the Bureau of Labor Statistics discontinued its monthly press briefing on the Consumer Price

Index and unemployment statistics. Similarly, while the Defense Department gave much attention to Viet Cong deserters, it avoided discussion of South Vietnamese deserters.

Collection of Information

Government officials can also affect public opinion, albeit indirectly, by not collecting information on certain issues. The lack of integrated information diminishes the public's ability to judge for itself whether a problem exists or the extent of that problem. For example, as of 1975 there was no centralized compilation of information on white-collar crimes like official corruption, corporate crime, and consumer fraud. Likewise, no major effort was ever made during American participation in the war in Vietnam to determine the true cost of U.S. involvement.

Obfuscation

At times public officials seem intent on obscuring the truth. Former White House Press Secretary Ron Ziegler once said the following about the Watergate tapes:

> I would feel that most of the conversations that took place in those areas of the White House that did have the recording system would, in almost their entirety, be in existence, but the special prosecutor, the court, and, I think, the American people are sufficiently familar with the recording system to know where the recording devices existed and to know the situation in terms of the recording process, but I feel, although the process has not been undertaken yet in preparation of the material to abide by the court decision, really, what the answer to that question is.[15]

Colonel David H.E. Opfer, former air attaché at the United States Embassy in Phnom Penh, Cambodia, once stated to reporters, "You always write it's bombing, bombing, bombing. It's not bombing. It's air support."[16] Other examples of official obfuscation of military tactics in Southeast Asia include "it became necessary to destroy the town to save it" and labeling United States air strikes "protective reaction."

Distortion

Even when officials present the facts, they may distort their significance. For example, sustained bombing of North Vietnam was begun after the attack on the United States barracks at Pleiku. However, the administration had already decided to bomb the North and was just waiting for the proper pretext.[17]

Statistics can be compiled to mislead. President Johnson once claimed that the 89th Congress had appropriated a record $9.6 billion for education under his guidance. What he failed to mention was that this figure included about $2 billion for military training plus the budgets of the Library of Congress, the Agricultural Extension Service, most of the Office of Economic Opportunity, and the Smithsonian Institution. Similarly, he claimed that the budget for fiscal year 1968 provided $26.6 billion for "poor people." Included in these figures were billions for social security benefits and veterans pensions, plus funds for highway construction and urban renewal.[18]

Presidents have also used tricks to make overall spending appear small. In his last year in office President Johnson introduced the "unified budget," which included trust funds previously *excluded* from the budget, such as those for social security, unemployment, highway construction, and retirement pensions of railroad workers. The fact that the trust funds were running a surplus allowed him to cut the size of the projected federal deficit—at least on paper. President Nixon introduced the "full employment" budget in fiscal 1972. His ruse was to calculate federal revenues not at what was expected but at what they would be if there were full employment (which there was not). This subterfuge allowed him to show a smaller overall deficit.

Information can be distorted not only by those at the top

but also by people at the middle and lower echelons of the bureaucracy. Both the public and top officials depend on those "in the field" for their information. In April 1975 the United States Embassy in South Vietnam forwarded to Washington lurid reports of communist atrocities in communist-occupied areas of the country. On the basis of these cables, Secretary of State Henry Kissinger asked Congress for more aid to South Vietnam. However, when *Newsweek* reporters tried to substantiate these reports, they found they could not. When questioned, the Embassy admitted that it had sifted through all the reports it had received based on interviews with refugees and culled only the most extreme cases to send to Washington. Moreover, it did not transmit interviews with refugees that cast doubt on the theory of a communist bloodbath.[19]

Attempts to distort information are not always successful. In 1971 the United States supported a South Vietnamese invasion of Laos. It was unsuccessful and the South Vietnamese retreated six weeks ahead of their own timetable for withdrawal. Nevertheless, the administration denied that there was a rout and the Deputy Assistant Secretary of Defense for Public Affairs, Jerry Friedheim, said the South Vietnamese were engaged in "mobile maneuvering" and proceeding according to plan. However, every night on television the American public could see South Vietnamese soldiers clinging to the skids of overloaded helicopters in an attempt to escape from their enemy.[20]

Prevarications

Overt lying is yet another means of trying to influence public opinion. The following were official United States claims subsequently proven false.[21]

1954   The United States had no role in the coup in Guatemala.

1960   The U-2 spy plane shot down over the Soviet Union was there by accident; it was unauthorized.

1961 The United States had no role in the Bay of Pigs invasion of Cuba.

1962 The United States had no information on Soviet missiles in Cuba.

1963 The United States had no role in the coup in South Vietnam which overthrew President Diem.

1963 The military-political situation in South Vietnam is bad, but the South Vietnamese government can cope with it. (On the very day he made this claim to the press, Secretary of Defense McNamara told President Johnson that the situation in South Vietnam was quite serious and the government might fall even with United States aid.)

1964 Two United States destroyers were attacked on August 4. (President Johnson told this to the American people when he knew there was considerable doubt at the scene that the attacks ever took place. His claim led to the Gulf of Tonkin resolution in which Congress granted the President broad authority for intervention in Vietnam.)

1965 A CIA agent never offered a $5 million bribe to the Prime Minister of Singapore. (Despite the official U.S. denial, the Prime Minister produced a letter from Secretary of State Rusk, predating the disavowal, apologizing for the bribe offer.)

1965 The United States invasion of the Dominican Republic was necessary to save American lives because some "1,500 innocent people have been murdered, shot, and had their heads cut off" and the United States ambassador phoned the President while sitting under his desk as bullets were whizzing overhead. (None of this was true. Moreover, the President also claimed our intervention was neutral, whereas it was actually designed to prevent a feared communist takeover.)

1965 The President had not considered whom he would appoint to the Supreme Court to replace Arthur Goldberg. (President Johnson told this to reporters the day before he announced the appointment of Abe Fortas.)

1967 The USS Liberty was stationed so close to the fighting in the Arab-Israeli war that it was attacked and sunk by our allies, the Israelis, and thirty-four Americans were killed.

When asked why the ship was stationed so close, the Pentagon replied that it was so the moon could be used as a passive reflector for communications. (This answer was an attempt to hide the fact that the *Liberty* was a spy ship monitoring battlefield communications.)

1969–1970 The United States was not bombing in Cambodia. (Air Force reports were falsified to cover up facts that contradicted the denial. Only a few approving members of Congress were informed of actual U.S. actions.)

1970 The United States was not providing air and logistical support for South Vietnamese operations in Cambodia after the United States invasion of Cambodia had ended.

1971 Secretary of Defense Laird showed the press a piece of pipe that had been severed from a Ho Chi Minh Trail fuel line during the United States-supported South Vietnamese invasion of Laos. (Later it was revealed that the pipe came from an earlier, unreported operation in Laos.)

1971 The United States was neutral in the war between India and Pakistan. (The President had, however, ordered a "tilt" toward Pakistan.)

1964–1972 A constant stream of official statements assured the American people that "our side" was winning the war in Vietnam. (These statements included inaccurate information on the effects of bombing, counts of enemy casualties, "secure" areas, United States losses of planes, and the ability of the South Vietnamese army.)

1972–1974 President Nixon and top administration officials had no role in the Watergate break-in or subsequent cover-up. (The President subsequently resigned and was pardoned by his appointed successor, Gerald Ford. His chief of staff, chief domestic adviser, personal attorney, White House counsel, two Attorneys General, leading campaign officials, and numerous other aides were convicted of a wide variety of crimes.)

1973 The United States made no attempts to prevent the election of Marxist Salvador Allende as president of Chile in 1970. (In 1977 former CIA Director Richard Helms was convicted on two counts of failing to testify fully about these activities before Congress.)

These examples reveal several patterns. First, lying is most common in the areas of foreign and military policy. It is more difficult for the public to challenge a statement about events in other countries (particularly military activity) than a report of activities American reporters can scrutinize. Second, lies are told not only to deny information to an enemy, but also to deny information to the American public. In virtually all the disproven claims cited relating to foreign policy—from the U-2 flight over the Soviet Union to the secret bombing in Cambodia—the "enemy" knew the truth. Third, the government risks embarrassment before world opinion when its lies are uncovered, such as in the U-2 or Bay of Pigs incidents. Fourth, the government may seek to maintain a lie for only a short time, presumably to avoid public panic or to confuse a foreign adversary, as in the Cuban missile crisis. Sometimes, as in reports about a President's appointments, speeches, or trips, officials lie to keep their options open until the last moment. Other lies reveal more about a leader's personal needs than about his public policy (e.g., Lyndon Johnson's disproven claim that his great great grandfather died at the Alamo).

No one really knows how many overt lies are made by government officials or how many official lies have significance for public policy. But in the face of several confirmed lies it is reasonable to assume there are many more that we don't know about. This conclusion is supported by the following two examples. In 1966 several reporters met with Assistant Secretary of Defense for Public Affairs Arthur Sylvester. One reporter raised a question about the credibility of American officials on the war in Vietnam. Sylvester responded, "Look, if you think any American official is going to tell you the truth, then you're stupid. Did you hear that?—stupid."[22] In 1974 Senator Edward Kennedy requested information on the commitments entailed in plans for military aid to South Vietnam. When he heard of this, the American Ambassador to South Vietnam, Graham Martin, cabled his superiors in the State Department that it would be foolish to give the senator an "honest and detailed answer."[23]

PUBLIC RELATIONS

In their attempts to mold public opinion, governments employ public relations campaigns modeled after those of commercial advertising firms. The public relations effort of the federal government is staggering in its magnitude. Even Richard Nixon, one of the most public-relations-oriented presidents in history, complained in the early years of his presidency about the great size of the public relations bureaucracy and ordered that it be reduced. A 1971 study by the Office of Management and Budget, using a narrow definition of public relations, found over 6,000 federal employees engaged in promoting government activity at an annual cost of $161 million. Half of them worked for the Department of Defense. The Department of Health, Education, and Welfare, the National Aeronautics and Space Administration, and the Office of Economic Opportunity also had substantial staff assigned to public relations. The Department of Defense runs a Defense Information School which graduates about 2,000 persons a year. The White House itself engages several dozen employees to advance public relations.[24]

This is only the tip of the iceberg. No one really knows how many federal employees work on public relations or how much money they spend. It is illegal for the government to hire "publicity experts" unless Congress specifically authorizes such positions (which it rarely does). Therefore, the various executive departments hire "information" experts. Many of these employees answer questions from the press and the public and prepare information about government programs. Others prepare advertisements asking citizens to join in such widely supported activities as anti-littering or fire-prevention. Still others promote compliance with federal laws like those effecting fair housing or equal opportunity employment. Yet others encourage persons to enlist in the Army, use ZIP codes, or ride the railroads. Nevertheless, the line between *information* and *propaganda* is vague and often crossed.

In addition to the "information" experts, many other government employees engage in public relations. Theodore H. White quotes President Johnson's 1964 comment that the federal government spends nearly $1 billion a year on public relations.[25] When President Nixon ordered a cutback in these activities in late 1970, very few persons actually lost their jobs; they simply received new titles.

The public relations of the government subsumes a large variety of activities. In 1969 the Department of Transportation printed and distributed 50,000 copies of a 73-page comic-book-type pamphlet called *Teachers Guide for SST*. The purpose of the pamphlet was to indoctrinate children on the virtues of the controversial supersonic transport.[26] (Congress later refused to authorize subsidies for the plane, so it was never produced.) The public relations of the Defense Department includes VIP tours; public dissemination of troop indoctrination films; Armed Forces Day demonstrations; the provision of war heroes for taped interviews with members of Congress; the use of installations, equipment, and manpower for Hollywood productions; military lectures on foreign policy for civilian audiences; and announcements of individuals' military activities in hometown newspapers.

The White House gives "information" packages on policies directly to local newspapers and radio and TV stations around the country. This technique, along with special meetings with regional media leaders, can shield the President's views from the more considered scrutiny of the national, Washington-based media. By early 1972 almost all the Cabinet departments had installed Spotmaster machines which hold audio and video tapes that radio or TV stations can rebroadcast via telephone as "live" interviews with top officials.

Staff aids of members of Congress also present their boss's activities in the best possible light, using newsletters and interviews taped for local TV and radio stations. A few members of Congress gain public attention by taking part in prominent hearings or by sponsoring controversial legislation.

Members of Congress who attempt to compete with the President in shaping public opinion may face formidable obstacles. In early 1967 while Senator Robert Kennedy was preparing to deliver a speech attacking President Johnson's policy towards Vietnam, the President engaged in a whirlwind of activity to divert attention: he suddenly called a press conference to announce the progress of United States-Soviet negotiations on anti-ballistic missiles, gave an address on civil rights at Howard University, and delivered a speech at the Office of Education about the state of the nation's schools. At the same time, Senator Jackson produced a letter from the President defending his Vietnam policy; Secretary of State Rusk dismissed Kennedy's proposals as nothing new; and General Westmoreland issued a rebuttal from South Vietnam. All of these activities and opinions were reported in the morning newspapers, which diminished the impact of the reports of Kennedy's opposition. An even more spectacular example of the executive's manipulation of events as a public relations move to counter opposition took place in early 1966 when the Senate Foreign Relations Committee was holding hearings on Vietnam. The hearings, which received wide publicity, were not supportive of the President's policy. He therefore hastily arranged a "summit meeting" in Honolulu with the leaders of South Vietnam.[27]

In addition to using PR campaigns to counter fully developed opposition, public officials rely on public relations to cover up activity that might provoke a negative public reaction. Less than three weeks after becoming Secretary of the Interior, Rogers Morton hired Harry Treleaven, Jr. to improve the department's image. (Treleaven was one of the most important public relations men in President Nixon's 1968 campaign.) In his report to Morton (done at taxpayers' expense but not made public), Treleaven listed the following as one of the objectives of the Secretary's Office of Information: playing "a key role in helping develop new programs to mold public opinion in support of the Secretary and the administration . . . and to head off or counteract adverse publicity resulting from events and activities that could put the Department in a bad light (such as mine disasters, accidents in National Parks, etc.)."[28]

In his book on the massacre of Vietnamese civilians by United States soldiers at My Lai, Seymour Hersh reports that the Army correspondent who covered the attack knew most of the dead were civilians. Nevertheless, he wrote his story of the episode based on the false, official version. He gave it to the brigade press officer who thought it looked "fishy" but dictated a similar story to division headquarters. The brigade press officer said he would have lost his job if he had let others know of the civilian massacre.[29]

Sometimes public relations experts go to extraordinary lengths to influence public opinion. When President Nixon made the decision to mine Haiphong harbor in 1972, his re-election committee spent $8,200 on telegrams and advertisements to make it appear as though there were widespread support for his decision. When the *New York Times* opposed the decision in an editorial, the committee placed an ad in the paper entitled "The People vs. the *New York Times*." It was signed by ten people who supposedly paid thousands of dollars of their own money for it. Actually, the money came from the same secret fund that paid the "hush money" to the Watergate burglars.[30]

HARASSMENT OF THE PRESS

Politicians consider some members of the press to be common gadflies and try to neutralize the impact of critical coverage in various ways. President Nixon was particularly active at harassing the press. He sent Vice-President Spiro Agnew on a speaking campaign to influence public opinion against the press, ordered the FBI to initiate an investigation of CBS reporter Daniel Schorr (and later had the White House falsely claim it was considering him for a job), prompted the Justice Department to file anti-trust suits against the three major commercial television networks, and spearheaded his administration's attempt to decentralize (and presumably weaken) the public television network.

When the Nixon administration perceived the *Washington Post*'s investigation of Watergate as a real threat, the White

House began excluding the *Post* from covering social events at the Executive Mansion and many on the White House staff refused to talk to the *Post*'s veteran White House correspondent, Carroll Kilpatrick. Presidential aide Charles Colson told a reporter for the *Washington Star,* the *Post*'s chief competitor, that after the 1972 election the White House planned to deny news to the *Post* while providing it freely to the *Star.* In addition, several persons long associated with the President filed charges with the Federal Communications Commission against two of the *Post*'s television stations in Florida.[31]

MANIPULATION OF SYMBOLS

Language has a subtle but important influence on political thought. We all use metaphors, generally quite unconsciously, to describe political events and issues. Figurative language helps us understand the new or unknown by relating it to something known. But through our choice of metaphors we highlight certain aspects of an issue or event and conceal others. The metaphoric mode of describing complex political issues and events encourages citizens to filter new information to fit a previously adopted metaphor.[32]

Because of the importance of metaphors in shaping mass attitudes, policymakers frequently attempt to select the metaphors by which people will describe policies and events. At the birth of our nation, those politicians who favored a strong central government adopted the name of Federalists to combat charges that they were trying to destroy the states and establish an all-powerful central government. They also dubbed their opponents anti-Federalists, thus associating them with a negative image. In this century Roosevelt's "New Deal," Harry Truman's "Fair Deal," John Kennedy's "New Frontier," and Lyndon Johnson's "Great Society" have been powerful symbols of their administrations. More specifically, every U.S. president from Roosevelt to Nixon presided over a military draft which forced young men to involuntarily serve in the armed forces. Many citizens found the draft objectionable, but the government cavalierly termed it "selective service."

When Congress enacted the Model Cities program, it called the project the Demonstration Cities program. But President Johnson had his administration refer to it as Model Cities to prevent problems caused by people confusing the program with political protests.[33] He was no less sensitive to public opinion when he declared a "War on Poverty" rather than using a phrase indicating a less-than-complete commitment to the elimination of poverty in America. President Nixon went to great lengths to have the public see the January 1973 peace agreement ending the involvement of American troops in Vietnam as "peace with honor" despite the fact that the war in Vietnam continued for two and a third more years and ended under less than honorable conditions for the United States. He also claimed his administration represented "law and order," but his successor issued him a pardon for offenses committed while in office.

Metaphors were also important in the debate over United States policy toward Cambodia in 1975. Proponents of further military aid to that country said their opponents either supported "surrender" or sought to push Cambodia into a "bloodbath."[34] In labor issues, those who oppose compulsory union membership for employees have a powerful symbol in the phrase "right to work" as do those favoring a "minimum wage."[35] Each of these labels reflects only part of the issue, but each is an effective device for putting opponents on the defensive and influencing public opinion.

Sometimes politicians use expressions calculated to change the focus of an issue. Opponents of federally funded medical care for the aged fundamentally altered debate on the issue when they labeled the plan "socialistic." Discussion no longer focused on the substance of the proposed legislation; proponents now had to contend with the larger issues of socialism. During the Watergate controversy, President Nixon repeatedly referred to his unwillingness to fully cooperate with Congress and the Special Prosecutor as necessary to protect the office of the Presidency, not himself as a particular president.

Another use of labeling would have the public view certain government decisions as "professional" rather than political. Groups of government employees, like welfare workers, police, the military, highway engineers, and school administrators, claim that their activities are purely professional and therefore require no oversight by bodies composed of laymen. "Private" groups also encourage the public to view their activities as nonpolitical. Professionals, from doctors to barbers, are licensed by state boards composed completely or largely of those practicing the occupation they are licensing. In theory, the governmental power delegated to private organizations is to be used in a "professional" manner. In practice, this power has sometimes been used for economic and political ends, such as to limit the number of people practicing an occupation. However, the fact that professional groups use their power for political ends has provoked little public criticism because most citizens believe the boards are nonpolitical.

Governments may appeal for support by raising the symbol of an external threat. They may do this to win approval for an increase in defense expenditures or for intervention in the affairs of other nations, or the tactic might have a wider target. National defense has been used as a rationale for federal aid to education (the National *Defense* Education Act)[36] and the interstate highway system (authorized in the Interstate and *Defense* Highway Act).[37]

The courts also manipulate symbols. The wearing of black robes and the couching of decisions in legal terms encourage the belief that judges are neutral arbiters seeking to implement the values embodied in the Constitution. The image of neutrality increases public acceptance of policy set by the courts.

Sometimes the use of symbols can backfire. Daniel Moynihan writes that the Nixon administration used explicitly conservative rhetoric to cover its more liberal actions on civil rights while advising liberals to "watch what we do and not what we say." But, Moynihan argues, words are at least as important as deeds, and it is difficult for the general public to differentiate between the two. Moreover, symbolic rewards are immediate while programmatic rewards come in the longer run or not at all, and blacks needed symbolic rewards to maintain their organizations.[38] Thus, the Nixon administration alienated blacks despite its efforts to aid them.

REDUCTION OF COGNITIVE DISSONANCE

At times government policies cause a gradual change in public opinion. When people are forced to behave in a manner contrary to their attitudes, as most Southerners were forced to do during the civil rights movement in the mid-1960's, they may change their attitudes to make them congruent with their behavior. People do not like to behave in a manner contrary to their attitudes. They therefore tend to bring attitudes into line with behavior in order to reduce what psychologists term "cognitive dissonance."[39] In 1963 the Gallup Poll reported that only 31% of adult Southern whites agreed that white and Negro students should attend the same schools. By 1973, after ten years of substantial school integration in the South, 65% of Southern whites favored integrated schools.

Not all change in public attitudes can be attributed to legally imposed changes in behavior. For example, the vocal support for integration of many middle-class religious, educational, business, and civic leaders undoubtedly had some influence on public opinion. Nevertheless, the theory of cognitive dissonance does help us understand one cause of change in the attitudes of the general public and the influence of policymakers on this change.

SUMMARY

Policymakers are not content to follow public opinion. They use several techniques to influence it, including information control, public relations, harassment of the press, the manipulation of symbols, and the reduction of cognitive dissonance. To the extent that officials are successful in their attempts to influence the public, they limit the import of public opinion as a determinant of public policy. While officials may limit the public's influence, however, they do not eliminate it. Imperfect as such devices as elections, public opinion polls, interest groups, and political parties are, they do much to set the boundaries of discretion within which officials operate.

NOTES

1. See, for example, Eugene J. Rossi, "Mass and Attentive Opinion on Nuclear Weapons Tests and Fallout, 1954-1963," *Public Opinion Quarterly* 29 (Summer 1965); Robert S. Erikson and Norman R. Luttbeg, *American Public Opinion: Its Origins, Content and Impact* (New York: Wiley, 1973), p. 155 and works cited therein.

2. William McGaffin and Erwin Knoll, *Anything but the Truth* (New York: Putnam's, 1968), p. 79.

3. David Wise, *The Politics of Lying* (New York: Vintage, 1973), p. 57.

4. *Ibid.,* pp. 66–69.

5. "SST Report," *Congressional Quarterly Weekly Report,* August 28, 1971, p. 1830.

6. Jack Anderson, "A Blueprint for Recreation," *Washington Post,* July 21, 1974, Section C., p. 7.

7. James S. Coleman, *Policy Research in the Social Sciences* (Morristown, N.J.: General Learning Press, 1972), pp. 13–14.

8. Wise, *The Politics of Lying,* p. 101.

9. Testimony of William G. Florence before the House Subcommittee on Foreign Operations and Government Information, June 24, 1971. Cited in Richard L. Worsnop, "Secrecy in Government," *Editorial Research Reports,* August

18, 1971, p. 648. See also Theodore C. Sorensen, *Watchmen in the Night* (Cambridge, Mass.: MIT Press, 1975), p. 104; and Patrick McGarvey, *CIA: The Myth and the Madness* (Baltimore: Penguin Books, 1973), p. 233.

10. United States Department of State, *Freedom of Information* (Washington, D.C.: U.S. Government Printing Office, 1974).

11. "'Top Secret' Tag Routine Jury is Told," *Washington Post,* April 24, 1973, Section A, pp. 1 and 15.

12. Quoted in Norman Dorsen and Stephen Gillers, eds., *None of Your Business: Government Secrecy in America* (New York: Penguin Books, 1974), p. 73.

13. Raoul Berger, *Executive Privilege: A Constitutional Myth* (Cambridge, Mass: Harvard University Press, 1974), pp. 254–255.

14. For a full discussion of this question see *Ibid.*

15. Israel Shenker, "Obfuscation Foes Against Zeigler and an Air Attaché," *New York Times,* November 28, 1974, Section 1, p. 35.

16. *Ibid.,* p. 1.

17. Wise, *The Politics of Lying,* p. 41.

18. McGaffin and Knoll, *Anything but the Truth,* p. 162.

19. "Will There Be a Bloodbath?," *Newsweek,* April 28, 1975, p. 22.

20. A similar sequence of events occurred during the 1968 Tet battle. See Donald Oberdorter, *TET!* (Garden City, N.Y.: Doubleday, 1971), p. 159.

21. On this general point see Wise, *The Politics of Lying;* Joseph C. Goulden, *Truth Is the First Casualty* (Chicago: Rand McNally, 1969); Phil G. Goulding, *Confirm or Deny* (New York: Harper & Row, 1970); and McGaffin and Knoll, *Anything but the Truth.*

22. Quoted in McGaffin and Knoll, *Anything but the Truth,* p. 86.

23. Carl P. Leubsdorf, "Kennedy Tells of Envoy Cable," *New Orleans Times-Picayune,* April 3, 1974, Section 1, p. 3.

24. Wise, *The Politics of Lying,* Chapter 9.

25. Theodore H. White, *The Making of the President—1964* (New York: Atheneum, 1965), p. 57.

26. Wise, *The Politics of Lying,* pp. 306–307.

27. Bruce Ladd, *Crisis in Credibility* (New York: New American Library, 1968), pp. 174–173; Chester L. Cooper, *The Lost Crusade: America in Vietnam* (New York: Dodd, Mead, 1970), p. 301.

28. Wise, *The Politics of Lying,* p. 299.

29. Seymour M. Hersh, *My Lai 4* (New York: Random House, 1970), pp. 77–78.

30. Carl Bernstein and Bob Woodward, *All the President's Men* (New York: Warner, 1975), pp. 293–294.

31. *Ibid.,* pp. 246–247.

32. For a more complete analysis of the manipulation of symbols to influence public opinion, see Murray Edelman, *The Symbolic Uses of Politics* (Urbana: University of Illinois Press, 1964); Murray Edelman, *Politics as Symbolic Action: Mass Arousal and Quiescence* (Chicago: Markham, 1971); and Murray Edelman, *Political Language: Words That Succeed and Policies That Fail* (New York: Academic Press, 1977).

33. Edward C. Banfield, "Making a New Federal Program: Model Cities, 1964–68," in *Policy and Politics in America,* ed. by Allan P. Sindler (Boston: Little, Brown, 1973), p. 140.

34. Tom Wicker, "Two Scare Words," *New York Times,* March 16, 1975, sec. IV, p. 19.

35. William R. Keech, "Electoral Politics and the Meaning of Partisanship in Federal Minimum Wage Policy" (paper

presented at the Annual Meeting of the American Political Science Association in San Francisco, September 4, 1975), pp. 8–11.

36. Norman C. Thomas, *Education in National Politics* (New York: David McKay, 1975), p. 24.

37. Governmental leaders do not always fully exploit the symbol of a foreign threat. President Johnson never tried to mobilize the country behind U.S. efforts in the war in Vietnam because he feared arousing the emotions of the mass of citizens. See, for example, Doris Kearns, *LBJ and the American Dream* (New York: Harper & Row, 1976), p. 324.

38. Daniel P. Moynihan, *The Politics of a Guaranteed Income* (New York: Vintage, 1973), pp. 157–158.

39. For a full discussion of cognitive dissonance see Leon Festinger, *A Theory of Cognitive Dissonance* (Stanford, Calif.: Stanford University Press, 1957).

RATIONAL DECISIONMAKING

In Part I we outlined the reasons why public opinion often does not serve as the basis for policy decisions. In Part II we examine a second potential criterion for policymaking: rational analysis.

To review briefly, rational decisionmaking would include the following stages:

1. Identify a problem and its cause(s).
2. Clarify and rank goals.
3. Collect all relevant options for meeting each goal and all available information on them.
4. Predict the consequences of each alternative and assess them according to standards such as efficiency and equity.
5. Select the alternative that comes closest to achieving the goal and is most consistent with the standards of evaluation.

If policymakers followed this model of decisionmaking they would presumably choose policies that came as close as possible to meeting their goals (and those of the public) for the least cost. Unfortunately, decisionmakers rarely realize this ideal. Nevertheless, by scrutinizing the failures of the rational model we can learn a great deal about why policy decisions are made as they are.

Policymaking is not an orderly process. While one group of officials administers an established policy according to set procedures, a second group of officials may be drafting changes in that policy and a third group may be finding unmet needs that suggest the necessity for additional changes. Each group of officials is probably trying to respond to the demands and expert advice of different interests from outside the government. Disagreement over both the problems that exist and the best way of dealing with them is likely. Although all this activity may take place simultaneously, it is possible to distinguish individual phases in policymaking to facilitate an analysis of the process. The isolation of stages results in some distortion of what really happens, but to good purpose, and the warpage of reality is not great.

Identifying the Problem, Setting the Policy Agenda, and Clarifying and Ranking Goals

4

To decide on the "best" means to a given end, policymakers must have a clear notion of the end they desire to achieve. They must also know what priority the goal in question has in relation to other goals because it is often necessary to choose between various goals as well as between alternatives for achieving a single goal. But before they even reach the stage of clarifying and ranking goals, decisionmakers must identify the problem that will be the target of policy and discover its cause or causes. They must also place the issue on the policy agenda for governmental consideration. Although this last step is not part of their rational analysis, it is an essential stage in decisionmaking, for without it the process cannot proceed.

IDENTIFYING THE PROBLEM

It is no simple task to identify a problem. That something is wrong may be clear to all, but exactly what is wrong is generally not clear. No one defines problems for policymakers;

they must determine the nature of the problems meriting their attention by observing, assessing, and abstracting from reality. This ambiguous process often generates differing conclusions and sharp political conflict.

The conflict that surrounds the definition of a problem suggests the importance of this stage of the process. How problems are defined has important implications for which agencies will deal with them and how those agencies will define their goals and policies. If government officials regard urban riots strictly as a breakdown in law and order, they will assign responsibility for dealing with the problem to law enforcement agencies who may well decide that additional police and stiffer penalties are the best means to quell the unrest. If, however, policymakers link the problem to poverty and racial discrimination, they will also seek solutions through social agencies having wider-ranging goals than the simple control of dissent. In macroeconomics, the type of inflation policymakers perceive influences their choice of policies. If they consider rapidly rising costs to be the cause of inflation, they may try to curtail increases in the wages demanded by unions or in the profits of corporations. If they see excessive demand as the cause of the problem, they may try to limit the purchasing power of consumers. The view that inflation results from inadequacies in the structure of the economy may give rise to policies giving rule-making discretion to regulatory agencies, whereas the judgment that the causes of inflation are psychological may produce a campaign to restore consumer confidence.

The Existence of Problems

The political culture of citizens and policymakers, including their beliefs, values, and attitudes toward behavior and conditions in the world, affects what they see as problems. In the United States citizens hold the freedoms of speech and religion in high esteem. An obvious deprivation of these freedoms is likely to arouse widespread concern and be seen as a problem calling for government action. In many other countries these freedoms are either ignored or given only lip service. Similarly, political culture influences whether poverty or racism are seen as just or unjust, inevitable or correctable. If they are viewed as unjust and correctable, then they are likely to be seen as problems requiring governmental action. However, if they are considered just or inevitable, policymakers will not treat them as targets for policy.

Among American cities having similar levels of actual air pollution the issue of air pollution is most likely to arise in those cities where issues such as government reorganization, water pollution, sewage disposal, and mass transit are also on the agenda. Like the abatement of air pollution, solutions to these other issues benefit all citizens collectively. Air pollution is less likely to be on the agenda in municipalities where the prominent issues are business and industrial development, the elimination of poverty, and the provision of welfare services. These policies benefit one interest more than another. Issues on a city's agenda may be linked by a comprehensive political orientation or ethos (e.g., concern for public or private interests) that determines which conditions in a city are considered problems. Moreover, once a certain issue activates people, these people may in turn generate other, similar issues.[1]

Professor Karl Deutsch argues that orientations to time differ from culture to culture in ways that influence the perception of problems. Thus, Great Britain, which places more importance on the past than the United States, initiated old age pensions in 1908, twenty-seven years ahead of the United States. Conversely, the more future-oriented United States instituted substantial national government support for public higher education in 1862, a century ahead of Great Britain.[2]

Political culture also affects the attitudes and images that guide people's views on international relations. A capitalist society identifies its friends and enemies differently than a socialist one. The leaders of many countries did not view a communist victory in South Vietnam as much of a threat to

their national interest whereas for the anti-communist leaders of the United States, it became a problem calling for
government action.

Other factors besides political culture influence how
people perceive problems. Technical disagreements and
economic self-interest also play a role. In disputes concerning the regulation of drugs or food additives, some scientists
warn the public about a product they consider dangerous,
while those who manufacture the product argue that research has not proven any danger exists. In the debate over
whether the fluorocarbons used in many aerosol sprays destroy part of the ozone layer which surrounds the earth and
protects us from the sun's rays, some asked the government
to ban the use of chemicals while others claimed that no
problem warranting governmental action had been shown to
exist.

Technical disagreements also emerge over issues originating in the social sciences. The question of whether pornog-
raphy and violence in the media produce antisocial behavior
are far from settled. Yet the answers will largely determine
whether or not there is a cause for governmental action. The
conclusions of the special commissions that have studied
each of these questions have generated both praise and criticism. People on both sides of the issue appear to have made
up their minds without referring to the evidence.

Sometimes problems arise only after their solutions become feasible. Putting a man on the moon became a problem
for policymakers only after it became technically possible to
do so in the late 1950s. Pollution is another such issue. It has
been a long-standing feature of our environment but has
achieved status as a problem only as we have acquired the
technology and affluence to handle it.

Measuring the Symptoms of Problems

In addition to determining whether or not a given situation
constitutes a problem suitable for governmental action,
policymakers must measure the extent of the problem. Fail-

ure to quantify a measurable problem (such as civilian casualties in the war in Vietnam) can make it easier for policymakers to ignore the problem.

Policymakers often decide on policy with only a very general idea of the problems they are trying to solve. When Lyndon Johnson declared a "war on poverty," his staff aides had only the vaguest notion of how many people were poor and who they were. The initial $3,000 poverty line was based on a 1955 Department of Agriculture survey showing that the average family spent a third of its income on food and a 1961 study on the cost of a nutritionally adequate "economy food budget." The measure obtained by multiplying the amount a family spent on food by three did not take into account such factors as family size, family assets, temporary "poverty" (e.g., students' standard of living), extraordinary expenses (such as medical bills), geography, or inflation; but it was the best that could be done with the information and technical capabilities available. Economists have subsequently raised the poverty line in response to inflation, and taken family size into consideration, but their calculations of how many people live in poverty have not taken into account a variety of substantial in-kind transfers such as food stamps, medical aid, and public housing.[3]

When considering the 1965 Elementary and Secondary Education Act, policymakers had only a general notion of the nature, extent, and distribution of educational disadvantages among children from poor and minority families. And in 1966 when analysts at the Department of Health, Education, and Welfare began examining the health care of American children, they found it extremely difficult to gather information on the prevalence of serious illnesses and handicaps among children. It was also hard to learn of the need for vocational rehabilitation because there was little information available on disabilities among adults.[4]

Those particular gaps in information have been remedied to some extent by surveys and studies. But even these investigations have provoked criticism. Some people, particularly the poor and young adults, tend to be missed or fail to respond to surveys. Moreover, some questions in a survey,

such as those on income, are often answered incorrectly or
not at all. Many surveys are one-shot efforts to collect information and do not tell us what happens to people over time.
Do the poor eventually move out of poverty? Do those who
perform poorly in school at one point in time also perform
poorly at a later date?[5] Are general conditions becoming
better or worse? These are important questions, and the inability of policymakers to answer them clearly invites attacks
from those who do not support their policies.

Crime Statistics.   There are serious problems with the information on crime that is available to policymakers. The principal source of data is the *Uniform Crime Reports* of the Federal Bureau of Investigation, which compiles statistics
provided by over 13,000 local police departments. A police
department may try to justify its own budgetary requests by
padding statistics on certain types of crime; or it may under-
report the incidence of crime to meet the needs of a mayor
seeking re-election. Moreover, the police in many small
communities are not equipped to engage in detailed statistical reporting, and there is considerable variation in the
recordkeeping of police departments. Some departments do
not submit any data on crime to the FBI (but we have no
information on how nonparticipating departments differ
from those that do report).

   For crimes such as gambling, prostitution, blackmail, and
selling illegal drugs, both the criminals and the victims have
incentives to hide their activities. This is also true for rape;
many of the victims do not report a rape because of the
embarrassment and humiliation they would suffer as a consequence of public knowledge, official investigation, and a
trial. (Indeed, disdain for legal procedures and publicity inhibits the reporting of many crimes.) The Law Enforcement
Assistance Administration (LEAA) has filled part of this gap
between reported and unreported crimes through its surveys
of citizens (generally finding that unreported crimes exceed
those reported). Yet because of variations in the definitions
of crimes used by the FBI and the LEAA, it is "virtually
impossible to compare the two sets of figures and glean more

information."[6] Finally, there is no central source of information on the incidence of white collar crimes, which makes it difficult for policymakers to gauge the size of the problem and the rate of its increase.

There are a number of additional problems with the statistics available on crime. The FBI's Crime Index only carries information on about one-half of all the crimes committed, and the "sample" is not representative of all crimes or even serious crimes. Rather, it contains those crimes the FBI considers most serious, most frequent and/or most likely to be reported to the police. However, the crime rates for all types of crimes do not necessarily move in the same way. In addition, the FBI compilation weighs all crimes equally. Therefore, a bicycle theft and a homicide contribute equally to the aggregate Crime Index. The crime statistics also do not take into consideration factors such as inflation which causes more goods to be worth at least $50 and thus artificially increases the number of serious crimes; the increased availability of cars to be stolen and the increased number of persons in the car-stealing age bracket; and the improved capacity of the police to identify crime. Finally, crime statistics tell us little about the number of people associated with each type of crime or the number of crimes perpetrated by individuals or groups.[7]

In the words of Ronald Gainer, the director of the Justice Department's Office of Policy and Planning, "[T]here is not in this country a fairly good idea of what kind of crime exists. That's a ridiculous way to run a criminal justice system. . . . We operate on hunch, on war stories, on personal experiences, on what we presume to be logic. . . . "[8]

Consumer Price Index. Governments expend considerable effort to measure the symptoms of some problems. Nevertheless, the results are far from perfect. The Bureau of Labor Statistics (BLS) compiles a monthly Consumer Price Index to measure the rate of inflation. The index affects the incomes of about half the country's population because Social Security payments, certain other pensions, many labor contracts, and a wide variety of other rates and benefits are pegged to its fluctuations.[9] Compilation of the index requires the services of 350 BLS employees and costs about $3.5 million annually.

Despite its widespread use, the Consumer Price Index represents the experience of only about 55% of the urban population and less than 45% of the total United States population. It measures changes in the prices urban wage earners and clerical workers pay for goods and services. Thus, the index is probably inaccurate for the country as a whole because the prices it analyzes may rise faster or more slowly than the average for the entire nation. Some economists believe that pensioners receive larger incomes on the basis of the Consumer Price Index than they would on the basis of an index that measured their own spending patterns. If that is true, the index itself is a cause of inflation.

Another source of inaccuracy in the index is the uneven rate of price fluctuation, particularly the unusually rapid rise of prices for some goods. In 1973 and 1974 the rate of increase in food prices showed unusual spurts. Because low-income consumers spend a greater percentage of their income on food than the average household surveyed by the Bureau of Labor Statistics, the index did not reflect the real problems of the poor. A third technical problem concerns changes in the *quality* of products. Stable or decreasing prices may hide decreases in quality whereas increasing prices may actually reflect the cost of improving the quality of goods or services, and not inflation *per se*.

A further technical problem is simply mistakes in computation. The BLS Commissioner has said that an error of only 0.1 percent could lead to the misallocation of more than $100 million because of provisions in labor contracts for the escalation of wages. One error in 1974 resulted in overestimates of from 0.1 to 0.3 percent in seven monthly indices.

Technical errors account for only part of the distortion of the Consumer Price Index. Because the index can pinpoint problems, political interference is inevitable. In March 1971 the Bureau of Labor Statistics discontinued its monthly press briefing on the Consumer Price Index (and unemployment statistics), perhaps to cover up the ominous record of unfavorable economic news. In September of the same year the Bureau was reorganized in what many again viewed as a political move. Finally, in 1972, Geoffrey Moore, the Commissioner of the BLS, resigned at the request of the White House.

Private groups are equally anxious to have the Bureau of Labor Statistics serve their special purposes. Because much of the existing Consumer Price Index is based on surveys of shopping and spending habits conducted in the early 1960s, the Bureau began to update the index in the early 1970s. The Bureau originally planned to use new data, and new sampling and computer techniques to publish one new index reflecting the spending of 80 percent of the American population instead of the 45 percent it now covers. Although the update was a perfectly reasonable idea, the decision elicited considerable criticism from organized labor and groups representing the elderly. Labor liked the old index because it more accurately reflected the experience of working people; and the National Council of Senior Citizens, which desires a separate index for the elderly, complained that the proposed index, by including more high-income people than the present index, would not accurately reflect the inflationary pressures on the elderly. The end result of this political pressure was that the Bureau retreated and decided to begin publishing two updated indices beginning in April 1977 (later delayed until the fall of 1977): the existing one and an aggregate one for the broader population. Moreover, Congress directed that the existing index must have first claim on the Bureau's resources.

Unemployment Statistics. Like attempts to compute the rate of inflation, efforts to measure unemployment encounter problems with important consequences. National and state compilations serve to identify unemployment and trigger federal aid. The 1973 Comprehensive Employment and Training Act, for example, favors areas with the greatest unemployment as do other programs offering public service jobs and expanded unemployment benefits. Until 1974 the BLS relied primarily on unemployment claims in determining unemployment figures for specific areas within the nation. This method of computation left much room for error. A new system updates estimates for industries not covered by state laws, classifies jobless persons by where they live rather than by where they work, adjusts for persons holding several jobs, and also uses statistics from the Bureau of Census' Current Population Survey (which aids in identifying persons who are unemployed but who do not qualify for compensation and thus do not apply). Although the new system is an improvement over past methods, many states have complained that the new estimates are too low, causing them to lose federal aid. New Jersey filed suit to stop use of the system, and officials from other states and representatives in Congress brought pressures on the Bureau.

Some experts also claim that unemployment figures overstate unemployment by about 0.2 percent because the base for calculating percentages is the civilian labor force, which excludes the military. Most of the military workforce is young so that this bias overstates most the unemployment figures for teenage males. Although there have been improvements in the means of computing unemployment statistics, an increase in unemployment might reflect a liberalization of eligibility requirements for unemployment insurance (creating incentives to say one is seeking a job) or an increase in the size of the labor force as well as a decrease in the availability of jobs. Economist Milton Friedman has argued that the announced high levels of unemployment in 1974 and 1975 overstated that recession in comparison with those of the past.[10] Conversely, statistics may understate unemployment because some people give up job-hunting in despair and are therefore not officially unemployed; others are counted as employed although they have only part-time jobs.

There are many other indicators which are far from perfect and many other potential problems about which we know very little. The Gross National Product (GNP) does not reflect the work of millions of wives or the value of homemade goods. The Wholesale Price Index relies on list prices and not the lower transaction prices often in effect, and uses anachronistic seasonal adjustment factors.[11] No one really knows how many people are covered by pension plans other than Social Security and how much of a pension they will get. Moreover, we are unable to translate the data we do have into figures analyzing family or household pension earnings.[12]

Poor measurement of problems means not only that some problems will be overlooked but also that sometimes actions will be taken for perceived problems that don't really exist. Professor Thomas Sowell has argued that the federal government's efforts at "affirmative action" in hiring faculty for institutions of higher education was a response to a problem of racial and sexual discrimination which did not and does not exist. He presents data showing that even before affirmative action programs went into effect the proportion of academic positions held by women and blacks was higher than the proportion of the Ph.D.s received by those two groups, and that neither women nor blacks have been discriminated against in promotions and salaries. It is only married women, who spend less time on their work than unmarried women because of family responsibilities and tend to interrupt their careers for childbearing and relocate to further their husbands' careers rather than their own, who do less well.[13]

Statistics on crime, prices, and unemployment have their faults, but they nevertheless seem relatively simple to compile. Measuring specific acts of crime, purchasing power, and the number of jobs is easier than measuring equal opportunity, freedom, personal satisfaction, or other abstract concepts that American citizens value highly. We lack useful measures for these and many other important concepts.

Even the best of statistics do not reflect the "human" side of problems. Unemployment statistics do not measure the consequences of being out of work. Some unemployed persons may have little need for income-producing jobs, while others who are employed may actually live in poverty because of their low wages. Similarly, the poverty line remains fixed in that it represents a constant purchasing power over time. But poverty is a relative concept—especially in the minds of the poor—as well as an absolute, and the poverty line does not take into consideration rising aspirations at the bottom of the economic scale or increasing affluence in the middle. Thus, the poverty line is a decreasing percentage of the median family income, and figures on the number of those below the poverty line do not reflect the fact that those just above the line can share in a smaller and smaller percentage of the American dream or that those just below the line are relatively less well-off than their counterparts in former years.[14]

The failure of indices to capture important aspects of a problem is due not only to the difficulty of measuring those aspects, but also to the lack of a clear notion of what is being measured. For example, poverty can be considered an absolute deprivation, a relative deprivation, or a mode of behavior (i.e., a "culture"). Different measures are required to analyze each of those concepts and different types of policies are likely to result from the use of each measure. Policies designed to provide the basic necessities of life logically follow from measurement of absolute deprivation, policies aimed at increasing the equality of income distribution follow from measures of relative deprivation, and policies emphasizing social work follow from measures of the culture of poverty.[15]

Sometimes the only information available on the dimensions of a problem is in the hands of private interests who refuse to cooperate with the government. At various points in the "energy crisis" that began in 1973 the government wanted information on the magnitude of petroleum reserves. However, the oil companies claimed "proprietary" interest in this information and refused to supply it. Of course, their refusal to cooperate hampered the fashioning of a national energy policy and, it is important to note, regulation of the oil companies.

There are times when the government does possess vital information on a problem, but it is not in the hands of those who must make crucial decisions. When the *U.S.S. Pueblo,* a naval intelligence ship with 83 crew members aboard, was captured by the North Korean Navy in January 1968, there was a delay of two hours in sending the news to the White House; this may have been long enough to prevent early action to keep the crew from a North Korean prison.

Distilling Problems from Symptoms

Even when there is consensus that "something is wrong," policymakers must distill conceptions of problems from the symptoms they see. For example, most observers accepted urban rioting as a sign of severe difficulties. What was less clear was the nature of the underlying problem(s). Was it a breakdown of law and order, racial discrimination, unmet expectations, poverty, black power, alienation, urban disorganization, lawlessness on the fringe of otherwise peaceful reform movements, incipient revolution, unemployment, an inadequate educational system, unresponsive political and economic elites, or some combination of these? The answer was not obvious. President Johnson appointed a special commission to advise him about the underlying problems. Later, when the Commission cited "white racism" as a major cause of the riots, the President refused to accept this conclusion.

The analysis of the urban riots provoked numerous political conflicts about the question of "What is wrong?" as well as about "What should be done?" Conservatives tended to see the problem in terms of law and order, incipient revolution, and unrealistic expectations (brought about by the inflated promises of liberal politicians). Liberals, on the other hand, who generally felt the conservatives were responding only to symptoms, saw the problems in terms of the environment in which rioters found themselves: racial discrimination, poverty, unemployment, and inadequate education. (In the summers of 1967 and 1968 some of President Johnson's advisers spent a few days in black neighborhoods in Northern cities to learn how the persons who lived there felt. In the words of one high White House aide, "[i]t was a desultory way of getting information about the black poor to the President."[16])

It is sometimes difficult to decide whether there is a single large problem or many separate problems independently causing the observed symptoms. Does poverty result from one overall problem such as racial discrimination, or is it caused by several problems like inadequate education for the young, inadequate retirement income for the old, inadequate welfare payments for members of broken families, and low earnings and lack of employment opportunities for the unskilled? If poverty is considered the result of discrimination, then it is tempting to focus on the passage of civil rights legislation. However, policies such as occupational training, social security adjustments, guarantees of jobs, or adjustments in the minimum wage may be more appropriate to meet each of several discrete problems.

THE POLICY AGENDA

Whether or not a consensus develops over the nature of a given problem or the extent of its symptoms, persons who desire governmental action on an issue must have it placed on the policy agenda. By *policy agenda* we mean the *items receiving active and serious consideration by important policymakers.* There is a limited amount of time, money, and personnel to handle policy problems. Issues must compete for a position on the agenda and when one issue gains in prominence, it may bump others.

"Old" Issues

At any given time there are many "old" items already on the policy agenda, including national and state budgetary matters, which legislators must consider at prescribed intervals. The importance of the budget and its linkage to deadlines set by the fiscal year force it onto the agenda at about the same time each year. Two other annual items that reach the agenda at a predictable time are the President's State of the Union address and his annual Economic Report, each of which serves as a vehicle to discuss problems and offer proposals.

Some items appear on the agenda every year or two. Adjustments in social security payments was such an issue before the payments were pegged to the cost of living; filibuster reform in the U.S. Senate, tax reform, and economy and efficiency in government are currently recurring issues. They have established places on the agenda because of their importance to the public (taxes, social security), to interest groups concerned with controversial issues (filibuster), or to politicians seeking publicity on a popular issue (economy in government). Certain issues gain a place on the agenda because of demands to renew programs about to expire, for example, speed limits, the 1965 Voting Rights Act (renewed in 1970 and 1975), and revenue-sharing.

The policy agenda is clogged with issues. After an issue has achieved a place on the agenda, the agencies dealing with it have an interest in drawing attention to and developing support for proposed programs. Once the government begins to act on a problem, the problem itself is given publicity and "respectability." A likely result is more demands for action on that same problem. Because the agenda has so many old items on it, it is not easy to find a place for new issues. As a result, supporters of new issues may attempt to classify them as issues already on the agenda. Thus, proponents of medicare articulated it as an extension of social security, and supporters of federal aid for college classroom construction claimed it was simply an extension of aid for college housing.[17]

Sources of New Problems

There are many sources of new problems for the policy agenda. Any of the following can trigger unforeseen problems requiring governmental action: natural catastrophes (floods, fires, air inversions, mine explosions); unanticipated human events (assassinations, air hijackings, riots); technological changes in the environment that create heretofore undiscussed issues (air and water pollution, air travel congestion); imbalances or biases in the distribution of resources (leading to civil rights protests or strikes); demographic changes (population growth and change in the age distribution of the population, migration of blacks to northern cities); the availability of state or federal grants (requiring the adoption of certain policies); innovation in weapons technology (ABM, MIRV); wars or military actions involving the United States (Vietnam, *Pueblo* incident); international conflict not directly involving the United States (Mideast, Cyprus); requests of other nations (sale of wheat to the Soviet Union); competition in international trade (leading to demands for protective tariffs); and changing patterns of international alignments (the revolutions in Chile and Portugal, the civil war in Angola).[18]

Incipient problems must vie for attention with other issues on the policy agenda. To obtain immediate consideration they must strike policymakers as urgent. In fact, how policymakers and the public perceive problems is more important than actual events. If many people believe there is an improper distribution of resources, for example, some people will act to alter this situation, whatever the "truth" of the matter.

Converting Problems into Agenda Items

New issues do not automatically win a place on the policy agenda. A prominent figure, the mass media, or an interest group must elevate a perceived problem into an issue that warrants space on the agenda.

Policymakers themselves may place problems on the agenda. When John F. Kennedy campaigned in the West Virginia presidential primary of 1960, he was sufficiently impressed by the poverty of the mountain people to initiate what became a regional development commission for Appalachia.[19] Kennedy's own perceptions seem to have been more important than contributions of interest groups or the media in putting the issue on the policy agenda.

Shortly after Lyndon Johnson became president he received a briefing on the emerging concept of a war on poverty from Walter Heller, then chairman of the Council of Economic Advisers. Johnson seized upon the idea as a program he could take to the voters as his own.[20] Similarly, Richard Nixon set in motion plans for opening negotiations with Communist China in 1969.

Members of Congress have elevated some issues to a place on the policy agenda. Senator Estes Kefauver used committee hearings to publicize his efforts to regulate the safety, effectiveness, and pricing of drugs. Likewise, Senator Edmund Muskie boosted pollution control and Congresswoman Leonore Sullivan promoted food stamps.

Most foreign policy issues, from outright war to innovations in weapons technology, are placed directly on the policy agenda by officials in the national executive branch. In crises, however, the issues may originate with actors outside the United States. Most often, domestic American interests do not create foreign policy issues. There are exceptions, as when the plight of Russian Jews came to the agenda via Jewish groups and sympathetic members of Congress, and when the pressure of Greek organizations forced the cut-off of American aid to Turkey during 1974–1975. One reason for the short route to the agenda of many foreign policy issues is that they are frequently perceived as crucial to the nation's security and are therefore more difficult to bypass than other problems.

Because policymakers have more or less control over the agenda, they are sometimes tempted to manipulate it to serve their own interests. Morton Halperin cites the example of General Earle Wheeler, Chairman of the Joint Chiefs of Staff, requesting 205,000 additional troops for the war in Vietnam in 1968. Although he wanted to use these troops for invasions of Laos and Cambodia, he did not raise these issues with the President when he made his request for troops. He limited the agenda item to the "easier" decision and saved the question of the invasions until conditions were more favorable for an affirmative decision.[21] Similarly, Professor Doris Kearns writes that the Joint Chiefs of Staff knew from the start that the bombing in Vietnam would not make it possible to avoid sending troops, but they refrained from voicing this view in early 1965 when pessimism regarding the consequences of bombing might have persuaded Johnson to do nothing. They made their requests for troops gradually, in easy incremental steps, and the U.S. mission was expanded as the number of troops increased.[22]

Policymakers can place items on the agenda through the collection and dissemination of data. By measuring and announcing to the public the current cost of living or the correlation between cigarette smoking and cancer, the issues of inflation and smoking receive widespread publicity and become topics of debate.

Often it is not government officials who take the initiative in placing items on the policy agenda. Government agencies have insufficient personnel to look for problems, too few resources to devote to new programs, and a desire to avoid provoking new conflicts that would upset delicate agreements reached in other matters. For these reasons they generally give low priority to identifying new problems. Moreover, when agencies do identify problems, they do so while under the influence of prior experiences and commitments. Thus, they are likely to look for problems only within what they view as their primary area of responsibility. Furthermore, when they do see that a situation presents problems requiring governmental action, agencies are likely to define the problems in terms of the solutions they are able to offer. The military tends to see military problems in a situation whereas the State Department tends to see political problems in the same situation.

In lieu of policymakers placing an issue on the policy agenda of their own initiative, widespread public interest can force their hand. If an event is widely viewed as a crisis, the coincidental attention of officials and citizens can elevate the issues triggered by the crisis to a choice spot on the agenda. The 1973 Arab Oil embargo, the harsh treatment of civil rights demonstrators in the 1950s and 1960s, the assassination of political leaders, urban riots, floods, mine disasters, attacks on United States civilians or its armed forces, the

1969 oil slick off Santa Barbara, and the problem of "thalido-mide babies" of the early 1960s all gained governmental attention in this manner.

Those were dramatic events that thrust themselves upon the public consciousness, bypassing the necessity for the time-consuming process of raising mass and elite awareness of particular problems. Yet some of the issues engendered by these crises were not able to sustain the interest of the public or government officials. The public and legislators may be greatly concerned about gun control after a political assassination or about mine safety after a mine explosion, but without the organization to carry an issue through the decisionmaking process and maintain support in the face of organized opposition, an issue may soon lose prominence.

Sometimes a single person outside government can raise an issue to the agenda. Although the issue of auto safety had existed for years in a dormant state, it was Ralph Nader's book, *Unsafe at Any Speed*, and the exposure of General Motors' investigation of his private life that gained publicity for the issue and forced legislative attention. Similarly, Rachel Carson's *Silent Spring* and Michael Harrington's *The Other America* brought wide public attention followed by gov-ernmental action to the issues of environmental protection and poverty. This process is not new. At the beginning of this century Upton Sinclair's *The Jungle* helped publicize and provoke regulation of sanitary conditions in the food pro-cessing industry.

The mass media often play a crucial role in forcing policymakers to add an issue to the agenda. Sometimes the media initiate discussion of a problem. Examples include the Watergate affair, atrocities in Vietnam, excess Pentagon spending on public relations, hunger among the poor of America, the plight of migrant workers, and the problems resulting from overworked air traffic controllers.[23] The mass media also serve as a conduit for policymakers and interest groups who wish to bring problems to the public's attention. When President Johnson announced the War on Poverty in January 1964, the news media were inundated with facts and rhetoric from the White House on the plight of the poor.

The mass media also stimulate the public to write officials, structure public discussion of issues, and bring issues to the attention of policymakers. Witness the experience of a congressman attempting to get committee hearings on a subject he regarded as highly important:

> He had been making speeches on the floor and writing the committee chairman for months, to no avail. Then an editor for a minor magazine noticed it and asked him to write an article. When the article . . . appeared, the editor of an important newspaper in the district of a senior committee member picked it up and wrote a prominent editorial. That committee member, in turn, inquired of this congressman and became a leading advocate of hearings. Then the editor of another newspaper, this time in the district of another committee member, also picked it up and wrote a prominent story. That committee member called the congressman, asking for a copy of his bill, and eventually introduced it. Finally, after the chairman's initial reluctance, hearings were scheduled. As is so often the case, nothing happened until well-placed media decided to play up the story, which in turn forced congressmen to respond in some fashion.[24]

On many issues, groups pressure officials to place an item on the agenda by arousing latent support in the community. They rely on direct appeals for support and attempts to dissuade the opposition. If these means fail, they may attempt to provoke another group or governmental agency into action against them in order to obtain public sympathy. Some civil rights and anti-war groups have used this tactic, demonstrating in anticipation of clashes with the police and other opponents. Groups also use demonstrations to show the public the size of their constituency, the strength of their commitment, or their potential for disruption. The mass media are an essential part of any demonstration: group leaders rely on the media to carry their messages to the public through coverage of appeals, provocations, and rallies.

The media are not omnipotent in their efforts to arouse public attention. Their restricted coverage of public affairs, the selective perceptions of their clientele, and the fact that the public does not always rely on the mass media for its views limit the clout of the media. Television in particular devotes little attention to public affairs. The script of the national evening news program of a major network contains only as much text as one page of the *New York Times*.

Limiting the Range of Agenda Issues

In addition to asking why and how some issues achieve a place on the policy agenda, it is necessary to ascertain why certain issues do not. Some aspects of the policymaking process suppress certain issues.[25] If policymakers can kill an issue before it gets on the agenda, they and those of their constituents who oppose the change necessary to resolve the problem will not have to worry about the issue reaching a broader public and sympathetic policymakers. Attempts to limit the agenda are particularly likely to occur on issues that challenge values of high priority to persons and interests in society, but opposition within an agency or a legislative committee to seemingly unimportant programs may keep them from being presented to other policymakers.[26]

Sometimes force is used against activists seeking to put issues on the agenda, for example, against civil rights workers and anti-war demonstrators. Other sanctions government or private interests use to suppress action on controversial issues include firing blacks who register to vote; revoking draft deferments for those opposing the war in Vietnam; subjecting the members of "radical" organizations to scrutiny and harassment (including opening their mail, auditing their taxes, tapping their telephones, and providing their employers with derogatory information); and attempting to create internal disharmony in the organizations themselves.

Sometimes officials and interests opposed to letting an issue on the policy agenda offer benefits to potential backers of the issue. Often these benefits are only cosmetic, designed to cover rather than cure a problem. The creation of organizational units to deal with a problem, the labeling of issues as matters for "professionals" or for "private" resolution (and therefore not for public concern), and the labeling of policy demands as "un-American" (and therefore not worthy of public consideration) have been used, sometimes effectively, to keep issues off the policy agenda. Another tactic is to *co-opt* the leaders of a group making undesirable demands. By giving leaders a position in established agencies, those opposed to fundamental change may silence some opponents of the status quo.

There are also more subtle, long-range ways of keeping certain items off the policy agenda. Business groups support public relations efforts that stress the advantages of capitalism while other interests stress the importance of keeping America a first-rate military power. Established public authorities seek to build citizen support for American political institutions via required civics classes in the schools and public displays of patriotism (e.g., saluting the flag, singing the national anthem, and observing national holidays). The fact that existing political institutions make it difficult to bring about fundamental change because of the multitude of "veto points" in our decentralized system of checks and balances is seldom stressed in these long-range efforts to build citizenship.

Attempts to influence attitudes in order to suppress certain demands also take the form of public relations campaigns directed at more specific targets. Oil companies provide films showing the great risks they take in searching for petroleum; investor-owned utilities advertise the benefits received from private (as opposed to public) ownership of utilities; and the Association of American Railroads hires a former astronaut to describe the fine work of the railroads. Unlike most advertising, none of these campaigns asks for business. They seek instead to create a favorable image for particular industries to preempt demands for sterner tax or regulatory policies.

Delaying tactics can also be used to keep certain issues from the agenda. Officials can deflect weakly organized groups (who find it difficult to sustain pressure on policymakers) by assigning their demands to committees for study, by sending them through the labyrinth of routines that characterize most decisionmaking systems, by postponing consideration of the matter, by making token changes in established programs, by showing cooperation (to decrease political pressure) and then reverting to previous stances, or by pointing to perennial constraints such as a tight budget.

Not all the items that fail to reach the policy agenda are kept off by the conscious efforts of opponents. Some proponents of change believe that certain problems cannot be resolved by the established political process and therefore do not work to have them placed on the agenda. Or supporters of an issue may anticipate the battle to achieve a place on the agenda and decide that the potential benefits are not worth the costs.

After an Issue Gets on the Agenda

Just because an issue attains a position on the policy agenda does not mean it will stay there. New issues come to claim their share of policymakers' time and money. Civil rights and poverty do not receive the attention they did a decade ago but energy and environmental protection are considerably more prominent. Moreover, a group's success in putting an issue on the policy agenda does not guarantee that actual policy decisions will favor the group's stand on the issue. To understand this paradox, it is necessary to examine subsequent stages of the decisionmaking process.

CLARIFYING AND RANKING GOALS

Clarifying Goals

Once the problems have been identified and placed on the policy agenda, the next logical step is for decisionmakers to clarify their policy goals. According to the model of rational analysis, it is only after they have clarified (and ranked) their goals that policymakers can effectively propose and evaluate the options for meeting those goals. Clarification of goals may follow directly from the statement of the problem. If, for example, a breakdown in law and order is seen as the problem behind urban riots, the goal may be to reinstate law and order. Unfortunately, the answer is not always that simple. If policymakers decide that poverty is the cause of civil disorder, their goals may include alleviating the symptoms of poverty by guaranteeing everyone a minimum income and distributing economic resources equally. Or they may seek to solve the problems behind poverty through improved programs of education and job placement that would make it possible for everyone to compete on the basis of "equal opportunity."

Although it appears sensible to clarify goals, policymakers actually do so on very few issues.[27] There is wide consensus on most general objectives such as the avoidance of nuclear war, the protection of American interests abroad, effective public services, equal opportunity, the reduction of poverty, and the control of inflation. But "interests," "equality," "poverty," etc. are loosely defined concepts, and agreement over general goals usually dissolves in conflict over the specific decisions that engender actual policies. When is opportunity equal, for example? To answer this question people must agree on a definition of equality and a means of measuring it in society. Different policymakers will have different views of these questions, and those views will affect their choice of goals.

When it is difficult to agree on goals, policymakers may seek general improvements. Oftentimes they have a better notion of what they want to escape (poverty, war) than what they want to achieve. In the words of David Braybrooke and Charles E. Lindbloom:

> Policy aims at suppressing vice even though virtue cannot be defined, let alone concretized as a goal; at attending to mental illness even though we are not sure what attitudes and behavior are most healthy; at curbing the expansion of the Soviet Union even though we do not know what positive foreign policy objectives to set against the Kremlin's; at reducing the governmental inefficiencies even though we do not know what maximum level of competence we can reasonably expect; at eliminating inequities in the tax structure even

> though we do not agree on equity; at destroying slums even
> though we are uncertain about the kinds of homes and
> neighborhoods in which their occupants should live.[28]

The lack of agreement on precise goals is probably inevitable in a large, diverse country where people have different values. There may be consensus that inadequate job training is a problem but disagreement over the proper role of government in resolving the problem. Additional confusion results when debates over means (such as minimum wage laws) are treated as debates over ends (such as assuring a decent income for everyone). Furthermore, those who disagree about the existence or nature of a problem are even more likely to disagree about goals.

Because of difficulties in agreeing on goals, policymakers may skip the stage of clarifying goals and get right down to a discussion of policy options. This bypass has several distinct, albeit somewhat perverse, advantages. If policymakers do not precisely state their goals, they cannot be held accountable for the results of their policies. Also, if goals are vague, it is easier to change them in light of new facts.

Finally, emphasizing alternatives rather than goals makes it easier for different groups to support a program: each group can maintain its own conception of the goals the program is designed to realize. In the words of Lyndon Johnson, "(t)here is no getting around it. If the full implications of any bill were known before its enactment, it would never get passed."[29] For example, school board members can approve a policy to increase spending for totally different reasons. They may differentially pursue goals of: developing greater student knowledge, skills, and mental ability; equalizing opportunity for learning and livelihood; improving character and moral values; freeing parents for work; changing the social structure by fostering mobility; increasing student and staff productivity; creating jobs for minority teachers; financing school construction and equipment purchases; or building a better gym for the high school basketball teams.[30] The ambiguous goals of policymakers make it less threatening for groups to be on the losing side of a policy conflict and this may dampen their opposition.

Ranking Goals

After clearly stating their goals, policymakers operating in a perfectly rational system would rank them to determine which goals should receive the most attention and resources. Of course, if goals are vague, this task is difficult if not impossible. It is further complicated by the fact that there are many people ranking goals in any policymaking system and no two of them share exactly the same priorities.

Methodical ranking would consist in assigning a scalar value to each clearly stated goal. However, it is difficult for even one person to rank policy goals because there may be hundreds or thousands of them. The problems of the process are compounded by all the variables of the policymaking system. Different persons may agree on goals but rank them differently. There is continual debate over national economic policy between those who would give priority to reducing unemployment and those who would emphasize curbing inflation. The unemployed and marginally employed would like the government to emphasize jobs whereas investors and retired people on a fixed income want the emphasis on fighting inflation. Other conflicts in goal rankings pit pollution abatement against industrial development and highway construction against fuel conservation. People may agree over the merits of each goal but quarrel sharply over their relative importance.

Conflicts over the ranking of goals also emerge as discussion moves from the general to the specific. Most people support the goal of reducing poverty, but when President Nixon introduced a reform of the welfare system that included a form of guaranteed annual income, many members of Congress argued that his proposals would be detrimental to the preservation of self-reliance, a value they ranked higher than the reduction of poverty.

Sometimes even very basic goals are not ranked because policymakers want everything and do not want to choose between policies. President Johnson tried to satisfy the competing claims of those supporting the expensive Great Society programs and those supporting the equally expensive

war in Vietnam by giving both sides what they wanted instead of choosing between them. This approach was consistent with his past experience as a legislative leader in which
he compartmentalized his leadership and moved in different
directions at the same time.[31]

The process of ranking goals would be much easier if
there were consensus on the criteria for ranking them. Not
only are possible criteria such as "justice" and "equity" rather
nebulous, but there is also no agreement on the standards by
which to judge whether certain measures are more or less
"just" or "equitable." The concept of "public interest" fares
no better as it has no widely accepted definition, and policies
rarely if ever affect all members of the public the same way.

Because of all these difficulties, policymakers seldom rank
goals in a formal or explicit manner. Roughly defined
priorities may emerge over a period of years as a result of
organized political support for a policy. Ultimately, implicit
rankings of policies requiring funding are revealed in the
budget: some programs receive more than others or their
allocations increase faster than others. With the decentralized system of policymaking that exists in the United
States, however, these "priorities" may differ from one state
or locality to another and vary with changing circumstances.

The lack of methodically ranked priorities makes it possible for policymakers to support contradictory goals in different policies. Federal highway programs have sponsored
fast, safe, convenient highways to the suburbs that enable
middle-class (mostly white) families and commercial estab-
lishments to move out of the central city. Moreover, the Federal Housing Administration, in the Department of Housing
and Urban Development (HUD), and the Veterans Administration have made it easy for middle-class families to buy
homes in the suburbs. These policies produced further racial
segregation of housing and schools within the metropolitan
area and reduced the number of service jobs available to the
poor. Increased commuting has also augmented pollution,
congestion, and energy consumption. At the same time, the
Urban Renewal Administration (also in HUD) has helped
cities to lure suburbanites back into the city by tearing down

slums, displacing the poor, and encouraging the building of commercial facilities and middle-class apartments. The Environmental Protection Agency has sought to combat pollution, the Federal Energy Office has encouraged people to conserve fuel, the Department of Health, Education, and Welfare and the courts have tried to decrease segregation in the schools, HUD has worked to decrease segregation in housing, other agencies have tried to provide jobs for the poor, and the Housing Assistance Administration (in HUD) has assisted cities in building low-rent housing for the poor.[32]

SUMMARY

An examination of the first three stages of rational decision-making—identifying problems, setting the policy agenda, and clarifying and ranking goals—does not provide an optimistic view of rational analysis as the basis for policy. There is often disagreement about the existence or extent of a problem. There is difficulty in reaching agreement about the problems that lie behind observed symptoms. Even if a problem is identified, there is no guarantee it will find a place on the policy agenda. And once the agenda is established, it is difficult for policymakers to clarify and rank goals. We now turn to the next stage of rational decision-making—that of collecting options and information—to see if it fares any better in the real world.

NOTES

1. Matthew A. Crenson, The *Un-Politics of Air Pollution* (Baltimore: Johns Hopkins University Press, 1971), Chapter 6.

2. Karl W. Deutsch, *Politics and Government,* 2nd ed. (Boston: Houghton Mifflin, 1974), p. 238.

3. See Edgar K. Browning, *Redistribution and the Welfare System* (Washington, D.C.: American Enterprise Institute for Public Policy Research, 1975), Chapter 2; U.S. Department

of Health, Education, and Welfare, *The Measure of Poverty* (Washington, D.C.: Government Printing Office, 1976); and U.S. Congress, Congressional Budget Office, *Poverty Status of Families Under Alternative Definitions of Income* (Washington, D.C.: Government Printing Office, 1977).

4. Alice M. Rivlin, *Systematic Thinking for Social Action* (Washington, D.C.: Brookings Institution, 1971), pp. 12 and 14. See also Daniel P. Moynihan, *The Politics of a Guaranteed Income* (New York: Vintage, 1973), p. 19.

5. Rivlin, *Systematic Thinking,* pp. 11 and 15. For other problems with information on the poor see Martin David, "Strategies for Improving Policy-Relevant Data on the Poor, " *The American Statistician* 30 (August 1976).

6. Margaret Gentry, "Facts on Crime Hard to Pin Down," *New Orleans Times-Picayune,* February 14, 1977, Section 1, p. 16.

7. Judith Innes de Neufville, *Social Indicators and Public Policy,* (New York: Elsevier, 1975), pp. 102, 116–117.

8. Gentry, "Facts on Crime," p. 16.

9. The index also affects payments for food stamps and welfare, federal school lunch and breakfast programs, alimony and child support payments, rents and condominium charges, and royalty payments. We have drawn some of the information for this discussion of the Consumer Price Index from "Worries about Accuracy in Tracking Inflation," *Congressional Quarterly Weekly,* February 8, 1975, pp. 279–283.

10. "Where Has the Hot Summer Gone?" *Newsweek,* August 4, 1975, p. 63.

11. Peter H. Schuck, " 'National Economic Planning': A Slogan Without Substance," *The Public Interest* (Fall 1976), p. 72.

12. Peter F. Drucker, "Pension Fund Socialism," *The Public Interest* (Winter 1976), p. 38.

13. Thomas Sowell, "Affirmative Action Reconsidered," *The Public Interest* (Winter 1976).

14. See Arthur M. Ross, "The Data Game," in *Inside the System,* 2nd ed., ed. by Charles Peters and John Rothchild (New York: Praeger, 1973), p. 199.

15. For a different view see Robert A. Levine *The Poor Ye Need Not Have With You: Lessons from the War on Poverty* (Cambridge, Mass.: MIT Press, 1970), p. 17.

16. Harry McPherson, *A Political Education* (Boston: Little, Brown, 1972), p. 375.

17. James L. Sundquist, *Politics and Policy* (Washington, D.C.: Brookings Institution, 1968), p. 393.

18. See Roger W. Cobb and Charles P. Elder, *Participation in American Politics: The Dynamics of Agenda-Building* (Boston: Allyn and Bacon, 1972), pp. 84–85.

19. Daniel P. Moynihan, *Maximum Feasible Misunderstanding* (New York: Free Press, 1970), pp. 24–25.

20. John C. Donovan, *The Politics of Poverty,* 2nd ed. (Indianapolis: Bobbs-Merrill, 1973), p. 22.

21. Morton H. Halperin, *Bureaucratic Politics and Foreign Policy* (Washington, D.C.: Brookings Institution, 1974), pp. 117–118.

22. Doris Kearns, *Lyndon Johnson and the American Dream* (New York: Harper & Row, 1976), p. 275.

23. The influence of the media in making the issues it continually emphasizes salient to the general public is still uncertain. On this question see Robert G. Meadow, "Issue Emphasis and Public Opinion: The Media During the 1972 Presidential Campaign," *American Politics Quarterly* 4 (April 1976); David H. Weaver, Maxwell E. McCombs, and Charles Spellman, "Watergate and the Media: A Case Study of Agenda Setting," *American Politics Quarterly* 3 (October 1975); Maxwell E. McCombs and Donald L. Shaw, "The Agenda-Setting Function of the Mass Media," *Public Opinion Quarterly*

36 (Summer 1972); and Thomas E. Patterson and Robert D. McClure, *The Unseeing Eye* (New York: Putnam's, 1976), Chapter 4.

24. John W. Kingdon, *Congressmen's Voting Decisions* (New York: Harper & Row, 1973), p. 207.

25. On this point see Peter Bachrach and Morton S. Baratz, *Power and Poverty: Theory and Practice,* (New York: Oxford University Press, 1970), pp. 43–46.

26. For example, see Norman C. Thomas, *Education in National Politics* (New York: David McKay, 1975), p. 185.

27. For examples of the failure to clarify goals, see *Ibid.,* p. 52, and Sundquist, *Politics and Policy,* pp. 113–114.

28. David Braybrooke and Charles E. Lindbloom, *A Strategy of Decision: Policy Evaluation as a Social Process* (New York: Free Press, 1963), pp. 202–203.

29. Kearns, *Lyndon Johnson,* p. 137.

30. For some examples from foreign policy see Halperin, *Bureaucratic Politics,* p. 78; and Robert L. Gallucci, *Neither Peace nor Honor* (Baltimore: Johns Hopkins University Press, 1975), pp. 47–54.

31. Kearns, *Lyndon Johnson,* p. 283.

32. Thomas R. Dye, *Understanding Public Policy,* 2nd ed. (Englewood Cliffs, N.J.: Prentice-Hall, 1975), pp. 174–175.

5

Options and Information

After a goal has been selected, the next step in an orderly and thorough decisionmaking process is to list all the alternative means or options for attaining it and all the information that is available regarding those options. As we shall see below, this process is no more easily accomplished than the previous stages in policymaking.

OPTIONS AND INFORMATION FROM THE BUREAUCRACY

A primary source of options and information for policymakers is the bureaucracy. Yet it is not a neutral instrument. Among the factors that influence the options and information the bureaucracy presents to policymakers are bureaucratic politics (the competition among organizational units and personnel striving to attain authority or preserve their own interests), bureaucratic structure (the nature of formal relations among bureaucratic units and the standard operating procedures used in each agency), and assorted other constraints (including the characteristics of each policymaker) associated with the sprawling administrative units of most large governmental bodies.

Bureaucratic Politics (1): Organizational Parochialism

One source of bureaucratic politics is the inbreeding of points of view peculiar to the personnel of an agency. Sometimes a homogeneity of attitudes perpetuates itself through the selective recruitment of new staff. The Department of Health, Education, and Welfare, for example, tends to attract persons with liberal views who support active policies for social services. People attracted to the Departments of Defense or Agriculture are likely to support well-known established policies. The result is that each governmental unit tends to have a uniform environment for policymaking. In addition, the policy views of public employees as a group are more homogeneous than we might expect. Bureaucrats of national, state, and local governments in the United States tend to have attitudes which are more liberal on social, domestic, and foreign policy issues than those of the general public.[1]

Aside from the initial recruitment of like-minded personnel, other aspects of organizational life foster parochial views among members of governmental units. Except for a few high-level policymakers, most bureaucrats spend the greater part of their careers within one agency or department. This long association encourages parochialism. People want to believe in what they are doing. A recent study found that agency affiliation is a better predictor of most of the policy attitudes of upper-level civil servants than the personal background of the officials.[2] One result of all this cliquishness is that intraorganizational communications pass mainly among persons who share similar frames of reference and who reenforce bureaucratic parochialism by their continued association.

David Truman illustrates this trend toward provincialism in his discussion of the businessmen who came to Washington to serve on the staff of the War Production Board or the Office of Price Administration during World War II. They began their service fuming against bureaucrats and their creations. After a while, however, they began to defend their agency to friends in the business world.[3]

The distribution of rewards within each organization creates further pressure to conform. Staff who do not share basic organizational goals are less likely to be promoted to important positions.[4] We shall discuss this point in more detail later.

Another cause of the parochial views of governmental agencies is the narrow range of each agency's responsibilities. The civilian and military leaders of the Defense Department do not deal with the whole budget for the national government, but only that part which pertains to defense. It is their job to recommend to the President and Congress what is best for defense and to let others worry about the trade-off between defense and education, health, or housing as well as the impact of defense spending on the overall economy. With each department focusing on what is best for its own programs, the general picture has few spokesmen.

Influences from outside an agency also encourage parochial views among bureaucrats. When interest groups and congressional committees support an agency, they expect continued bureaucratic support in return. Since these outsiders generally favor the policies the bureaucracy has been carrying out right along (which the outsiders probably helped initiate), what they really want is "more of the same."

Because of this externally supported parochialism, presidents distrust the objectivity of their departments (especially those oriented to a well-organized constituency, like Labor and Commerce). Their distrust forces them to rely on units in the Executive Office (such as the Council of Economic Advisers and the Office of Management of Budget), or independent individuals (such as university professors) for new options.[5]

Parochialism can lead policymakers to see different faces

on the same issue. In 1977 President Carter asked Congress for an authorization for a 20 percent cutback in wheat acreage and the placing of several million tons of food and feed grains in reserve. This proposal followed an intense internal debate in which the Department of Agriculture, reacting to the demands of farmers, wanted an even bigger cutback; the Treasury Department and the Council of Economic Advisers opposed any cutback out of concern for future consumer prices and the export potential of the United States should food shortages develop; and the State Department was concerned about the proposal's effects on international negotiations regarding an international grain reserve. In other words, policymakers in different bureaucratic units with different responsibilities saw the same policy in a different light and reacted differently to it.

Bureaucratic Politics (2):
Maintaining the Organization[6]

As a result of parochialism in the bureaucracy, career officials come to believe that the health of their organization and its programs is vital to the national interest. In their eyes, this well-being depends in turn on the organization fulfilling its missions, securing the necessary resources (personnel, money, authority), and maintaining its influence. Organizational personnel can pursue their personal quests for power and prestige, the goals of their organization, and the national interest all at the same time without perceiving any role conflicts. Moreover, policymakers in different organizational units are prone to see different faces in the same issue because of their different organizational needs.

The singlemindedness of policymakers attached to various agencies causes them to raise options and gather information that support the interests of their organization and avoid or oppose options and information that challenge those interests. In this way, the goals of maintaining an organization may displace the goals of solving the problems for which the organization was created. As one former high

White House official has written, "[f]or many cabinet officers, the important question was whether their department would have the principal responsibility for the new program —not the hard choices that lay hidden within it."[7]

Within most organizations there is a dominant view of the *essence* of the organization's mission and the attitudes, skills, and experience employees should have to carry out that mission. Although different groups within an organization have different primary functions (e.g., the Strategic and Tactical Air Commands within the Air Force), most organizations have some functions they clearly consider secondary. The United States Department of Agriculture sees serving the needs of farmers as its essential mission and not managing the Food Stamp program; the United States Army views ground combat operations as its essence and not air defense or advisory misssions; and for the United States Foreign Service, representing the United States abroad, negotiating, and political reporting are its primary functions, not managing foreign aid and military assistance programs or developing information services. Generally, agencies allocate fewer resources and less time to those functions they perceive as marginal.

Organizations usually propose options they believe will build upon and reenforce the essential aspects of their organizations. Although its bombing campaigns had not had unqualified success in previous wars,[8] the Air Force lobbied for strategic bombing and deep interdiction as its missions in the war in Vietnam. One way to do this was to argue for bombing as a central feature of U.S. policy in order to show its utility. Moreover, the lack of success of bombing in Vietnam[9] only reenforced the Air Force's efforts to step up bombing even further; the Air Force never admitted it was not accomplishing its objectives.[10] The National Air Pollution Control Administration fought the Department of Transportation for responsibility for research on alternatives to the internal combustion engine.[11] An organization will also vigorously resist efforts of others to take away, decrease, or share its essence and the resources deemed necessary to realize that essence.

Sometimes organizations do not seek new functions (which become options) because they fear the new missions may dominate those currently constituting the essence of the organization. The Air Force has long viewed long-range strategic bombing as its essence. Thus, it showed little interest in ballistic missiles until the mid-1950s, although they were technologically feasible earlier. Blinded by its attachment to the manned bomber, the Air Force saw ballistic missiles as a low priority weapons system which would be feasible only in the far future. It was only after the responsibility for developing missiles had been transferred to a new organization that was able to bypass the established review and control points within the Air Force and thereby avoid delays, obstruction, and inadequate funding that rapid progress was made.[12]

An organization may seek a secondary function, however, if not having it might jeopardize a more critical function. In the case of the Air Force and ballistic missiles, the Air Force exerted considerable effort to prevent another service from obtaining responsibility for ballistic missile development despite its own lack of interest. It did not want another service to have separate control of weapons capable of performing strategic bombardment.[13] Similarly, the Navy insists on transporting troops rather than allowing the Army to perform that function, partly to preserve the Marines' "essence" of coming ashore first. And the Air Force opposes Army efforts to provide close-in tactical support for its ground troops by fixed-winged aircraft to keep the Army from gaining a toehold in flying.[14]

Bureaucracies also try to rid themselves of functions that might dominate their essential roles. After World War II many officers in the Army urged creation of a separate Air Force as a safeguard against domination by flyers who had recently gained prestige.

In their struggles over roles and missions, bureaucrats may distort the information and options provided to senior officials. In Vietnam, the Air Force and Navy were each concerned that the other might encroach on its bombing missions; the Navy was also concerned about justifying the high cost of its aircraft carriers. Thus, they competed in their efforts at air warfare: over targets (with each service demanding its share of choice ones); over the number of missions flown (providing an incentive for flights regardless of their utility); over the number of MIGs downed (with the Air Force insisting the areas of responsibility be altered to bring its pilots into contact with more MIGs); and over the number of planes from each service downed by MIGs (leading to trade-off agreements between the services before meetings of the intelligence committee keeping track of downed American planes). The aspect of this interservice competition that was most damaging to the accuracy of the perceptions high-level decisionmakers had of American success in the war was the battle over the relative effectiveness of each service's air warfare. Each was concerned for future budgets and missions and could not let the other get the upper hand. Thus, each exaggerated its own performance and expected the other to do likewise.[15]

Budgets are another vital component of strategies to maintain an organization. This is true for grant-awarding agencies like the Department of Health, Education, and Welfare as well as for agencies with large operational capabilities like the military services and the Department of Agriculture. Because staff within governmental organizations generally believe their work is vital to the national or state interest, and because conventional wisdom stipulates that a larger budget enables an organization to perform its functions more effectively, units normally request an increase in funding and fight decreases. The size of a group's budget not only determines the resources available for its services but also serves as a sign of the importance others attach to the organization's functions.

Agency personnel also examine any substantive proposal to ascertain its impact on the budget. They rarely suggest adding a new function to their responsibilities if it must be financed from monies already allocated for ongoing activities. Moreover, components of large organizations, like units in the military or the Department of Health, Education, and Welfare, are concerned about maintaining or increasing their percentage of the larger unit's budget.

An organization's staff are likely to raise and support options that give them autonomy. In their view they know best how to perform their essential mission. They resist options that would place control in the hands of higher officials or require close coordination with other organizations. This desire for autonomy helps explain the military's opposition to foreign bases not under United States control, multinational military forces, and multiservice weapons systems. It also elucidates why both the Air Force and the Navy prefer that the Air Force retain independent control of strategic bombers and land-based missiles while the Navy retains exclusive control over Polaris missiles; neither force supports the idea of sharing responsibility for a combined strategic force. Similarly, both the State Department and the Treasury Department prefer that the Treasury conduct negotiations on trade while the State Department handles political relations with foreign governments. Finally, several agencies independently gather and evaluate national security intelligence from their own perspective.[16]

Because organizations seek to create and maintain autonomous jurisdictions, they rarely oppose each other's projects. This self-imposed restraint reduces the conflict between organizations and correspondingly reduces the options and information available to higher decisionmakers. In dealing with their superiors, the leaders of an organization often guard their autonomy by presenting only one option for a new program. The rationale is that if higher officials cannot choose among options they cannot interfere with the organization's preference.

Organizational leaders use several tactics to enhance morale among their subordinates. They raise and support options that would (1) maintain or increase their organization's functions (indicating the importance of its roles and its contributions to the national interest); (2) aid their organization in controlling its own resources; and (3) provide for and protect advancement for career officials. To attain this third goal, organizational leaders seek to ensure that the top jobs in their organization are held by career officials (reserving ambassadorships for Foreign Service Officers and not outsiders); resist efforts to decrease the number of jobs available for senior personnel; and oppose discrimination in assignments that have the most potential for advancement (combat assignments in the military).

Bureaucratic Politics (3): Organizational and Personal Influence

To achieve the policies they desire, organizations and individuals seek influence. In pursuing power, officials often further distort the processes of generating options and gathering information. One way for organizations to increase their influence is to defer to one another's expertise. The operations of all large-scale organizations, including governments, require a considerable degree of specialization and expertise. Those who possess this expertise, whether within executive agencies or congressional committees, naturally believe they know best about a subject in their field, and they therefore desire primary influence on the resolution of issues in their subject area. Because each set of experts has a stake in deference to expertise (they each receive benefits from it), reciprocal deference to expertise becomes an important theme in policymaking. Deference to expertise appears between senior officials within a department or in different departments, within and between legislative committees, and between levels of state and federal judicial systems. One result of this reciprocity is that fewer challenges to expert views are aired than might otherwise occur.

For several decades there has been an implicit agreement between the Departments of State and Defense that each would stay out of the other's affairs. During the war in Vietnam the State Department often took no part in shaping war policies and refrained from airing its views on many of them. Contributing to this restraint was Secretary of Defense McNamara's adamant belief that the State Department should not challenge the military's appraisal of the actual progress of the war. Once when Roger Hilsman, Director of the Department's Bureau of Intelligence and Research, attempted to do so, McNamara forcefully elicited a promise from Secretary of State Dean Rusk that such a challenge would not recur. He thus deliberately blocked the flow of information on the war. This meant that policymakers had to defer to Defense Department assessments that were often inaccurate and biased towards military rather than political solutions.[17]

An example of deference to expertise within a department took place in the preparation of Special Intewligence Estimates during the war in Vietnam. Although the Army and the Air Force each had considerable doubts about the other's operations, neither challenged the other's claims of success in their respective efforts (fighting a land war for the Army and bombing for the Air Force).[18]

Expertise is also suspect when the experts base their calculations on simple rules of thumb, standard operating procedures, compromises, and simple guesswork. The work of the scientists who set the performance goals for the first American ICBMs is a case in point. The goals were the explosive yield of a one-megaton warhead, a range of 5,500 nautical miles, and a capability for striking within a five-mile radius of the target. These goals were based on a round number, a quarter of the earth's circumference, and the upper level of an optimistic scientist's estimate.[19]

Although deference to expertise is not always a satisfactory way of resolving conflicts in policymaking, it is often the only possible course of action. Governmental agencies are the sole source of data and analysis on many issues. As their work becomes more and more specialized, it becomes more and more difficult to check their information and evaluations. This problem is exacerbated by a need for secrecy on most national security policies, which makes it necessary to limit even further the number of participants in the policymaking process.

Deference to expertise occurs in legislatures as well as in bureaucracies. Because legislators cannot even begin to develop expertise on the wide range of proposals they must consider, they often simply follow the lead of party colleagues serving on committees that have dealt at length with the various issues of policy.[20]

Of course, officials do not always defer to expertise. The recommendations of the experts are less convincing if there are conflicting opinions (leading experts such as those in the military services to compromise before they announce their views); if the experts offer advice on a policy outside their field of expertise (such as a nuclear physicist speaking on arms control or Dr. Spock on the war in Vietnam); if the policy conclusions attendant on expert advice run contrary to the interests of several officials in the policymaking process; if the experts have not considered relevant factors from areas where their expertise does not apply (such as teachers discussing the size of educational budgets while ignoring the trade-offs in taxes or funding for other policies); or if the experts themselves have a conflict of interest (such as lawyers on no-fault insurance proposals).

To take full advantage of deference to expertise and to further increase their influence, organizations seek to prevent their own experts from disseminating conflicting information and options. Contrary information and evaluations undercut the credibility of a unit's position. Moreover, by presenting several real options, a unit increases the range of possible policy decisions and commensurately decreases the probability that the option favored by the unit's leaders will be selected. Thus, the Joint Chiefs of Staff rarely disagree in their recommendations. One analyst calculated that they were unanimous on more than 99 percent of all issues between 1966 and 1969.[21]

If there are disagreements among the experts of an organizational unit, efforts to produce an appearance of unanimity can reduce the experts' recommendations to broad generalizations. A record of agreement on the least disputed common denominators usually fails to mention many controversial points that may be crucial to the ultimate success of the policy at issue. When compromise positions reach a high-level executive in a form that suggests a unified, consensual judgment, they can give the ultimate decisionmaker a false sense of security; the policymaker receiving the watered-down proposals may lack an awareness of the potential problems buried within the recommendations. For example, in the early days of bombing North Vietnam the Army wanted to show infiltration was increasing (to bolster its requests for more troops) while the Air Force wanted to show success in stopping it. They worked out a compromise in which the Defense Intelligence Agency (DIA) each month reported that "[e]nemy infiltration continued at a rate higher than last month; however, the cumulative effect of United States bombing has seriously degraded his ability to mount a large-scale offensive." It should be noted that there was no evidence the enemy was considering such an offensive.[22]

For bureaucrats interested in their own careers, the prospect of a deferred promotion or even dismissal makes them reluctant to report information that undercuts the official stands of their organizations. The example of Ernest Fitzgerald, an Air Force efficiency officer who was himself fired as an "efficiency measure" after he reported large cost overruns on the C5A, is not quickly forgotten in the bureaucracy. Nor is that of the Foreign Service Officers who frankly (and accurately) reported on the strength of the Communists in China during the late 1940s. They were driven from the Foreign Service for allegedly pro-Communist sympathies. Twenty years later, the Foreign Service's memory of these incidents may have inhibited candid reporting on the weakness of the South Vietnamese regime and the strength of the Viet Cong.[23] In addition, senior officials at the State Department are still complaining about the Foreign Service's lack of creativity.[24]

The hierarchical organization of the military and its norm of discipline make it especially susceptible to the stifling of dissent. A common expression at the Defense Intelligence Agency (DIA) is that it exists to provide justification for what Operations (the action arm of the military) wants to do. This protective role can result in distorted information and unfortunate policies. In 1966 the Air Force mistakenly bombed a North Vietnamese leper colony after Operations had pressured the DIA into labeling it a possible military headquarters; the DIA did not clearly contradict General Westmoreland's view that ships in Haiphong harbor were carrying war material and therefore should be bombed, despite information the agency possessed to the contrary; in 1968 it chose men to participate in the Paris peace talks who would not make waves with the Joint Chiefs' hard line; it did not go out of its way to impress on Operations that the information upon which a North Vietnamese installation at Son Toy (which the Army wanted to raid) was labeled a prisoner of war camp was highly tenuous (when raided, no prisoners were found); and in 1968 the DIA watered down its estimates of the Tet offensive because they contradicted the Joint Chiefs of Staff's view that it had been a total defeat for the enemy.[25]

If the anticipation of sanctions does not deter dissent within an organization, superiors can take more direct action to silence those who refuse to tow the line. When Lt. Col. John Vann left Vietnam with information disagreeable to his superiors, he was not debriefed, and he was not allowed to address the Joint Chiefs of Staff.[26] Neither the State Department's Bureau of Intelligence and Research nor the CIA's Intelligence Branch were informed of the impending invasion of the Bay of Pigs and thus they had no chance to give the President their pessimistic views of its success.[27] Certain DIA officials were not allowed to present a paper to the Joint Chiefs of Staff and General Westmoreland, our commander in Vietnam, which (it turned out) correctly predicted the focus of the enemy's massive Tet offensive.[28]

Some actions to stifle dissent are more subtle. Several people working in the State and Defense Departments who voiced doubts about the war in Vietnam witnessed a gradual decline in their influence which eventually forced them to resign.[29]

Sometimes the President will try to stifle dissent in the entire executive branch to prevent alternative views from being raised in broader arenas. In 1976 the Senate Select Intelligence Committee issued its final report on U.S. intelligence agencies. In the report the committee presented evidence of efforts by the Nixon administration to reverse an intelligence evaluation made by CIA director Richard Helms regarding the Soviet Union's new missiles with multiple warheads. The report also contained evidence that Helms had deleted judgments about both Soviet intentions to seek a first-strike capability to destroy U.S. strategic forces and the potential success of the U.S. invasion of Cambodia, judgments which the administration did not share. Helms and others denied that they had tailored their intelligence estimates to meet political demands, but the committee, along with John Huizenga who had chaired the board of national intelligence estimates, concluded that CIA directors are reluctant to engage in confrontations over substantive findings with others in the intelligence community, and they therefore avoid difficult issues.[30]

At times an illusion of competition conceals a basic consensus. Rivalry among the military organizations has reached legendary proportions, but much of it is superficial. Interorganizational competition among the armed services has primarily been over jurisdictional matters (which service should do what) rather than over questions of substantive policy.[31]

Experts also create an illusion of competition when they agree to compare their preferred action to infeasible alternatives.

> In the summer of 1964 the President instructed his chief advisers to prepare for him as wide a range of Vietnam options as possible for post-election consideration and decision. He explicitly asked that all options be laid out. What happened next was, in effect, Lyndon Johnson's slow-motion Bay of Pigs. For the advisers so effectively converged on one single option—juxtaposed against two other phony options (in effect, blowing up the world, or scuttle-and-run)—that the President was confronted with unanimity for bombing the North from all his trusted counselors. . . .[32]

As another means of seeking influence, organizations act to protect their reputations. Thus, some hedge against their estimates being wrong. Intelligence agencies tend to overestimate the probability of crises, and operating agencies tend to hedge by asking for more resources than they actually need, which makes an option appear more expensive or difficult than it actually is. Conversely, agency officials may be reluctant to bother senior officials about possible problems for fear of predicting problems that will not materialize. Either way, concern for organizational and/or personal reputations affects the information policymakers receive.[33]

In protecting their reputations organizations try to avoid reporting efforts that have failed. The CIA can serve as a good example of this point. One former official reports that the CIA criticized most U.S. programs in Vietnam except the pacification program—which it was running. After the Army received control of the program, the CIA evaluated it negatively too. When the CIA chief in Saigon was told that the local police were using the CIA informant system for their own purposes (sometimes leading to the death of innocent people), he replied that the program was "funded in the budget, and we're not going back to Washington and tell them it isn't working."[34]

Individual bureaucrats also act to gain the esteem of their colleagues. High federal officials "recognize that their ability to operate effectively in the bureaucracy on issues of paramount concern to them depends on being known by other participants for effectiveness with the President."[35] In the words of former Secretary of State Dean Rusk, "the real organization of government at higher echelons is . . . how confidence flows down from the President."[36] To avoid having their advice rejected, officials may not strongly advocate positions they consider sound if they know the President is unlikely to adopt those positions.

Because aides to high-level decisionmakers are dependent upon one person and probably desire to perpetuate their position, they may also refrain (perhaps unconsciously) from giving their superiors "unpleasant" information or from fighting losing battles. Or they may become overprotective of their reputations, knowing they can get high-paying jobs after successful tenures as executive aides. These tendencies are reenforced by an executive like Lyndon Johnson, who cut off access to aides who upset him with options and information he did not like. Former presidential press secretary George Reedy reports that the White House under

Johnson had an inner political life of its own: the staff carefully studied the President's psyche to gain and maintain access to him.[37] All of these strategies help distort a decisionmaker's view of reality.

Bureaucratic Structure (1): Hierarchy

The structure of administrative organizations is one of the factors that impedes the flow of options and information to higher-level decisionmakers. Most bureaucracies have a hierarchical structure, and the information on which decisions are based usually passes from bottom to top. At each step in this ladder of communication personnel screen the information from the previous stage. This is necessary because decisionmakers cannot absorb all the detailed information that exists on an issue. Some policymakers, like President Eisenhower, have demanded that subordinates summarize and synthesize information as it proceeds upwards. The longer the communication chain, the greater the chance that judgments will replace facts; nuances or caveats will be excluded; subordinates will paint a positive face on a situation to improve their own image or that of their organization; human error will distort the overall picture; and the speculations of "experts" will be reported as fact.[38]

Anthony Downs illustrates how information becomes distorted in his discussion of tests carried out to appraise the combat capability of a certain aircraft by means of radar bombing scores. Each bombardier had an incentive to do as well as possible (for his personal record) and some cheated in reporting their scores. Each squadron commander was motivated by competition (and the prospects of future promotions) to report squadron scores as favorably as possible. Often they did not inform their superiors that impressive scores were accomplished on sunny days with no strong winds and lots of visual assistance. The wing commanders in turn knew that the aircraft was competing with other weapons for money. Thus, they summarized scores reported to them as optimistically as possible before forwarding them to their superiors, leaving out such qualifying facts as the number of air aborts. By the time the summary of data reached the top of the hierarchy, the sum of these cumulative distortions had greatly exaggerated the aircraft's capabilities.[39]

This example reveals that screening, summarizing, and human error are not the only pitfalls in the transmission of information. When subordinates are asked to transmit information that can be used to evaluate their performance, they have a tendency to distort information to put themselves in the most favorable light. Body counts of killed enemy soldiers in Vietnam, made by the troops who had faced them in combat, were notoriously unreliable and became even more so as they were padded at each higher level of the military hierarchy to demonstrate successful operations.[40] Equally inaccurate were the estimates of bombing damage, made by the pilots flying the bombing missions.[41]

Although officials in stable bureaucracies, such as the military, could learn to understand and compensate for the biases of their subordinates, they usually do not. As in the above examples, those at each level may have an incentive to distort information themselves or pass on information they know to be distorted. Even if this is not the case, controlling for others' biases is inevitably a crude procedure.

Distortion can take place on a continuous and widespread basis. Throughout the war, official information from military headquarters in Vietnam was biased in the direction of excessive optimism, and was further distorted after receipt in the Pentagon. The reports were structured to bolster the military's view. Accurate reports of Viet Cong strength and North Vietnamese infiltration were diluted to show the Army was doing well; military setbacks became arguments for reinforcements.[42] South Vietnamese information was even worse. Their units attacked targets where Vietcong were known not to be in order to inflate statistics on attacks initiated against the enemy (while not suffering casualties). There were also fraudulent statistics on strategic hamlets and villages under government control. In the words of one

South Vietnamese general, "Your Secretary of Defense loves statistics. We Vietnamese can give him all he wants. If you want them to go up, they will go up. If you want them to go down, they will go down."[43]

Sometimes the distortion of information is quite ingenious. Officials can structure or transmit reports so that senior policymakers will see only certain information. Selectively forwarding information through different channels is one means of controlling reception. Some information channels lead directly to the top, and American commanders in Vietnam skillfully used this fact to their own advantage. In the mid-1960s when they desired a greater number of American troops, they wanted the President to see every bit of evidence that enemy infiltration was increasing. Reports of such activity were emphasized in General Westmoreland's daily cablegrams, which received high priority in Washington. Data from field reports on contacts with enemy units arrived weeks later via less visible channels. In 1967 the generals wished to emphasize victories. Therefore, the emphasis of Westmoreland's reports switched to "body counts" and the pacification of villages while enemy infiltration and recruitment figures were sent with mundane data through routine channels.[44]

Subordinates sometimes distort facts by not reporting those which indicate danger. President Eisenhower was not warned of the growing concern that the Soviet Union would be able to shoot down a U-2.[45] And President Kennedy was not apprised of the following problems with the contingency plan for the Bay of Pigs: the men participating in the invasion had not been told to go to the mountains if the invasion failed; there was a large swamp between the beach and the mountains which supposedly offered refuge; and only one-third of the men had received guerrilla training. Instead, he was simply informed that if the invasion failed, the men would go to the mountains and carry out guerrilla warfare.[46]

There are yet other problems in the bottom-up transmission of information resulting from the hierarchical arrangement of organizations. Because of the great amount of information that flows upwards in most organizations and the limited time high-level decisionmakers have to examine it, subordinates may exaggerate statistics and analyses to capture a decisionmaker's attention.[47]

The requisite specialization of roles within a hierarchy is another source of problems. People performing specialized tasks within an organization develop their own systems to classify, analyze, and communicate about their area of responsibility. If information does not fit into the classification scheme of a specialized vocabulary, it may not be transmitted.[48] Moreover, information that is transmitted outside the organized channels is difficult for nonspecialists, such as legislators, to understand.[49]

There is also the problem of information gatherers being so far removed from decisionmakers in the upper strata of the hierarchy that they fail "to transmit information upwards simply because the subordinate cannot visualize accurately what information his superior needs in order to make decisions."[50]

An additional feature of hierarchy of concern to us here is the different resources, status, and skills of participants in policymaking. These differences can affect the effectiveness of an official's arguments on policy alternatives. Higher status, experience in advocacy, and superior resources may be more important than the inherent strength of a proposal in influencing decisions. Those favoring escalation of the war in Vietnam were at the peak of the government, were in daily contact with each other, and had access to substantial staff and secret information. They could therefore coordinate their activities, prepare elaborately detailed predictions of the consequences of escalation, and be sure of a serious hearing. The dissenters from this view generally worked at lower levels in the hierarchy, did not coordinate their activities with those of other dissenters, and proceeded without adequate staff assistance. They could only offer personal judgments on various aspects of the war and hope someone would listen.[51]

The *absence* of hierarchy can also hinder the effective use of options and information. Unlike the executive branch, the legislature does not have a hierarchical structure. Consequently, the sum of the information available to the legislature as a whole is not a synthesis of the information available to each legislator. The legislature as a whole does not ask questions, individual members do; thus, not all members receive the answers. The lack of hierarchy therefore means that there is probably no integration of information.[52]

Even in the executive branch, there is no guarantee that information will eventually be centralized. There was a great deal of information pointing to the Japanese attack on Pearl Harbor, for example, but it was never fully organized.[53] No one brings forward all the political, economic, social, military, and diplomatic considerations of a policy in a recognizable manner for the deliberation of top decisionmakers[54] because the bureaucracy relevant to any policy is too decentralized and too large, and produces too much paper to coordinate information effectively.

Top decisionmakers may attempt to compensate for the problems of hierarchy by sending personal aides or outsiders to assess a situation directly and propose options. However, the person assigned to the task may determine the nature of the report more than the situation itself. When President Kennedy asked Dean Acheson to advise him on what action to take during the 1961 Berlin crisis, the answer was predictable for those familiar with Acheson: a hard-line stand emphasizing military force.[55] When the President sent General Maxwell Taylor and Walt Rostow on a fact-finding mission to South Vietnam, their recommendations for military action could have been predicted on the basis of their views before they left on the trip.[56]

Sometimes decisionmakers seek to supplement the positive reports of bureaucrats in the field with special questions posed directly from the top. However, Roger Hilsman reports that when the American Commander in Vietnam (General Harkins) was asked certain questions by the National Security Council, he answered as instructed by his superiors in the Pentagon, who had advised him of the proper answers even before he had received the questions.[57] Thus, hierarchies have defenses against end runs.

Some executives are tempted to evade intermediate unit

heads in the hierarchy and contact low-level personnel close
to a situation. However, this technique has many problems.
It may take a great deal of time to find a subordinate with
good information and the capacity to make a candid appraisal of a situation. Also, executives cannot bypass senior participants very often without lowering their morale and under-
cutting their operational authority.

President Kennedy's chief White House national security
adviser, McGeorge Bundy, ordered that cables to the State
Department, CIA, and Pentagon be sent directly to the
White House,[58] and not just to the Washington headquarters
of those departments where they could be summarized and
analyzed for transmittal to the White House. But this practice could not correct the distortion that may have gone into
the cables in the first place, and someone had to summarize
and synthesize the tremendous volume of information before it reached the President.

Bureaucratic Structure (2):
Standard Operating Procedures

Organizations use routines or standard operating procedures (SOPs) to gather and process information in a methodical fashion. However, the character of the SOPs may delay
the recognition of critical information, distort the quality
of information, and limit the options presented to policymakers.

In his case study of the Cuban missile crisis, Graham Allison shows that several weeks before the president was aware
of the missiles there was a good deal of information in the
United States intelligence system pointing to their presence.
But the time required by SOPs to sort out raw information
and double check it delayed recognition of the new situation.[59] Organizational routines also masked signs forecasting
the 1974 leftist coup in Portugal. Officials from the intelligence services of the CIA, the Defense Department, and the
State Department testified after the event that their routines
did not focus much attention on Portugal, and they could
not shift personnel rapidly to new areas of concern.[60]

SOPs affect not only *if* and *when* information is collected, but also the substance of the information. In Vietnam the military's concentration on the technical aspects of bombing caused it to substitute a set of short-run physical objectives for the ultimate political goals of the war. Military reports emphasized physical destruction per se rather than the political impact of such destruction. The enemy's capacity to recruit more men or rebuild a structure never seemed to enter into the calculations.[61]

Standard operating procedures give disproportionate weight to information entering the system from regular channels. For example, in the early stages of the Vietnam War, the routines gave undue credence to the reports of South Vietnamese officials without questioning whether the information favored South Vietnamese interests more than those of the United States and without giving proper weight to the opposing views of journalists and others outside the regular flow of information.[62]

SOPs structure the process of decisionmaking by pre-selecting those who will be asked for advice and pre-determining when they will be asked. There are routine ways of invading foreign countries and of determining agency budgets. Some persons will be involved at earlier stages than others, and some will be viewed as having more legitimate and expert voices in policy discussions. When Lyndon Johnson limited his circle of personal advisers on the war in Vietnam to a half-dozen top officials, those at a lower rung in the foreign policy hierarchy found it harder to have their dissents heard. In addition, there was little opportunity for others in the Cabinet to challenge the war policy because they were not in the right decisionmaking channels.[63]

Purely analytic units often have problems in being heard. According to Henry Kissinger, "unless you sit at a strategic point at which action is not possible without your office, there is a danger that you become simply an abstract, academic adjunct to an operating agency."[64] Thus, information is most likely to influence policymaking if the position of those who have it ensures they must be consulted before a decision is made.

Standard operating procedures also affect the nature of

the alternatives proposed by organizations. The original mission of the Economic Development Administration was to aid economically depressed *regions* such as Appalachia, principally by developing the economic infrastructure (including roads and electric power) and attracting industry. When the agency tried to aid the *city* of Oakland, it based its proposals on what it considered standard alternatives. But Oakland was in a prosperous area with a highly developed economic infrastructure, a great deal of manufacturing, and plenty of capital. The city's problems were those of unemployed minorities, and the SOPs of the Economic Development Administration did not allow the agency to deal with those types of problems.[65]

In 1975 Congress' Office of Technology Assessment charged that the Energy Research and Development Administration was pursuing a "narrow, hardware-oriented approach" that overemphasized costly technology (the sort of gadgetry that appeals to scientists and engineers) at the expense of energy conservation programs.[66] The Bureau of Reclamation has been criticized for not considering alternatives to reclaiming land through the large projects (such as major diversion dams) with which it is best equipped to deal,[67] and the Army Corps of Engineers has similarly been criticized for relying on structural alternatives for flood control.[68] Some people have even argued that Congress uses a regulatory approach to public policy rather than one that relies on analyses of the market and the price system, because the approach stressing economic incentives is less familiar to lawyers (who dominate Congress) than the regulatory approach which is based on a system of rights and duties.[69]

Inappropriate SOPs also occur in foreign policy. The Agency for International Development views economic development from the perspective of economists and avoids anthropological or political analyses.[70] In Vietnam the Army relied primarily upon the strategy of "search and destroy," the traditional attack mission of the infantry, and largely ignored winning the support of the population of South Vietnam, clearing populated areas of the enemy, and creating noncommunist enclaves. It also neglected unconventional approaches to warfare like that of the Green Berets, acting as if there was nothing special about counterinsurgency warfare.[71] These examples illustrate the traditional saying that the military is always prepared to fight the last war.

As a result of problems with established routines, top officials create special task forces of "outside" experts to develop new programs. Such bodies, brought together for a new purpose, are less likely than established agencies to be blinded by SOPs.

Constraints of Time

The diverse obligations of busy policymakers impose severe constraints on the amount of time they can give to generating and evaluating options and information. Sometimes they are simply too busy to deal with an issue at all and therefore do not give their views on it. Sometimes deadlines make it necessary for them to cease their search for more information and options and make a decision. Because of such time limits, the less controversial parts of elaborate policies often receive too little attention and contain too much logrolling.[72]

If a study about an issue is not available when policymakers must make a decision, the report will go unread.[73] If the report is required by a certain date and more than one person has been engaged to produce it, there is an incentive for the participants to "soften" their views in order to reach a consensus. This in turn can mask problems inherent in the policies recommended.[74] Or, the pressure of hammering together a report under a strict deadline may make it quite incoherent.[75]

Advisers as well as decisionmakers face time limits. Overloaded advisers may rely on others, equally overloaded, to bring crucial information to the attention of top policymakers. Several of President Truman's advisers believed there was a serious danger of Chinese intervention in the Korean War if the President attempted to reunite all of Korea under a non-Communist government. However, no one went to him to argue that he should reverse General MacArthur's orders. Each person thought that someone else would do it.[76]

Policymakers can use time constraints for their own purposes. Richard Nixon announced an early August deadline for the preparation of the first domestic program and thereby forced his advisers to get moving.[77]

Ignoring Available Information

Sometimes accurate information is available to decisionmakers, but they choose to ignore it. Critics of United States involvement in Vietnam charge that top U.S. officials, including the President, consistently ignored CIA reports that the military effort was not going well, that the bombing of the North was of limited value, and that the conflict was essentially a political one requiring political measures. It appears that there was too much organizational momentum and presidential commitment to the contrary for policymakers to make objective use of the information.[78]

Information is only as good as it appears in relation to information pointing in another direction. Decisionmakers often ignore good information if it is transmitted by an inarticulate adviser (frequently a problem in technical questions) or if complex problems of political feasibility make information supporting contrary courses of action more appealing. Officials may also not follow good advice because it is necessary for them to find short-run solutions to either satisfy public demands, gain re-election, or compensate for lack of time. Such short-term solutions preclude paying much attention to pre-empting crises destined to result from such problems as insufficient energy, food shortages, and overpopulation. Other times useful information may remain unnoticed because it is lost among the plethora of irrelevant information or "noise" that exists in most organizations.[79] In the area of national security, where many organizations exist to collect information, it is often impossible to make rational use of all the information collected.[80]

Sometimes an agency ignores information collected by another agency. Four days before the 1973 Mideast war erupted the National Security Agency learned the exact time and place of the planned Egyptian attack in the Sinai. The NSA passed this information on to the rest of the intelligence community on each of the days preceding the attack, but the other intelligence groups failed to give it sufficient weight because they underestimated Egypt's intentions.[81] They discounted it as one of the many misleading indications that circulate in the international intelligence community (some of whose members are always at work trying to mislead their counterparts in other countries). Both American and Israeli experts were operating with conceptions of Egyptian timidity that blinded them to the possibility of a major attack. Thus, on the morning of Yom Kippur, Israel and the United States were caught by surprise.[82]

Secrecy

Because only decisionmakers directly responsible for a policy are normally consulted on "secret" matters, fewer advisers contribute to secret deliberations than to debate on more open issues. This reduces the range of options that are considered in a secret decision and limits the analysis of the few options that are considered. The secrecy of President Johnson's Tuesday lunch group, which made the important decisions on the war in Vietnam, prevented an advance agenda. Thus, decisions were made without a full review of the options beforehand.[83] Secrecy also makes it easier for those directly involved to dismiss (intentionally or unintentionally) the dissenting or offbeat ideas of outsiders as the products of ignorance,[84] which is unfortunate because secret information is often inaccurate or misleading.[85] President Kennedy wished he had not been successful in persuading the *New York Times* not to publish the plans for the Bay of Pigs invasion; he afterwards felt that publicity might have elicited some useful critiques.[86]

Personal Characteristics of
Bureaucrats and Elected Officials

Managing Inconsistency. The structure of the policymaking system and the general patterns of bureaucratic behavior are not the only factors that affect the presentation and consideration of information and options. The personal traits of policymakers also leave their mark. The environment in which top decisionmakers operate, as we have already seen, is complex and uncertain. Yet the human mind is not comfortable with these characteristics. It has certain cognitive needs and prefers stable views, not continuous consideration of options. Lyndon Johnson's biographer writes that the President became obsessed with the correctness of his views on the war in Vietnam. He simply had to feel he was right or else he would have to open himself to the pain of reliving his old decisions and options.[87] The mind simplifies in order to deal with the complexities of the world, and resolves uncertainty by ignoring or deemphasizing information that contradicts existing beliefs.

These mental activities occur through unconsciously operating inference mechanisms which function to some extent in everyone's mind. Those mechanisms may have as great an influence on a person's beliefs as objective evidence. Consequently, most policymakers remain unreceptive to a major revision of their beliefs in response to new information. Moreover, they are unlikely to search for information that challenges their views or for options contrary to those they advocate.

An analysis of the consideration of alternatives during the war in Vietnam provides some prominent examples of mechanisms used unconsciously by policymakers to reduce the inconsistency—and thus the uncertainty and complexity—in their environment.[88] One relatively simple technique consists in attaching very negative consequences to alternatives, as top policymakers did to the option of "scuttle and run" from Vietnam. By concluding that the role of the United States in international relations would be seriously diminished by such action, decisionmakers dismissed an alternative that was widely advocated outside the government.

Related to this mechanism of predicting undesirable consequences is that of making inferences based on selected indicators to show that a particular situation could not possibly occur. If policymakers accept this inference of impossibility, there is no need for them to consider information pointing to the "impossible" situation, or alternatives to prevent or respond to it, or what effect it would have on the alternatives that *are* being considered. Before the massive North Vietnamese Tet offensive in early 1968, planning regarding the war was based on the assumption that no such offensive was possible; top U.S. officials paid little heed to information that contradicted this assumption. Data on the size and firepower of South Vietnamese forces, the number of hamlets pacified, and the number of communists killed provided welcomed positive feedback on U.S. policy and were accepted as signs of progress; policymakers never realistically weighed those indicators against the size of the task at hand. Another, classic example of the inference of impossibility was the belief that the Japanese could not attack Pearl Harbor. Because they were not expecting an attack, U.S. officials did not notice the signs pointing towards it. Instead, they paid attention to signals supporting their current expectations of enemy behavior.[89]

Another means of reducing inconsistency and thereby decreasing the pressure to consider alternatives is similar to what we commonly term "wishful thinking." Information inconsistent with ongoing policy is deemphasized by believing that undesirable conditions are only temporary and will ameliorate in response to current policy. Officials used this type of reasoning to garner support for the continued escalation of the war in Vietnam. All that was needed to force the enemy to succumb, they argued, was to keep up the pressure.

Yet another means of resolving uncertainty and simplifying decisionmaking is reasoning by analogy. Metaphors, as we have seen in our discussion of symbols in Chapter 3, simplify a complex and ambiguous reality by relating it to a relatively simple and well-understood concept. If a metaphor is then used as the basis of an analogy, the possibilities for error are considerable. The theoretical underpinning for the war in Vietnam was often characterized as the "domino theory" of international relations, which holds that the United States must prevent countries from falling to the communists because once one country falls, the one next to it will fall, and then the next—just like falling dominoes. An analogy frequently used to support opposition to the imperialistic ventures of other nations is "Munich," referring to the attempts of the allies to placate Hitler by legitimizing his control over Czechoslovakia. The beliefs supported by this type of reasoning seem to have strength independent of the available evidence, probably because the analogies simplify and provide a coherent framework for ambiguous and inconsistent information.

Discrediting the source of information and options is another means of reducing the complexity and resolving the contradictions with which policymakers have to deal. At first, President Johnson handled the critics of his war policy quite well, inviting them to his office and talking to them for hours. But as opposition increased and polls indicated a dip in his popularity, he responded to criticism by discrediting its source. He maintained that Senator William Fulbright (the chairman of the Senate Foreign Relations Committee) was upset at not being named Secretary of State; the liberals in Congress were angry at him because he hadn't gone to Harvard, because the Great Society was more successful than the New Frontier, and because he had blocked Robert Kennedy from the Presidency; the columnists opposed him to make a bigger splash and to follow James Reston and Walter Lippman; and the young were hostile because they were ignorant. According to Professor Doris Kearns, toward the end of his term, President Johnson saw the criticism of the war as a giant conspiracy. Indiscriminatingly piecing together bits of information, he developed a fantasy world of heroes and villains. Concentration on the conspiracy squandered a large amount of the President's energy and intruded suspicions and fears into every aspect of his daily work.[90] His attitude toward criticism of America's war policies undermined the impact of that criticism on the conduct of the war during his presidency.

Sometimes there is a devil's advocate on the inside who does not share the common views. In the Johnson Administration George Ball stood out for his contrary views on Vietnam. His objections, however, were discounted even before they were delivered because everyone assumed he was playing a predictable role.[91]

President Johnson went to considerable lengths to minimize the dissent with which he had to deal. Although he was hungry for information when things were going well, when he was under heavy criticism, he gave "signals" as to what he did and did not wish to hear from his advisers.[92] When this sytem failed to shield him, he dismissed his Undersecretary of State, his Special Assistant for National Security, and his closest White House aide. He also went so far as to reduce contact with such key people as Secretaries of Defense Robert McNamara and Clark Clifford and Vice-President Hubert Humphrey.[93] As the war progressed he even began bypassing the National Security Council and relied for information on a Tuesday lunch group of five or six people, all of whom were in basic agreement with his war policy.[94]

Each of the cognitive processes that reduce uncertainty and complexity can be a reasonable response to a situation. The point is that people are likely to rely on them not by conscious choice but because of the human need for certainty and simplicity. In each of the examples cited above policymakers made use of an inference mechanism to divert attention from vital information and ignore appropriate options. Potential actions that were considered disastrous would have been far less so than those that were taken, situations thought to be impossible actually occurred, hoped-for results from policies never materialized, inferences were based upon inappropriate analogies, and worthwhile criticism was rejected. Thus, the management of inconsistency clearly jeopardizes rational decisionmaking.

Maintaining Self-Esteem. In addition to simplicity and certainty, policymakers have other psychological needs for which they must provide. One of the most important of these—the need to maintain self-esteem—was identified by

Freud. We all have egos and we all have defensive mechanisms to protect them.[95] A policymaker may manifest those mechanisms by denying that his actions caused a problem or that there is a problem, assertions that make it unnecessary to reconsider policies or examine new options. Lyndon Johnson's discrediting of the sources of criticism served to protect his self-esteem. The more his popularity plunged, the more he needed evidence that *he* was not at fault. The intellectuals, the press, the liberals, and the Kennedys provided convenient scapegoats for the causes of his problem, and his feeling of martyrdom temporarily increased his self-esteem. He found protection in the world of his imagination.[96]

According to his top domestic adviser, Joseph Califano, when the 1965 Watts riot broke out, Johnson at first refused to look at the cables, take calls, or make decisions about how to deal with the crisis. He simply refused to acknowledge that it was happening. His first perceptions of the rioting seemed to be in terms of the harm the rioters had done to *him,* indicating a connection between the event and Johnson's ego. Although he sometimes seemed to understand the frustrations behind the rioting in Watts and other cities, he never seemed to understand that he might bear partial responsibility for the conditions causing those frustrations.[97]

Decisionmakers also reduce uncertainty (and its accompanying doubt and anxiety) and sustain self-esteem by operating as part of a group. In a cohesive group, particularly one that operates under stress, is insulated from outside experts, and has a leader who actively promotes his own alternatives, unconscious processes sometimes occur that produce what one author has termed "groupthink."[98] Under conditions of groupthink, a group's members become excessively optimistic about the effectiveness and morality of their decisions while underestimating the difficulty of their task or discounting the skill and morality of those opposing them. As a result, they disregard warnings that would force them to reconsider their assumptions and thereby take greater risks than they would agree to take individually.

To protect itself from uncertainty and anxiety the group

may develop an illusion of unanimity. It may also impose direct pressure on any member who challenges the group's illusions or commitments. More subtle self-censorship of deviation from the group's apparent consensus may take place, and self-appointed "mindguards" whose task is to protect the group from adverse information may emerge.

These group dynamics bolster the personality characteristics that incline leaders to overlook the unfavorable consequences of their actions. The tendencies toward conformity are usually strongest in those who are most fearful of disapproval and rejection. And the more threats there are to the self-esteem of members of a cohesive group, the more it will tend to seek consensus at the expense of critical thinking.[99]

Other Psychic Needs.   Policymakers have many other psychic needs that may affect their consideration of information and options. Much remains unclear about this subject, but the scope and significance of these needs are great. For example, the bombing of North Vietnam may have satisfied several of President Johnson's psychological needs. It provided relief from the pressures and debates of decisionmaking; it was an action that accomplished something. The bombing also helped him ease his fear of appearing weak, and it supported his self-deceiving conjecture that the end of the war was in sight, which would enable him to free funds for his Great Society programs.[100]

Individual Perspectives and Abilities.   In addition to the intellectual mechanisms that provide consistency and support to a policymaker's psychological environment, there are other personal factors that inhibit the presentation of divergent viewpoints.

A decisionmaker with heightened fears of security leaks may place loyalty above either competence, independence, or openness as a criterion for recruitment of advisers. He also may control the information flow tightly and keep even insiders in the dark.[101] (One of the reasons President Johnson relied so heavily upon the Tuesday lunch group is that he felt the National Security Council leaked too much information.) Congressional liaison chief Lawrence O'Brien and Vice-President Hubert Humphrey had been in constant contact for months before they became aware of each other's views on Vietnam. Because President Johnson equated criticism with disloyalty, even the highest officials in the White House kept their dissent to themselves.[102]

Sometimes advisers find it difficult to disagree with a decisionmaker because of the latter's strong, dynamic, and/or magnetic personality. Former White House Assistant Chester Cooper writes that President Johnson polled his foreign policy advisers one at a time to discover their views of alternative policies for winning the war in Vietnam. Each would say "I agree" although Cooper, and probably others, did *not* agree and even dreamed of saying "no." But he never did.[103] Moreover, because the Secretaries of State and Defense spent more and more time in the White House as the war progressed, they became more and more dependent on the President and more submissive to him. Johnson was always at his best, argues Professor Kearns, when other people had independent power and he was forced to pay attention to the necessities of bargaining and modify his drive to dominate by the realistic perception of the limits of his resources. But when these external limits were gone, Johnson fell back on his need to dominate all.[104]

Some policymakers want a range of options but are unable to preserve group solidarity and accept the interpersonal tensions inherent in an advisory system of close give and take. President Nixon opted to work alone from written reports of diverse options. He did not take advantage of face-to-face confrontations between advocates who could pinpoint their critiques of each other's positions or raise follow-up points. In contrast, Presidents Franklin D. Roosevelt and John F. Kennedy recognized the value of heated discussion and seemed to thrive on pitting divergent advisers against one another.

The substantive views of top officials also influence their processing of information. They provide a frame of reference for raising and evaluating options. During the Cuban missile crisis President Kenendy precluded diplomatic and nonmilitary responses to the situation at the outset and actually considered a fairly narrow range of military options (contrary to much conventional wisdom). He believed that the presence of Soviet missiles in Cuba greatly increased the threat to the national security of the United States and that the Soviet Union would remove the missiles only if forced to do so by the threat of American military sanctions.[105]

Decisions about U.S. participation in the war in Vietnam were also molded by the views of top officials. The premises they shared included the contentions that a non-Communist Vietnam was important to the security and credibility of the United States; the war-torn country was a critical testing ground of U.S. ability to counter communist support for wars of national liberation; communism was a world conspiracy; and South Vietnam would fall to the North without American aid. When these views were coupled with President Johnson's more general premises that all problems were solvable and that the United States could do anything, U.S. intervention was a foregone conclusion.[106]

A decisionmaker's view of a problem and proposed response to it is especially likely to foreclose consideration of alternatives in a crisis when there is a premium on rapid and decisive action. The North Korean invasion of South Korea in 1950 and the civil war in the Dominican Republic in 1965 were seen by Presidents Truman and Johnson, respectively, as threats to the United States, and they decided virtually immediately that American armed forces would be employed in those countries.[107]

The substantive views of advisers are another factor determining what information and opinions are presented to decisionmakers. There are numerous examples of top advisers failing to consider or pass on to the President information contrary to their own views and not allowing people whose opinions contradict their own to have direct access to the President.[108] This problem is particularly critical when decisionmakers rely heavily upon regular channels of information and have only a very few persons reporting directly to them, as was true in the Truman, Eisenhower, and Nixon presidencies.

An adviser's conception of his job influences his delivery of information and options. President Eisenhower's Secretaries of Defense, Charles Wilson and Neil McElroy, considered themselves managers of the Department and did not become involved in disputes over foreign policy or strategic doctrine. By contrast, Secretary of Defense Robert McNamara adopted an aggressive stance as an adviser. But McNamara's colleague, Secretary of State Dean Rusk, did not consider it his job to participate in policy disputes with his colleagues or the President. In fact, many observers thought he did not effectively present State Department views on Vietnam or other foreign policy issues.[109]

ACCESS OF PRIVATE INTERESTS TO POLICYMAKERS

Many important options for achieving a goal originate outside of government. Because private interests have a significant role in policymaking, it is important to examine the governmental access available to them.

Governmental Structure

Several features of government in the United States greatly enhance access to policymakers. First, the federal system offers interests a choice between several levels of government. Each interest can seek access to those policymakers who are most likely to support the policies it desires. If an interest loses at the national or state level, it can try again at the other.

Historically, business interests have argued for state regulation of business activity. Each state has a narrower set of interests than the country, and many state and local governments are more conservative than the federal government. Moreover, several states lack the administrative capacity to regulate business effectively. One problem with the state regulations currently in effect however, is a lack of uniformity. A national corporation may have to cope with fifty different sets of regulations.

Federalism need not imply conflict between the nation and the states. Rather the system fosters competition between interests seeking favorable access to policymakers at different levels of government. Terms such as "states rights" and "local autonomy" represent the manipulation of symbols for the purpose of influencing public policy. Civil rights advocates and their opponents have continually fought over whether national or state government should make and enforce antidiscrimination laws, with civil rights advocates favoring the federal level. Labor unions have also found policymakers at the national level to be the most receptive to their demands.

Not only does the United States have a multilevel system of government, it also maintains a separation of powers at each level. As a result, different interests find some branches more receptive to their demands than other branches. Elected chief executives take a broader view of public policy questions than legislators because a broader electorate puts the executive in office. For many years liberal and conservative presidents of both political parties have tried to reduce aid to "federally impacted" school districts. The program offering this aid was originally set up to ease the educational burden of a sudden influx of children of federal employees into a school district. But the aid, which has continued long after the temporary adjustment periods have passed, frequently goes to very wealthy school districts. However, Congress has consistently refused to end a program that aids the constituencies of so many of its members. Judicial support for civil rights since 1954 offers another example of the distinctive orientation of each branch of government. Blacks turned to the courts to achieve school integration when the other branches of government were unwilling to take the lead.

The lack of strong, tightly disciplined political parties also facilitates access to government officials. Officials gain office largely on their own and not at the leave of their party, and the chief executive stands regardless of losses in the legislature. Federal judges have lifetime appointments, and many state judges have long terms and/or run on nonpartisan tickets. All of this inhibits party discipline and means that there is no sustained cohesive force in government that can overcome its decentralized structure and exclude interests from access to policymakers.

In addition, each branch of government offers multiple points of access. Legislatures are composed of two houses (except in Nebraska) and numerous committees. In Congress alone there are nearly 400 different committees and subcommittees. The executive branch has hundreds of departments, bureaus, agencies, and commissions. In many state governments the heads of departments are elected independently of the governor; they may even be political adversaries who have an incentive to provide hearings to groups unfriendly to the governor. The judicial branches of both federal and state governments are composed of several largely independent tiers of courts.

The sprawling governmental units of the United States often defy coordination. The undisciplined political parties are seldom able to enforce a common line on their members in the legislature, and civil service regulations insulate executive branch employees from much political pressure. Presidents and governors are potential coordinators but cannot intervene in all of the activities of their executive branches or concentrate their efforts to cover all the issues being considered by the legislature. Usually chief executives give special attention to only high priority issues. Administrators and legislators who work outside those priority areas have great freedom from executive surveillance. This makes them prime targets for interest groups seeking access to policymaking.

Another feature of the separation of powers is the veto that each branch has over the actions of the others. This potential for halting action not supported by an overwhelming majority of officials makes it difficult to alter the status quo. Substantial change requires the active support of different branches that represent interests in different ways.

What is really required for change is not just a simple majority of the population, but extraordinary majorities occuring simultaneously in different governmental arenas.

Democratic Norms

The broad access of interest groups to American policymakers rests on widely shared political norms, including respect for popular access, acknowledgment of minority preferences, and voluntary compliance with government regulations. Policymakers generally believe that they should confer with interested parties. They also believe that minority preferences should be protected and not lost in simple majority rule. Finally, policymakers view coercion as distasteful and inefficient and attempt to negotiate policies that interest groups will support.

Some norms are written into statutes. Laws provide for some 1,400 governmental advisory bodies (at the federal level alone), require administrative units to give advance notice of policy changes, and allow interested parties to express their views on changes. In addition, agencies establish numerous conferences to provide interested parties the opportunity to express themselves, and legislative hearings are normally open to all. In some settings policymakers enact their "rules" only after interested parties have agreed on their content.[110]

Interest groups enjoy regular opportunities to express their views on administrative appointments, especially to group-oriented units like labor, commerce, education, agriculture, and regulatory agencies. Groups also have influence on the composition of advisory commissions. When the Surgeon General of the United States set up a commission on television violence in the early 1970s, the candidates for membership were subject to veto by the television networks. CBS did not exercise a veto, but NBC and ABC vetoed seven persons. Two of the twelve members ultimately chosen were network directors of research. Three other positions went to scholars currently or previously under contract to the networks.[111]

Use of Channels of Communication

Despite the availability of a variety of channels through which interests can communicate their demands and preferences, many groups do not make effective use of this ready access to policymakers. A study of foreign trade legislation found that business interests took little advantage of opportunities to communicate with legislators.[112] On the other end of the socioeconomic spectrum, the failure of the poor to use such channels is even more pronounced.[113]

Policy Triangles

Because of the pervasive compartmentalization of the policymaking process and the multiplicity of opportunities for private groups to gain access to decisionmakers, many important decisions are made by "policy triangles." In the words of John Gardner, a former Secretary of Health, Education, and Welfare, and more recently president of Common Cause:

> Questions of public policy . . . are often decided . . . by a trinity consisting of representatives of an outside lobby, middle-level bureaucrats, and selected members of Congress, particularly those concerned with appropriations. In a given field, these people may have collaborated for years. They have a durable alliance that cranks out legislation and appropriations on behalf of their special interest.[114]

Policy frequently reflects the interests of the groups directly affected. Private groups provide political support for public officials and the officials provide policies that serve the interests of the groups. Moreover, those interests favored by current policies oppose new ones and those with special access to certain arenas fight to maintain their access. They do not want competing pressures or the unknown consequences of new organizational arrangements. Thus, when President Johnson wanted to merge the Labor and Commerce Departments, he was opposed successfully by groups

with access to each. Similarly, merchant shipping interests
opposed moving the Maritime Administration from Commerce to the new Department of Transportation. At times
the relationships between groups and agencies transgress
normal guidelines. In mid-1975 the people of Louisiana
learned that a lobbyist for the state AFL-CIO was being paid
$18,000 per year by the state government to serve as a con-
fidential assistant to the state commissioner of labor.[115]

Some groups work to effect policy that does not directly
benefit their members. For example, the Army, Navy, Air
Force, Marines, National Guard, and the Reserves have all
spawned separate interest groups, composed primarily of retired officers, which seek to benefit their former services.
There are even groups associated with subunits, such as the
Airborne Association for former paratroopers. Although
some such groups are primarily social and focus their ener-
gies on periodic reunions, others support the requests of the
departments around which they organize. When the Navy
League holds its annual convention, the Secretary of the
Navy, the Chief of Naval Operations, and several members
of the Congressional Armed Services Committees usually
put in an appearance.

Other groups seek to influence policy for reasons of
economic self-interest. The interest groups that represent
defense contractors work closely with members of Congress
on the armed services committees and defense appropriations subcommittees, and with personnel in the Defense Department to form a policy triangle concerned with defense
budgets and the development of new weapons systems.
There are further links along the sides of this triangle.
Executive branch personnel who support a strong defense
posture frequently "retire" to well-paid positions in the defense industries. Members of the key defense committee in
Congress seek both a strong defense policy and contracts for
industries in their districts; several of them also achieve high
rank in the military reserves.

Other policy triangles push for the development of rivers
and harbors, land reclamation, agricultural commodities,
civil aviation, highways, veterans' benefits, health services

and research, patents, federal grazing lands, forest products, education, and merchant shipping.[116] Moreover, smaller, two-sided subgovernments center around regulatory commissions. Nearly 30 percent of the persons appointed to the commissions since 1960, and over 50 percent of the appointees since 1970, have come from the regulated industry. Thirty-two of the eighty-five persons who left these commissions between 1960 and 1975 were employed at some time in the five years after they left the commission by the industry regulated by the agency that formerly employed them.[117]

What is missing from these ongoing, mutually supportive relationships are representatives of more general interests. For example, citizens or groups concerned with cutting defense expenditures, or opposing a certain type of weapons system or the expansion of the federal highway system typically stand outside these closed relationships.

Subgovernments may be particularly influential in shaping distributive policies, which authorize a decentralized distribution of funds to recipients in the form of contracts, tax provisions, or direct payments to individuals. These policies do not affect interests competing with each other, are not particularly visible to the public, and lend themselves to logrolling and compromise in the legislature.[118]

SUMMARY

The rational model of decisionmaking dictates that decisionmakers consider a complete range of options and full information on them. Yet policymakers rarely attain this goal. Several aspects of bureaucracies foil rational analysis: organizational parochialism and the goal of maintaining the organization; the search for organizational and personal influence; the constraints of hierarchy; standard operating procedures; limited time; the failure to use available information; and secrecy. The emotional needs and demands of key policymakers also affect the quality of information that actually shapes decisions. Although the decentralized nature of government and widely shared democratic norms provide numerous opportunities for private interests to present their views, groups do not use the available channels of communication with equal skill or frequency. As a result, these channels often transmit a limited range of views to the officials who make critical policy decisions. This problem is aggravated by the desire of those composing policy triangles to have only one side of an issue heard.

NOTES

1. See Kenneth John Meier and Lloyd G. Nigro, "Representative Bureaucracy and Policy Preferences: A Study in the Attitudes of Federal Executives" (paper presented at the Annual Meeting of the American Political Science Association at San Francisco, September 4, 1975); Kenneth John Meier, "Representative Bureaucracy: An Empirical Analysis," *American Political Science Review* 69 (June 1975), pp. 540–541; and Herbert Kaufman, *The Forest Ranger: A Study in Administrative Behavior* (Baltimore: Johns Hopkins University Press, 1960).

2. Meier and Nigro, "Representative Bureaucracy and Policy Preferences."

3. David B. Truman, *The Governmental Process* (New York: Knopf, 1951), p. 454.

4. See Kaufman, *The Forest Ranger,* pp. 182–183.

5. Joseph Califano, Speech given at Princeton University Conference on Advising the President, Princeton, New Jersey, October 31, 1975.

6. Our main source for this section was Morton H. Halperin, *Bureaucratic Politics and Foreign Policy* (Washington, D.C.: Brookings Institution, 1974), Chapter 3.

7. Harry McPherson, *A Political Education* (Boston: Little, Brown, 1972), p. 298.

8. See, for example, *U.S. Strategic Bombing Survey* (Washington, D.C.: Government Printing Office, 1947).

9. See Raphael Littover and Norman Uphoff, eds., *The Air War in Indochina,* revised ed. (Boston: Beacon Press, 1972) and sources cited therein; and Robert L. Gallucci, *Neither Peace nor Honor: The Politics of American Military Policy in Vietnam* (Baltimore: Johns Hopkins University Press, 1975), pp. 61–64.

10. Gallucci, *Neither Peace nor Honor,* pp. 48–49, 78–80.

11. Charles O. Jones, *Clean Air: The Politics of Pollution Control* (Pittsburgh: University of Pittsburgh Press, 1975), p. 61.

12. Edmund Beard, *Developing the ICBM* (New York: Columbia University Press, 1976). The author also shows that somewhat similar situations occurred regarding the Minuteman missile (Air Force), Polaris missile (Navy), continuous aim gunnery (Navy), and the strategic bomber (Army), pp. 211, 217–218, 230–232.

13. *Ibid.*

14. *Ibid.,* pp. 38–39.

15. Morris J. Blackman, "The Stupidity of Intelligence," *The Washington Monthly* 1 (September 1969), p. 26; Gallucci, *Neither Peace nor Honor,* pp. 80–86; Patrick J. McGarvey, *C.I.A.: The Myth and The Madness* (Baltimore: Penguin Books, 1973), pp. 131–132; and Doris Kearns, *Lyndon Johnson and the American Dream* (New York: Harper & Row, 1976), p. 272. For an earlier example of distortion relating to bombing effectiveness see Harold L. Wilensky, *Organizational Intelligence* (New York: Basic Books, 1967), p. 30.

16. For a different type of example see Jerome T. Murphy, *State Education Agencies and Discretionary Funds* (Lexington, Mass.: D.C. Heath, 1971), pp. 22–23.

17. David Halberstam, *The Best and the Brightest* (New York: Random House, 1972), pp. 347–349, 257, passim.

18. *Ibid.,* p. 359.

19. Herbert F. York, *Race to Oblivion: A Participant's View of*

the Arms Race (New York: Simon and Schuster, 1970), pp. 88–90. See also pp. 91–92 for other examples of expert arbitrariness.

20. See, for example, John W. Kingdon, *Congressmen's Voting Decisions* (New York: Harper & Row, 1973), Chapter 3.

21. McGarvey, *C.I.A.,* p. 126. See also Gallucci, *Neither Peace nor Honor,* p. 89. For interesting discussions of attempts to reduce dissent on congressional committees, see John F. Manley, *The Politics of Finance* (Boston: Little, Brown, 1970), especially Chapters 2–4; and Richard F. Fenno, Jr. *The Power of the Purse* (Boston: Little, Brown 1966), especially Chapters 3–5.

22. McGarvey, *C.I.A.,* p. 130. See also pp. 28–30, 125.

23. James C. Thompson, Jr., "How Could Vietnam Happen?" in *Who We Are: Chronicle of the United States and Vietnam,* ed. by Robert Manning and Michael Janeway (Boston: Little, Brown, 1965), p. 200. See also McGarvey, *C.I.A.,* p. 9; and Gallucci, *Neither Peace nor Honor,* p. 99.

24. "The Secretary and the Foreign Service," *Department of State Newsletter,* No. 163 (December 1974), p. 9; and Nathaniel Davis, "Diplomacy for the 70s," *Department of State Newsletter,* no. 160 (September 1974), inside cover.

25. For these and other examples see McGarvey, *C.I.A.,* pp. 55–56, 126–127, 132–133, 149–151, 10–11, and 154–155. Also see Gallucci, *Neither Peace nor Honor,* p. 66; and Halberstam, *The Best and the Brightest,* pp. 359, 280–281.

26. Halberstam, *The Best and the Brightest,* pp. 204–205. See also p. 203.

27. Roger Hilsman, *To Move a Nation: The Politics of Foreign Policy in the Administration of John F. kennedy* (New York: Dell, 1967), p. 31.

28. McGarvey, *C.I.A.,* p. 128.

29. Halberstam, *The Best and the Brightest,* pp. 361–378; and Gallucci, *Neither Peace nor Honor,* pp. 132, 98–99.

30. "Divided Intelligence Panel Issues Final Report," *Congressional Quarterly Weekly Report,* May 1, 1976, p. 1020. See also McGarvey, *C.I.A.,* p. 14; and Sam Adams, "Vietnam Cover-Up: Playing with Numbers," *Harper's,* May 1975.

31. Francis E. Rourke, *Bureaucracy and Foreign Policy* (Baltimore: Johns Hopkins University Press, 1972), p. 24.

32. Thompson, "How Could Vietnam Happen?," p. 209. For other examples of the illusion of competing alternatives see Kearns, *Lyndon Johnson,* p. 280; and Gallucci, *Neither Peace nor Honor,* pp. 41–45.

33. Halperin, *Bureaucratic Politics,* pp. 145–146.

34. McGarvey, *C.I.A.,* pp. 12, 129.

35. *Ibid.,* p. 121. See also Thompson, "How Could Vietnam Happen?," pp. 201–202.

36. "Mr. Secretary: On the Eve of Emeritus," *Life,* January 17, 1969, p. 62B.

37. George E. Reedy, *The Twilight of the Presidency* (New York: New American Library, 1970). See also Halberstam, *The Best and the Brightest,* pp. 456–458; and Kearns, *Lyndon Johnson,* p. 322.

38. See McPherson, *A Political Education,* p. 292 for an insider's view of the synthesis of information at the White House.

39. Anthony Down, *Inside Bureaucracy* (Boston: Little, Brown, 1966), p. 123.

40. Alain C. Enthoven and K. Wayne Smith, *How Much Is Enough?: Shaping the Defense Program, 1961–1969* (New York: Harper & Row, 1971), p. 295.

41. Blackman, "The Stupidity of Intelligence," p. 24; and McGarvey, *C.I.A.,* pp. 112–113.

42. Bernard Brodie, *War and Politics* (New York: Macmillan, 1973), p. 211–212; Kearns, *Lyndon Johnson,* pp. 272–273; and Halberstam, *The Best and the Brightest,* pp. 186–188, 544–545, passim.

43. Halberstam, *The Best and the Brightest,* pp. 186–188.

44. Patrick J. McGarvey, "The Culture of Bureaucracy: DIA Intelligence to Please" *Washington Monthly,* 2 (July 1970), pp. 71–72.

45. Halperin, *Bureaucratic Politics,* p. 160.

46. Theodore C. Sorensen, *Kennedy* (New York: Harper & Row, 1965), p. 302.

47. Joseph Frankel, *The Making of Foreign Policy: An Analysis of Decision Making* (New York: Oxford University Press, 1963), p. 97.

48. James G. March and Herbert A. Simon, *Organizations* (New York: Wiley, 1958), p. 165.

49. See, for example, Thomas R. Wolanin, "Congress, Information and Policy Making for Postsecondary Education: 'Don't Trouble Me with the Facts,' " *Policy Studies Journal* 4 (Summer 1976), pp. 390–391.

50. Herbert A. Simon, *Administrative Behavior,* 2nd ed. (New York: Free Press, 1951), p. 163.

51. For example, see Kearns, *Lyndon Johnson,* p. 262. For other examples of inequalities in advocacy see McPherson, *A Political Education,* p. 231; McGarvey, *C.I.A.,* pp. 132–133; Roger Hilsman, *The Politics of Policymaking in Defense and Foreign Affairs* (New York: Harper & Row, 1971), p. 169; and Adam Yarmolinsky, "The Military Establishment (Or How Political Problems Become Military Problems," *Foreign Policy,* No. 1 (Winter 1970–1971), pp. 95–96. For a more elaborate discussion of this problem see Alexander L. George, "The Case for Multiple Advocacy in Making Foreign Policy," *American Political Science Review* 66 (September 1972).

52. Wolanin, "Congress, Information and Policy Making," pp. 386–387.

53. Roberta H. Wohlstetter, *Pearl Harbor: Warning and Decision* (Stanford, Calif.: Stanford University Press, 1962).

54. *Ibid.* See also McGarvey, *C.I.A.,* p. 111.

55. Arthur M. Schlesinger, Jr., *A Thousand Days* (Boston: Houghton Mifflin, 1965), pp. 381–384.

56. See Halberstam, *The Best and the Brightest,* p. 172 for an analysis of the Taylor-Rostow report.

57. Hilsman, *To Move a Nation,* pp. 492–493.

58. Sorensen, *Kennedy,* p. 372.

59. Graham T. Allison, *Essence of Decision: Explaining the Cuban Missile Crisis* (Boston: Little, Brown, 1971), pp. 118–123. There were also SOPs for determining when and where the U-2 surveillance flights (which discovered the missiles) should take place.

60. "NSA Hearings Postponed," *Congressional Quarterly Weekly Report,* October 11, 1975, p. 2184.

61. Kearns, *Lyndon Johnson,* p. 272.

62. Halperin, *Bureaucratic Politics,* p. 143. See also Adams, "Vietnam Cover-Up." For another example of acceptance of formal channels see McGarvey, *C.I.A.,* pp. 113–114.

63. Kearns, *Lyndon Johnson,* pp. 262 and 318–319.

64. Judy Gardner, "Kissinger Retains Principle Role in Foreign Policy," *Congressional Quarterly Weekly Report,* November 18, 1975, p. 2353. For a similar conclusion see Walter Williams, *Social Policy Research and Analysis: The Experience in the Federal Social Agencies* (New York: American Elsevier, 1971), p. 9.

65. Jeffrey L. Pressman and Aaron B. Wildavsky, *Implementation* (Berkeley: University of California Press, 1973), Chapter 7.

66. Peter J. Bernstein, "Energy: Overdoing the Complex," *New Orleans Times-Picayune,* November 16, 1975, Section 1, p. 18.

67. Steve H. Hanke and Richard A. Walker, "Benefit-Cost Analysis Reconsidered: An Evaluation of the Mid-State Project," in *Water Resource Research* 10, No. 5 (1974), p. 906.

68. Irving K. Fox and Orris C. Henfindahl, "Attainment of Efficiency in Satisfying Demands for Water Resources," *American Economic Review* 54 (May 1964), p. 204. See also McPherson, *A Political Education,* pp. 225–226.

69. Allen V. Kneese and Charles L. Schultze, *Pollution, Prices, and Public Policy* (Washington, D.C.: Brookings Institution, 1975), pp. 116–117.

70. Theodore Geiger and Roger D. Hansen, "The Role of Information in Decision Making on Foreign Aid," in *The Study of Policy Formation,* ed. by Raymond A. Bauer and Kenneth J. Gergen (New York: Free Press, 1968), pp. 361–362.

71. See, for example, Gallucci, *Neither Peace nor Honor,* pp. 115, 116, 119, and 124.

72. Wolanin, "Congress, Information and Policy Making," p. 387.

73. Halberstam, *The Best and the Brightest,* p. 358; Frank L. Lewis and Frank G. Zarb, "Federal Program Evaluation from the OMB Perspective," *Public Administration Review* 34 (July/August 1974), p. 314; Wolanin, "Congress, Information and Policy Making," p. 391.

74. Halberstam, *The Best and the Brightest,* pp. 358–359.

75. McGarvey, *C.I.A.,* p. 152.

76. Richard Neustadt, *Presidential Power* (New York: Wiley, 1960), pp. 144–146. For another example of officials assuming someone else would pass along vital information, see McGarvey, *C.I.A.,* p. 124.

77. Richard P. Nathan, *The Plot That Failed: Nixon and the Administrative Presidency* (New York: Wiley, 1975), p. 17.

78. Chester L. Cooper, "The CIA and Decision-Making," *Foreign Affairs* 50 (November 1972), p. 231.

79. See Wohlstetter, *Pearl Harbor,* especially p. 387.

80. McGarvey, *C.I.A.,* pp. 24 and 67–68.

81. "The Warning That Wasn't," *Newsweek,* October 13, 1975, p. 27.

82. For other examples of the problems of transmitting information between organizational units see Wohlstetter, *Pearl Harbor,* p. 395; and Gallucci, *Neither Peace nor Honor,* p. 128.

83. Kearns, *Lyndon Johnson,* p. 321. On this general point see also Wohlstetter, *Pearl Harbor,* p. 394.

84. See Cooper, *The Lost Crusade: America in Vietnam* (New York: Dodd, Mead, 1970), p. 416; and Jann Wenner, "Daniel Ellsberg: Part I," *Rolling Stone,* November 8, 1973, p. 37.

85. Wenner, "Daniel Ellsberg," pp. 36–37 and 47.

86. Theodore C. Sorensen, *Watchmen in the Night* (Cambridge, Mass: MIT Press, 1975), pp. 106–107.

87. Kearns, *Lyndon Johnson,* p. 310. For another view of Johnson's need for certainty, see McGarvey, *C.I.A.,* p. 17.

88. For the insightful discussion of inconsistency management which informed the discussion here, see John D. Steinbrunner, *The Cybernetic Theory of Decision* (Princeton, N.J.: Princeton University Press, 1974), pp. 114–121.

89. Wohlstetter, *Pearl Harbor.*

90. Kearns, *Lyndon Johnson,* pp. 312–317. Professor Kearns adds that the President was confirmed and not corrected in this view by the White House staff.

91. On this point see Reedy, *Twilight of the Presidency,* p. 11; and Thompson, "How Could Vietnam Happen?" p. 201.

92. Halberstam, *The Best and the Brightest,* p. 588; and Kearns, *Lyndon Johnson,* pp. 319 and 323.

93. Halberstam, *The Best and the Brightest,* p. 534. See also Cooper, *The Lost Crusade,* pp. 402 and 416.

94. Kearns, *Lyndon Johnson,* pp. 319–320.

95. See, for example, Fred A. Greenstein, *Personality and*

Politics (New York: Norton, 1975) for the importance of ego defense. On this general topic see also James David Barber, *Presidential Character,* revised ed. (Englewood Cliffs, N.J.: Prentice-Hall, 1977); and Alexander L. George and Juliette L. George, *Woodrow Wilson and Colonel House: A Personality Study* (New York: John Day, 1956).

96. Kearns, *Lyndon Johnson,* pp. 314 and 311–312.

97. Kearns, *Lyndon Johnson,* p. 305.

98. Irving L. Janis, *Victims of Groupthink* (Boston: Houghton Mifflin, 1972).

99. Janis, *Victims of Groupthink,* pp. 191 and 206.

100. Kearns, *Lyndon Johnson,* p. 263.

101. See Thompson, "How Could Vietnam Happen?" p. 200, and Cooper, *The Lost Crusade,* pp. 414–416.

102. Lawrence O'Brien, *No Final Victories* (New York: Ballantine, 1975), p. 228.

103. Cooper, *The Lost Crusade,* p. 223.

104. Kearns, *Lyndon Johnson,* p. 324.

105. Erwin C. Hargrove, "Presidential Personality," *American Journal of Political Science* 17 (November 1973), p. 826.

106. Kearns, *Lyndon Johnson,* pp. 196 and 263; and Galluci, *Neither Peace nor Honor,* pp. 42–43. For other examples see Yarmolinsky, "The Military Establishment, pp. 83–87; and Morton H. Halperin, "The Decision to Deploy the AMB: Bureaucratic and Domestic Politics in the Johnson Administration," *World Politics* 25 (October 1972), p. 78.

107. George, "The Case for Multiple Advocacy;" and Lyndon B. Johnson, *Vantage Point: Perspective of the Presidency, 1963–1969* (New York: Popular Library, 1971), pp. 187–205.

108. See James A. Meader, "Information, Organizational Structure, and Foreign Policy Formation" (unpublished

M.A. thesis, Tulane University, 1975); John Dean, *Blind Ambition: The White House Years* (New York: Simon and Schuster, 1976), pp. 35 and 314–315; and Fred I. Greenstein, "A President is Forced to Resign: Watergate, White House Organization, and Nixon's Personality," in *America in the Seventies: Problems, Policies, and Politics,* ed. by Allan P. Sindler (Boston: Little, Brown, 1977), p. 76.

109. Halperin, *Bureaucratic Politics,* p. 12; Halberstam, *The Best and the Brightest,* p. 345; Gallucci, *Neither Peace nor Honor,* pp. 32–33; I.M. Destler, *Presidents, Bureaucrats, and Foreign Policy* (Princeton, N.J.: Princeton University Press, 1972), pp. 236; and Hilsman, *The Politics of Policy Making,* p. 169.

110. Gilbert Y. Steiner and Samuel K. Gove, *Legislative Politics in Illinois* (Urbana: University of Illinois Press, 1960), p. 52.

111. "The New Violence," *Newsweek,* February 14, 1972, p. 66.

112. Raymond A. Bauer, Itheiel de Sola Pool, and Lewis Anthony Dexter, *American Business and Public Policy,* 2nd ed. (Chicago: Aldine Atherton, 1972).

113. Harold L.Wolman and Norman C. Thomas, "Black Interests, Black Groups, and Black Influence in the Federal Policy Process: The Cases of Housing and Education," *Journal of Politics* 32 (November 1970).

114. Cited by Kenneth R. Cole, Jr., "Should Cabinet Departments and Agencies be More Influential?," in *Has the President Too Much Power?,* ed. by Charles Roberts (New York: Harper's Magazine Press, 1973), pp. 129–130.

115. "Avant Serves in Dual Role," *New Orleans Times-Picayune,* August 15, 1975, Section 1, p. 3.

116. See Randall B. Ripley and Grace A. Franklin, *Congress, the Bureaucracy, and Public Policy* Homewood, Ill.: Dorsey, 1976) for a thorough discussion of subgovernments on the national level.

117. "Public Dislike for Regulatory Agencies Cited by Symposium," *New Orleans Times-Picayune,* November 9, 1975, Section 1, p. 24.

118. Ripley and Franklin, *Congress, the Bureaucracy, and Public Policy.* For an argument that the different types of policies cited here are intertwined see Dean E. Mann, "Political Incentives in U.S. Water Policy: Relationships between Distributive and Regulatory Policies," in *What Government Does,* ed. by Matthew Holden, Jr., and Dennis L. Dresang, *Sage Yearbook in Politics and Public Policy,* Vol. 1 (Beverly Hills, Calif.: Sage, 1975). See Robert S. Gilmour and John A. McCawley, "Environmental Preservation and Politics: The Significance of the 'Everglades Jetport,'" *Political Science Quarterly* 90 (Winter 1975–1976) for an example of how the organization of an interest can broaden the questions considered in a policy debate.

6

Assessing Alternatives

After assembling as much information as possible on alternative policies, policymakers following the rational model should assess each option's potential for maximizing their goals. In their evaluation they should first predict and analyze the consequences of each alternative to determine how completely it will accomplish the goals it is designed to meet. Secondly, they should compare the benefits and costs of alternative policies to discover which provides the most efficient means of achieving those goals. Finally, they should examine the equity of the distribution of the consequences of each alternative.

PREDICTING THE CONSEQUENCES OF POLICIES

It is necessary to predict the consequences of a policy alternative to assess its potential for achieving its goals. But it is difficult to make accurate predictions, and different people have different approaches to this aspect of policymaking. As a result, predicted consequences often form the basis of political conflict. For example, in 1974 and again in 1975 Congress passed and President Ford vetoed bills designed to protect the environment against strip mining. The President contended the bills would abolish thousands of jobs, mean higher utility costs for energy consumers, and increase American reliance on imported oil. Representative Morris Udall, the floor manager for the bills in the House, disagreed. He argued that the President had distorted the probable effects of the bills.[1]

The calculation of the consequences of policy must take into account numerous variables. Consider just a few of the judgments policymakers have been asked to make in recent years regarding the consequences of welfare provisions. Will a guaranteed annual income encourage able-bodied people to avoid work? If the working poor are allowed to keep a portion of their earnings and still qualify for some welfare benefits, just which of the many possible ratios between wages and welfare benefits will encourage recipients to do the most work? If large families receive more welfare benefits than small families, will this encourage the poor to have more children? If the federal government provides public jobs at respectable wages for those out of work, will this attract poorly paid persons who already hold jobs in the private sector? Does the fact that the public provision of social services is dependent upon income deter the recipients of those services from increasing their incomes?

Outside the field of welfare policy there are countless other questions concerning individuals, institutions, and technology about which policymakers must make predictions. Will a decrease in taxes cause people to spend more on automobiles, homes and major appliances, and therefore help ease a depressed economy? Will an increase in taxes provide individuals with an incentive to limit their spending, and thus decrease inflationary pressures? If so, just what levels of taxes will accomplish the desired results? (Similar questions are relevant for gasoline taxes and gasoline consumption and pollution taxes and the discharge of pollutants.) Will labor unions accept wage and price controls in the long run? How will local television stations use the added half-hour of prime time allotted them by the FCC? What will various national health insurance plans cost? Will interest-bearing checking accounts decrease the amount of money available for home mortgage loans in savings banks? Will nuclear reactors be a safe source of energy? Can their radio-active waste be stored safely for the proper length of time? Will the ABM system work? Will the B-1 bomber be obsolete as soon as it is built?

Prediction is also a risk of foreign policy. In 1974 Congress attempted to force the Soviet Union to liberalize its restrictions on the emigration of Jews and other Soviet citizens by making that a condition for the ratification of a treaty dealing with international trade. Similarly, in 1974 Congress cut off aid to Turkey in an attempt to influence the Turkish government to be less aggressive towards Greece and the Greek population on Cyprus. Both of these congressional tactics were contrary to the desires of the President, and both seem to have failed because the Soviet Union and Turkey did not respond as Congress had predicted.

The executive branch has its own problems predicting the future behavior of other nations. Its failures include predictions that the Chinese would not intervene in the Korean War, that the Cuban population would rise up and support the Bay of Pigs invasion, and that the North Vietnamese would succumb to continued American escalation of the war.

Predicting the Consequences of Ongoing Policies and Incremental Changes

Problems in prediction can occur with an ongoing policy. In fiscal 1975 the Basic Educational Opportunity Grant program spent only three-fourths of the federal scholarship money appropriated for poor college students. The administrator of the program reported that the formula for allocating the money was so complicated that it proved impossible to determine how many students would apply, how much each one would be entitled to, and how many of those who qualified actually attended schools.[2] In fiscal 1976 the program ran out of money as the Office of Education erred by 18 percent in predicting the percentage of eligible students who would apply for grants.[3]

Most "new" policies simply provide for incremental changes from existing policies. Therefore, it should be possible for policymakers to observe ongoing policies and discover what "worked" and what did not, and then predict the effects of quantifiable changes in those policies. Unfortunately, things are rarely that simple.

Consider some problems in setting educational policy.[4] Predictions generally rely upon correlations between aspects of educational policy and children's performance during a limited period of time: typically one school year. However, education is a cumulative process. Children move between classes, schools, and school systems, and may have a good teacher in one year and a bad one the next. What is really important for the child is the cumulative experience that comes from a variety of programs.

The variables used as components of educational policy also stymie accurate prediction. They are often easy-to-measure elements like the average size of classes, the number of books in a library, teacher's scores on verbal tests, the age of a school building, and the money spent on a school system. Such items may be less important than difficult-to-measure components like the selection of library books or the rapport between teachers and students.

A related difficulty in making inferences from educational studies is that the unit of observation is usually a school or a classroom. Even in studies of individual children, researchers assume that all children in the same grade or school have the same access to resources. Averaging things out in this way can mask significant relationships; it is nevertheless necessary because most school systems keep central books and have no way of knowing which resources are devoted to a given student at any given school.

The measurement of educational results entails other problems. The tests used to measure achievement may not measure what schools teach; students who take the tests may not care how they do on them; the tests may be poorly constructed, measure native ability rather than skills acquired in school, and be biased against students from certain cultural backgrounds; few studies follow students long enough with successive tests to discern the long-run effects of a program; and different school systems use different tests (making it difficult to compare them).

Even if there is some correlation between educational policy and educational results, the analytical methods of assessment may not uncover them. Variations between schools may be too small for clear differences in results to emerge. And varying one component of educational policy, like class size, may affect student performance only if it occurs in conjunction with changes in other factors such as the way teachers spend their time. Moreover, the relationship between policy and performance may hold only for certain types of students, like slow learners. Finally, it is frequently impossible to separate the effects of educational and socioeconomic factors on academic performance because middle and upper class children generally go to better schools. It is also difficult to separate the effects of one of several ongoing programs from the effects of the others.

These difficulties in assessing the effectiveness of various policies are compounded by the fact that programs are usually not organized to generate information about their effectiveness. Most school systems, for example, use test data mainly for grading individuals, not for evaluating programs. Many systems also fail to collect or use cumulative information on children's school experiences. Moreover, major federal programs often do not include such things as an experimental design, control groups, or attempts to define promising methods or approaches and try them out under different conditions.

Problems of bureaucratic politics may hinder the evaluation of policy. Those in charge may not want to be assessed. A National Assessment of Education was begun in 1969. It included a series of tests on various subjects to be administered periodically to national samples of children and adults. But it could not show how particular schools or school systems performed because school officials rejected all designs that would have permitted systematic comparisons between schools or school districts.[5] If promotions are based on student performance on tests, there is an incentive for principals and teachers to help the students "cheat" (perhaps by preparing them for the tests), and thereby inflate the test scores.[6]

The costs as well as the benefits of ongoing policies are difficult to predict. In 1975 some Office of Management and Budget officials concluded that by the year 2000 spending for federal income assistance programs would amount to about 33 percent of the Gross National Product (as compared to 9.3 percent in 1975). However, they based this conclusion on assumptions that new programs would be created, benefit levels would increase, and eligibility requirements would be liberalized and/or eligible populations would increase and make use of available benefits at the same rates as in the past. In other words, the calculations projected the continuation of a past rate of growth (over inflation). The Congressional Budget Office challenged these assumptions. The creation or liberalization of assistance programs is a matter of choice. If now new programs are added, spending for income assistance will increase only marginally by the year 2000—to about 10 percent of the GNP (based on estimates of the size, income distribution, and age structure of the United States population in the future). The Congressional prediction remains similar whether future benefit levels and eligibility requirements are assumed to be governed by current law, adjusted to reflect increases in the cost of living, or escalated to keep pace with expected growth in incomes.[7]

Policy Experiments

It is rare that major changes in policy are tested in a systematic manner. There are several reasons for this failure, but before discussing them it is useful to illustrate the utility of policy experiments by looking at two which did take place.

In the early 1970s the Office of Economic Opportunity

contracted with six private firms to test the educational success of "performance contracting," whereby school boards
contract with private firms rather than the public school system to teach school children. The firms are paid according
to the subsequent performance of the students on stand-
ardized tests. Those running the experiement concluded
that performance contracting did not provide a better education than conventional public school teaching.[8] This experimental evaluation of a policy alternative enabled policymakers to see its consequences and not have to speculate
on them.

A second experiment dealing with welfare policy tested
the economic impact of various forms of the negative income
tax. Different combinations of a guaranteed income and tax
rates on earnings were provided samples of poor families
having different social traits. These "experimental groups"
were compared with "control groups" that received no special benefits. The various studies concluded that a guaranteed income would not provide a disincentive for poor
families to work.[9]

One barrier to effective policy experiments is the pressure
to allow as many people as possible to participate in a promising alternative. The designers of the Headstart preschool
programs sought to provide disadvantaged children with
early education so they could compete more effectively when
they entered a regular kindergarten. The original plan was
to select relatively few children to take part in a year-long
program, but there was such pressure to include more children in the promising activity that the overall limit on funds
permitted only shorter programs. As a result, the policy
could not be tested as originally envisioned.[10]

A similar problem occurred with the Model Cities Program, originally conceived as an experiment to concentrate
funds on one central city to see if it was possible to rebuild
and rejuvenate it. But many cities wanted to be models. By
the time the bill left the executive branch it included provisions for 66 cities and Congress was unwilling to let the bill
pass without spreading the funds to 150 cities in the first
year and more than 250 cities by the second year. The avail-

able funds were therefore spread so thin that it was impossible to judge the program according to its original goals.

Experiments cannot be carried out on some policies because of constitutional and legal restrictions. It is not possible to set up systems of integrated and segregated schools in order to compare them, nor can officials establish experimental systems of harsh and lenient punishments for violators of criminal laws or economic regulations. Similarly, legislators cannot levy different rates of income tax on citizens of different states.[11] Even if these experiments were constitutional, they would not be politically feasible.

Other policies do not lend themselves to experimentation because they are of the "all-or-nothing" variety. Our economic system is too interdependent to allow researchers to carry out an experiment in monetary policy in just one of its segments. Policies affecting foreign affairs and national security are also of the all-or-nothing variety: it would be impossible to experiment with only the political aspects of our relations with a certain country, for example, without having that experiment affected by economic factors that were not part of the experiment. Moreover, policymakers and citizens generally consider economic and foreign policies too critical for experimentation.

The desire to minimize risks taken with individuals also limits experimentation. The areas of health care and medicine offer great risks and are subject to elaborate safeguards that minimize an experimenter's leeway. This is true not only for procedures and products, but also for experiments with health delivery and payment systems that might deny people access to medical care. Policies ranging from those determining national defense to those regulating education and child care also have a potential for harm that makes policymakers reluctant to experiment with them.[12]

Some people oppose the idea of distributing policy benefits by chance. But this random distribution is necessary if policymakers are to base their decisions on experiments using a cross-section of the target population and a control group denied the benefits under consideration. If participants "select" themselves into a program and if the personal characteristics that incline them to take part in the program are related to their post-program behavior, then the evaluation of the program will be biased.

Lack of political feasibility also militates against experiments that take too long. In fact, the time span between a program's conception and the analysis of its results may be several years; but most decisionmakers think in terms of months, which encourages broad action in the short-run. Other political drawbacks to experimentation include the reluctance of officials to admit they are not already sure of the consequences (they may not receive funds if they admit this) and the reluctance of officials to use money for an experiment rather than for the substantive policy itself.[13]

Political feasibility also affects the use of the results of experiments. Those who are politically accountable for policies, such as local school superintendents, do not wish to publish results indicating policy failures. Those who originally proposed alternatives attempt to suppress negative results of experiments in order to uphold their reputations for wise advice. Administrators of experiments may actually "juggle" results either because it is in their interest to do so (such as in educational performance contracting) or because they do not desire to be associated with a "failure"—which may impinge on their reputations as administrators. For all these reasons, program managers should not evaluate their own programs.

Even when it is feasible to determine the impact of a policy option by experimentation, there are many difficulties in designing a good experiment. Some people modify their behavior if they know they are part of an experiment. Clinical psychologists call this the "Hawthorne effect": people will change their behavior when interest is shown in them—independently of the form that interest takes. Second, participants in an experiment often act differently knowing that the situation is only temporary. Their behavior may be quite different in a similar, relatively permanent situation.

Another problem comes from people's interaction with those around them. It may be one thing when only a few people in a neighborhood receive a guaranteed income. If their neighbors work, those in the experiment may work because of social pressures. But the results may be quite different if everyone in the neighborhood receives a guaranteed income. The solution to such a problem may be to include the entire neighborhood in an experiment. Yet that would be very expensive, as it would be necessary to experiment with a variety of neighborhoods having persons with different social traits.

There are additional problems in experimental design. It is necessary to both replicate an experiment to validate its results and test the proposed policy under different circumstances and contingencies. The problem is that special cases always arise that were not anticipated prior to the initiation of the experiment. Moreover, variations between the execution of repetitions of the same experiment are inevitable because teachers, physicians, social workers, and other professionals resist programming by experimenters. If variations from one professional to another are too great, they will not allow reasonable comparisons between the overall results of the experiments on one possible policy with those of an alternative because the differences *within* the experiments on one policy may exceed those *between* alternatives.[14]

Another problem in experimentation with policy alternatives is the large number of variables that account for human behavior. We noted this obstacle earlier in connection with ongoing educational policies. There are so many factors affecting the educational success of children that it is often difficult to discern the effects of a new teaching technique. Positive or negative results may be caused by changes in family life or classmates rather than by the change in teaching. It is very hard to keep the factors not being assessed constant while the experiment is taking place for two reasons: many of them are beyond the control of the experimenters, and many experiments last a considerable time.

Sometimes analysts attempt to simulate the consequences of a change in policy. Simulation is frequently successful in assessing the impact of "mechanical" policies such as traffic control systems, but more complicated policies are harder to simulate. Using a sample of federal tax returns, for example, officials may estimate the increase or decrease in tax yield and the distribution of burdens among taxpayers that would accompany various changes in the federal income tax. What such a model cannot readily do, however, is identify how individuals will alter their economic behavior in response to an increase or decrease in their taxes.[15] The policymakers dealing with the new Bay Area Rapid Transit (BART) system in the San Francisco region wanted to forecast its patronage and revenues. However, the theory of transport choice was inadequate to the task and large errors were made in the estimates. This was especially unfortunate because the numbers became reified once they appeared in print and were accepted by political leaders, voters, and bond buyers.[16]

Unintended Consequences

In predicting the consequences of a policy, officials must be alert to effects other than those desired. New York State implemented a law in 1973 designed to decrease traffic in illicit drugs. The law provided for mandatory life terms for those convicted of selling any amount of narcotics like heroin or specific quantities of other drugs like LSD. The only kind of probation dealers convicted under this law could ever receive would be a strict probation for the rest of their lives. The law also provided strict punishments for selling marijuana and set strict limits on plea bargaining. Although one would think that law enforcement officials would strongly support this law, it actually received a good deal of opposition from them. They foresaw unintended consequences: If life sentences were mandatory and the death penalty no longer available, there was little to deter the sellers of illegal drugs from killing the policemen sent to apprehend them. In addition, the law indirectly increased the incentives for corrupting policemen and for recruiting juveniles (not covered by the new law) to push drugs.

Unintended consequences also result from government attempts to control prices. A classic example is rent control. By keeping rents lower than they would be in the free market, the policy is meant to provide inexpensive housing for low-income people. However, rent control has other effects, some of which contradict its primary intention. If landlords cannot raise the rents they collect above a set level, but there is no ceiling on the rising costs of building and maintaining apartments, the landlords have little incentive to invest in building new housing or maintain existing housing. Taxes also rise faster than controlled rents, with the result that some landlords simply abandon their buildings. If a policy does not compensate for all of these unintended consequences of strict rent control, they can help defeat its objectives.

The legal limits on the interest banks can charge borrowers and pay savers also have self-defeating consequences. First, banks add charges for loans under the rubric of "handling costs." Second, unrealistic limits on interest rates can prompt investors to shift their money to more profitable investments, causing a shortage of funds. As a result, the demand for funds may exceed the supply, making loans more difficult to obtain and allowing lenders to avoid the poorer risks, mostly poorer people. It is precisely these people, however, who are supposed to benefit from the limits on interest rates.

Other policies that have caused demand to exceed supply and thus produced a shortage in goods or services include the 1971 price controls which resulted in beef shortages as ranchers held their livestock off the market in anticipation of the end of the controls, and the price controls on natural gas which have kept its cost to consumers artificially low and thus encouraged its use while providing insufficient incentives for producers to explore for and develop new resources.

Other aspects of economic policy have also generated unanticipated consequences. Policies to encourage growth have increased the number of jobs and the size of incomes, but they have also produced pollution, noise, loss of parks and open spaces, and esthetic blight; overtaxed roads, schools, water supplies, sewerage systems, and police and fire departments; and perhaps caused a loss of individual privacy, human scale, community pride, neighborhood identity, and a concern for others.

Environmental policies also produce unintended consequences. The Army Corps of Engineers moved the entire town of Niobrara, Nebraska to higher ground because in 1957 it had built a dam in the wrong place on the Niobrara River. The dam slowed down the swift-flowing river, piled up silt at its mouth, raised Niobrara's water table, and slowly flooded the town. In March of 1975 the Environmental Protection Agency postponed the tougher auto-emission standards scheduled to go into effect for 1977 automobiles. Tests showed that the catalytic convertor the Agency had forced the auto industry to adopt emitted significant amounts of sulphuric acid—a serious pollutant.[17]

Social welfare policy is likewise replete with unintended consequences. What follows is a sampling.

1. A 1975 study by the staff of a subcommittee of the House Interstate and Foreign Commerce Committee found that patients receiving aid under the Medicaid program had almost two and one-half times as many operations as those in the general population.[18] Others have argued that the increase in hospital beds resulting from federal programs has also been a factor in the excessive use of hospitals.[19]

2. As part of its implementation of the Pension Reform Act of 1975, the Labor Department sent employers a long and complex form which asked them to describe their pension plans. It was so costly and time-consuming for employers to fill out the forms that the Labor Department had to withdraw them in response to employer threats to end the very pension plans the act was designed to protect.

3. Busing of schoolchildren has been widely utilized by the courts in the past few years to counter *de facto* segregation. There is mounting evidence, however, that busing has encouraged the "white flight" to the suburbs, the opening of private schools, and the increased enrollment in parochial schools. All of these

trends have led to a resegregation of urban schools resulting in nearly all-black public schools in many cities.

4. For many years a family could receive welfare payments under the Aid to Families with Dependent Children program only if there was no able-bodied male in the family, if the parent(s) had no job, and if the parent (as in the case of an unwed teenage mother) was not living at home. Moreover, the level of payments varied widely from state to state. These regulations provided (and often still provide) incentives for fathers to desert their families (so the families could receive welfare benefits); for recipients not to work (their pay may be less than their welfare payments), not to remain with their families, not to complete schooling, and not to prepare for self-support; for welfare workers to conduct "midnight raids" on the homes of welfare recipients (to enforce the regulations); and for welfare families to move to states that pay higher benefits (thus increasing the burden on those making generous payments).

The Russian Wheat Deal of 1972 illustrates unintended consequences of agricultural policy. The large, unprecedented, government-approved sale of wheat to the Soviet Union that year depleted surplus stocks and tied up transportation facilities. Governmental policy therefore produced significant rises in the prices of domestic wheat, flour-based products, beef, pork, poultry, eggs, dairy products, and transportation.

Transportation policy often has unintended consequences. Subsidies for highways, because they make highway use less expensive, have been a leading factor in the decline of railroads. Moreover, freeways, as well as some mass transit systems, by initially making transportation more convenient, have increased urban sprawl and the traffic congestion they were designed to alleviate.

Anytime regulatory bodies allow costs to determine prices and profit to be figured as a percentage of price, they give regulated companies (whether they be airlines or public utilities such as phone and power companies an incentive to increase their costs. If the costs are greater, then profits will be greater even though the rate of profit remains fixed. One way to increase costs is to invest in capital projects that create sizeable fixed costs.[20] These may or may not aid a company in providing better service to its customers, but they will definitely increase consumers' bills.

Foreign policy also produces unintended consequences. This was dramatically illustrated when former President Richard Nixon agreed with interviewer David Frost's assertion that the U.S. invasion of Cambodia in 1970 brought horrible consequences for many Cambodians and may have turned them against us, thereby aiding the Khmer Rouge in their efforts to establish communism.[21]

Judicial decisions also have unintended consequences. For example, the exclusionary rule is a device the courts have used to exclude from criminal proceedings evidence that was improperly obtained by the police. The rule was designed to encourage police not to violate the rights of citizens in their searches for evidence. The extent to which the rule has accomplished that goal is unclear. What is clear is that guilty persons have been allowed to go free or have received lighter sentences (the increased possibility of the guilty escaping conviction provides an incentive for prosecutors to plea bargain), the police have sometimes imposed their own extrajudicial punishment, the courts have been under pressure to lower the standards for probable cause for arrest (making subsequent searches justifiable), and the police have been hampered in their investigations of criminal activity.[22]

Some unintended consequences of policies directly affect the distribution of the benefits and burdens of those policies. We shall defer discussion of this type of unintended consequence until later in this chapter.

It is naturally easier to discuss unintended consequences *after* they happen than to anticipate them. Even when it is relatively certain that they are happening, however, it is not always possible to define them precisely. In the welfare example discussed above, for instance, we really do not know what part the welfare system has played in causing families to move to other states, recipients not to work, and fathers to desert their families. One step policymakers can take to avoid unintended consequences is to look beyond a program's objectives when assessing it. As we have seen, there are many "effects" of programs which are not expressed in their objectives. Aside from this, probably the most we can hope for is that policymakers be sensitive to the possibility of unintended consequences and be willing to suggest refinements in their programs to avoid or repair the worst of those consequences.

Long- and Short-Run Consequences

Policymakers have to consider both the short-run and the long-run consequences of policies. Sometimes the two will differ. For example, Headstart raised the educational performance of preschool children from poor families who participated in the program (in comparison with the performance of other preschool children). But after a few years the Headstart participants performed no better than other children from poor backgrounds.[23]

Matching Consequences and Goals

Because of the various problems in predicting the consequences of policy options, policymakers frequently rely on seat-of-the-pants judgments. In the words of HEW Secretary Joseph Califano, "the basis of recommendations by an American cabinet officer . . . nearly resembles the intuitive judgment of a benevolent tribal chief in remote Africa."[24] Title I of the pathbreaking Elementary and Secondary Education Act of 1965 (giving money to school districts for special projects to improve the education of poor or educationally deprived students) was passed largely on faith "that extra money would compensate for the lack of intellectual stimulation at home. No one really knew *how* to run a successful compensatory educational program." Therefore, local school districts received little guidance on how to spend their funds. (By granting local discretion Congress also avoided the appearance of federal control.) Likewise, Project Headstart was "undertaken with a hunch and a prayer" and local officials could proceed with their own ideas with little central guidance.[25] President Nixon advanced his Family Assistance Plan to reform the welfare system even though no one could anticipate its consequences.[26]

Because it is difficult for policymakers to predict the consequences of policy alternatives, it is also difficult for them to choose the policies that come closest to achieving their goals. Moreover, officials may not have even defined or agreed about specific goals. If a policymaker does not know what goals he is attempting to achieve, he will find it difficult to determine the most effective means for achieving them. Finally, many policies have several goals. Health policies seek to increase productivity and decrease mortality, morbidity, and disability. In assessing a policy with several goals, it is hard to predict its impact simultaneously along several dimensions.

EFFICIENCY

The strategy of rational decisionmaking requires officials to choose policies that will accomplish their goals most efficiently. This means the policies must maximize the potential for attaining those goals for the least possible cost. We have already discussed the problems associated with competing or ambiguous goals, a limited range of alternatives, and unclear consequences. Now we will consider the problems of identifying and measuring the benefits and costs of policies.

Benefits

The benefits of a policy are those results that people find favorable. The problem is how to identify and measure benefits. Creating a unit of measurement to express the quantity of benefits would be the ideal solution. In the private sector the market system assigns values to benefits by measuring the willingness of individuals to pay for them. If there are no "spillover effects" (benefits that go to someone other than the purchaser), the value of a good equals its price. Unfortunately, market principles apply to relatively few, if any, services in the public sector.

The prices people pay for toll highways or the treatment of industrial wastes do not measure the total benefits of those public policies because of spillovers which benefit more people than the direct users. Everyone benefits from a highway system that makes it easier to transport goods from one place to another and therefore increases the opportunities both for producers to sell their goods and for consumers to buy them.

Many public services, like toll-free highways, public recreational facilities, and public education, are utilized on an individual basis. Even when these services are paid for individually, the payments seldom cover the costs of the services. Moreover these services also have spillover benefits, like the widespread gains from the research pursued in public universities or the advantages everyone receives from an economy with abundant public transportation and education.

Some public policies have indivisible benefits; in other words, if one person benefits from them, all do. Such policies are known as *public goods*. Examples of public goods include national defense, police protection, medical research, and the abatement of air and water pollution. It is difficult to measure the benefits of these policies in standard units. Because their benefits usually cannot be purchased in the private sector, they have no standard price. There is thus no simple way to measure the benefits, for instance, from policies lowering the incidence of crime or disease, or lessening the possibility of nuclear attack.

Other policies cannot be purchased either publicly or privately, which makes it impossible to measure their benefits by price. Some of those benefits are divisible, like justice in the courts of law and equality in the use of public accommodations. Others are indivisible, like freedom from the fear of cruel and unusual punishment. It is extremely difficult to think of a unit of measurement for either type of nonpurchasable benefit.

Some analysts have suggested that the amount of money individual consumers or governmental units spend to obtain certain benefits provides an implicit measurement of the benefits' relative worth. Aside from being somewhat of a circular argument, there are several other difficulties with this approach. First, preferences are not stable. The amount that people are willing to spend on recreation, for instance, varies from year to year. Thus, the prices used as the basis of measuring benefits must be chosen somewhat arbitrarily in relation to a specific point in time, and both the time and the prices are certainly open to change. Second, the monetary values placed on the same benefit differ from policy to policy, providing little guidance for a general measure. In deciding how much to spend on making a highway safe, policymakers may implicitly value a human life at $5,000 or $10,000 whereas in the design of an ejection seat of a fighter bomber they may value it at over $1,000,000.[27] Third, consumers often make selections from ignorance on health, education, or other matters handled by professionals. They lack the background to evaluate the services of physicians or professors. Thus, their decisions form a tenuous basis for assigning benefits to policies. They also frequently pay less than they would be willing to pay for a service. Most people, for example, would pay more than the usual cost of a dentist's bill to have a toothache remedied. People may also be willing to pay more than they presently do for recreation, but the price is kept low by public subsidies. In neither case do we know what people would ultimately be willing to pay. Finally, it is not possible to measure willingness to pay for alternatives that would provide services which do not yet exist.

Another possible means of measuring the benefits of a policy is to estimate its effect on the incomes of its recipients. Education usually increases the skills and thus the incomes of those who receive it. Good health can increase productivity. Public works and agricultural price supports contribute to the incomes of those affected by them. Policies such as social security, welfare, and public funding for jobs are related directly to income so that some of their financial effects can be assessed in a straightforward fashion. The Department of Health, Education, and Welfare has utilized the above approach in some of its studies of complex programs, but it has not overcome the serious problem of inaccurate long-range forecasting. Most troubling is the lack of acceptable estimates of future earnings attributable to specific programs and not to other causes.

While calculating the income-increasing benefits of a policy, it is also necessary to assess the other, less tangible, benefits of that policy. Education may not only increase a person's income, but might also facilitate participation in and enjoyment of cultural experiences. Freedom from the ignorance and incommunicability of illiteracy is also a benefit, albeit difficult to calculate, just as freedom from disease and the humiliation of poverty are benefits of medical and welfare programs.

Many policies, like those designed to prevent gambling or protect voting rights or develop public recreational facilities, are not aimed at increasing incomes at all (or only tangentially). Their benefits are not primarily monetary and cannot be reasonably measured in terms of income. Moreover, if officials evaluate policy alternatives, such as those in the health field, only on the contribution they make to increased earnings, those programs which benefit primarily low wage earners or the nonworking aged will receive poor ratings even though they may provide more health benefits than other options.

In addition to the conceptual difficulties of measuring benefits, there are technical problems. The prices of agricultural commodities affected by subsidies cannot be used to estimate the value of publicly provided irrigation water. If they were, the water would be overvalued, because the government sets an artificially high price for the commodities it subsidizes.

In times of close to full employment, any benefits achieved by a policy are accompanied by *opportunity costs*, accrued because the policy displaces other projects (and their benefits) by bidding resources away from them. The same policy would provide more benefits in a time of high unemployment, because it would employ idle resources and displace fewer projects.

Evaluations of benefits change as people get more of them, according to the law of diminishing returns. The benefits of additional years of college beyond those sufficient to enable a person to enter his or her chosen occupation will generally be less than those of the preceding years. In other words, the *marginal utility* of each additional year of college, or each additional hospital, bomber, or road, after a certain point is less than that of the one before.

An additional problem in assessing benefits is how to attribute benefits to a particular policy. How much of our national defense is due to our aircraft carriers and how much to our tanks? Or, how much of our society's cultural advancement (assuming there has been some) is due to public education and how much to other factors?

Some policies are so vast and diffuse that any attempt at assessing their benefits runs into all of the problems outlined above. The space program is a good example. It has provided the benefits of jobs; knowledge and new techniques in the areas of health, geology, meteorology, national defense, and aviation; college scholarships; large but intangible doses of national pride; and perhaps some increments of international influence. Its benefits are both public and private, tangible and symbolic. However, because other policies are aimed at producing similar benefits, it is difficult to attribute all of these benefits to the space program alone.

Costs

The costs of a policy include the resources employed to plan and implement it and the unfavorable consequences of governmental action. Estimating government spending for policies seems like a straightforward procedure, but it has several pitfalls. The costs of programs whose end results are not in hand, such as medical research or the development of a new weapons system, are difficult to estimate in advance. Although it is easier to measure the costs of building roads and other programs that more or less repeat past activities, it is still difficult to anticipate fully the future costs of land, labor, and materials.

The Medicaid and Medicare programs, which provide money for people to purchase goods and services in the private sector, illustrate the difficulties of estimating the future costs of policies subsidizing activities that already take place. Their costs were difficult to estimate initially because no one knew exactly how many people would make use of services made virtually free by public subsidies or how the level of use would affect the cost of the services. An increase in demand generally increases cost; this is especially true for hospitals and physicians, whose supply cannot expand rapidly. Increased demand for medical care also increased the demand and thus the costs for more elastic components of medical care such as drugs, laboratory tests, x-rays, and special therapy as more services and more expensive services were provided. Moreover, hospital administrators, working on a cost-based reimbursement system, had an incentive to increase the length of a typical patient visit, and this in turn made it harder to deny the internal demands for wages, staff, or supplies on the grounds of insufficient funds. Meeting these also increased costs. Finally, Medicaid and Medicare added yet further costs to the federal budget by replacing a large part of various other free physician and hospital services to the indigent as well as a share of state and local expenditures for free public clinics and hospitals.[28]

Some programs cost a computable sum of money, but do not call for direct public expenditures. Tax incentives for various purposes cost the Treasury funds it would otherwise receive: Homeowners can deduct the interest payments on their mortgages from their income in figuring their federal income taxes. The result is the same as a direct subsidy given to each mortage-payer. In fact, such "tax expenditures" now appear as such in the federal budget.

More complicated is the problem of analyzing the costs of

tax cuts designed to stimulate economic growth. The short-run cost of revenue lost to the treasury may be offset by increased revenues in the long-run resulting from the successful stimulation of the economy. The 1964 tax cut generated increased revenues in this manner.

Some policies are too vast, diffuse, and complex, and have consequences that extend too far in the future for policymakers to develop accurate information on their cost. The war in Vietnam is an example. It is impossible to fully assess its costs, even now that it is over. Certain figures represent the American military's share of the cost of the war, but there are no figures available on the exact amount of economic and military assistance channeled to Vietnam since 1950. Even if such a grand total were available, it would only reflect a part of the true price of the war. The U.S. government will provide benefits to Vietnamese refugees and American veterans of the war for decades in ways still to be determined by future legislation.

Many policies impose indirect or *spillover costs* on society by increasing the prices people have to pay for goods and services. Medicare increased the cost of medical care for everyone by adding substantially to demands for services and by authorizing the government's willingness to pay inflated prices for the health care received by medicare beneficiaries. The sale of wheat to the Soviet Union in 1972 had the same affect by increasing dramatically the demands on a limited supply of grain. On a larger scale, government spending is a primary cause of inflation, which raises prices for nearly all goods and services. Similarly, actions by the Federal Reserve Board to increase or decrease the money supply can influence the prices of many goods and services. Such policies may lower the real incomes of millions of people. Yet the economy is complicated and it is often difficult to know how much of an increase in prices should be attributed to any one change in policy.

Other spillover costs are in the form of intangibles like the offensiveness of an ugly public building. The war in Vietnam illustrates the problems of determining nonmonetary costs. Human lives, disabled bodies, displaced persons, devastated countryside, social disruption, and political alienation in the United States and abroad were important costs of the war, but defy simple measurement and inclusion in a budgetary analysis. Although it may be possible to quantify the value of a human life in terms of lost earnings, most people would agree that a person's life has many other, intangible values. Similarly, there is no way to compute the cost of political alienation.

Other policies less drastic than war also carry with them profound but intangible costs. Government policies that cuase recession, for example, impose the costs of anxiety, humiliation, frustration, and insecurity in addition to lost earnings.

There are also *opportunity costs*. Because governments do not have sufficient resources to carry out all proposed programs, every expenditure of resources (including money and manpower) precludes carrying out a potential policy whose benefits therefore cannot be received. Resources spent on national defense are resources that are not available for national health insurance, child care, or the space program. The cost of a policy thus includes lost benefits which would have resulted from alternative policies. It is not easy to measure those lost benefits both because they have not occurred and because there is no assurance that the "foregone" programs would have been enacted in the absence of those actually chosen. Even more difficult is measuring the opportunity costs of transfering resources to the public sector from the private sector, where the range of possible uses is enormous.

Other technical problems hinder the measurement of costs. If there is substantial unemployment, for example, the opportunity costs that arise from employing a unit of labor in some activity are smaller than in times of full employment. Also, insofar as the market costs of certain resources reflect monopolistic pricing, they fail to reflect the true alternative values of the resources used.

Some policies impose costs on the people they are trying to aid. If the federal government cuts off funds to a school district whose officials fail to comply with orders to integrate, the students deprived of education pay the major costs.

Likewise, withholding funds from nursing homes that fail to meet government standards causes the aged clients to suffer as much as the operators of the nursing homes. If a regulatory agency refuses to grant a public utility a badly needed rate increase because of poor service in the past, consumers may suffer because of the utility's continued inability to perform well. Each of these costs is difficult to measure.

Some policies directly increase the costs of other policies. This occurs when government-induced inflation increases the costs of everything purchased by all levels of government. It also happens when the construction of inland waterways increases the cost of highways because of the bridges required over the waterways.

A problem encountered in figuring the costs of many long-term projects is that of *discounting*. Because recipients prefer benefits in the present and value them less the longer they take to occur, and because of inflation, the amount of money that must be spent on a program in the future does not have the same relative value as an equal amount of money spent in the present. Thus, future expenditures have to be "discounted" to make them comparable with those of the present. (The same is true for monetary benefits that will occur in the future.) The process of discounting consists of multiplying future expenditures (or benefits) by the fraction of the current costs (or benefits) they represent. However, because there is seldom consensus on what rate of discount to apply, policymakers can manipulate the appearance of a program's total costs by their choice of discount rate. The calculations can also be altered by assumptions about the life of projects. Since costs generally are incurred disproportionately at the beginning of projects and benefits occur after the project has been completed, the longer the assumed life of a project, the greater the benefits are likely to be in relation to costs.

As with benefits, rational policymakers should know the *marginal cost* of each additional unit of a policy as well as the average cost of all the units. This requirement complicates the analysis of policy because marginal costs depend on a variety of factors. Additional units of a policy may cost *less* than the average because of economies of scale;

extending the administrative responsibilities of a bureaucracy that already exists can result in such economies. Conversely, additional units of some policies cost more than those which preceded them. This holds true for most attempts to eliminate air pollution. Cleansing the air of 50 percent of a certain type of particle is less expensive than removing the remaining 50 percent of the pollutant.

Nonmonetary costs can also increase in a nonlinear fashion. Thus, the diversion of a certain amount of income into taxes may be a small burden for most taxpayers, but to divert double that amount of income to taxes may cause more than twice the burden. Depending on one's income and personal situation, the higher taxes may cut into fundamental expenditures for food, shelter, or medical care.

Benefit-Cost Analysis and Decisionmaking

Despite the problems of measuring the benefits and costs associated with a policy, benefit-cost analysis can be a useful tool. If officials are aware of the variety of benefits and costs possible, they can use benefit-cost analysis to clarify the implications of each alternative considered. Even if estimates include only a portion of total benefits and costs, they can indicate what values unreported benefits must attain for the benefits of a policy to outweigh its calculable costs. The more quantifiable the benefits and costs of an alternative, the "harder," or more firm, the estimates of them are likely to be.

Benefit-cost analysis is probably most useful in analyzing the costs of means to a given end. This type of analysis is termed "cost effectiveness" and has been widely used in defense policy. There the basic goal (national defense) is given and the accomplishment of a program is stated in terms of minimal acceptable level of performance, such as the speed of a fighter plane, and not in terms of its contribution to national defense. The decisional problem then becomes choosing the most efficient means of achieving that level. Yet as we have seen above, effectiveness remains a difficult concept to measure for most policies.

Even though benefit-cost analysis is a useful tool, not

everyone takes advantage of it. Members of Congress decide on many programs without explicitly considering the programs' objectives, alternative policies for attaining those objectives, or the benefits and costs expected from the policies. And when Congress is interested in the relative effectiveness of programs, the bureaucracy may be unresponsive. During the Senate Finance Committee's 1972 deliberations on welfare reform, for example, Senator Abraham Ribicoff asked officials from the Department of Health, Education, and Welfare to produce a comprehensive listing of social programs and to indicate which were the most effective, which overlapped with one another, and where reforms were needed. What the committee received was a list of programs and little more. HEW officials said it was not feasible to evaluate programs in relation to each other.[29]

Several other problems deter those members of Congress who want to carry out benefit-cost evaluations. Many of their colleagues are not interested in this work, which is technical, time-consuming, and offers few political payoffs. Those who are interested receive inadequate assistance. Most members of Congress have too few professional staffers to analyze a wide range of policy issues, and committee staffs usually work under the direction of committee or subcommittee leaders (who may be among those uninterested in benefit-cost analysis). The establishment of a Congressional Budget Office may help, but its Director predicted that there will not be enough depth in its staff to evaluate specific policies intensively.[30] Congressional staff tend to have close relationships with staffs in the bureaucracy and are not prone to challenge them. Finally, the committee structure has a built-in bias towards higher budgets, especially when a liberal Democratic Congress is in competition with a Republican Administration. Members of the committees which authorize and appropriate funds generally support the policies they helped to initiate.[31]

Despite the drawbacks, benefit-cost analysis of projects affecting water resources is highly developed. The Bureau of Reclamation uses benefit-cost analysis to assess proposals for dams and irrigation. Its rule of thumb is that benefits must exceed costs by a certain amount for a project to proceed. However, several outside experts have criticized the Bureau's use of benefit-cost analysis. Using the same tools as the Bureau's analysts, theses experts have reached widely divergent conclusions, leading them to charge that the Bureau uses benefit-cost analysis to mask the political origins of water projects.[32]

Critics also charge that the Bureau often overestimates benefits and underestimates costs. They say that the Bureau ignores opportunity costs; discounts benefits over time at an artifically low rate; overlooks adverse effects of projects on the rest of the agricultural economy; and employs subsidized support prices in calculating the value of crops to be grown on reclaimed land.[33] By taking advantage of the ambiguities in benefit-cost analysis, practitioners can bend an analysis in any direction. They can focus only on quantifiable products and ignore other values, or they can make up needed benefits with intangible "underlying social benefits." The Bureau's positive recommendations find support among the Bureau's interest group and congressional allies.[34]

The ultimate limitation of benefit-cost analysis is its subordination to noneconomic values. Even with benefit-cost data for policy alternatives, officials do not simply choose to devote more resources to the alternatives with the most favorable benefit-cost ratios. Their decisions also depend on the noneconomic values attached to the benefits of each policy. Officials may select a job training strategy to attack poverty over a simple income maintenance alternative, even if income maintenance is more efficient, because they value self-reliance. Or their decisions may depend on vague standards of minimum effectiveness and maximum cost. An efficient alternative which does not meet the minimum goals of policymakers or whose costs exceed available resources will generally not be a viable policy option. Similarly, a potentially efficient policy which cannot attract voluntarily participants will be of little utility to society.

Although some criteria for choice seem reasonable, their requisite conditions may never occur. For example, *pareto optimality*, in which a change in policy is considered desirable if no individual will perceive himself to be worse off after such a change and at least one will see himself as better off, is an appealing criterion, but different people assess the same set of circumstances differently. Even if a person is objectively better off, he or she may *feel* worse off, either because of a sense of relative deprivation in comparison with others or because of disappointment over unmet expectations. Moreover, few policies improve everyone's lot, and if only a few benefit, the policy may well have high opportunity costs.

Thus, benefit-cost analysis is not a substitute for the hard task of establishing priorities and determining the trade-offs between goals and alternatives. In making their decisions policymakers must weigh the preferences of different people because different people place different values on different benefits and costs. Their choices are generally motivated by political, and not technical, considerations.

EQUITY

Most policies distribute their costs and benefits unequally. Farm programs, social security, and welfare all benefit most those who receive payments. Education, roads, and parks benefit most those who make use of them. On the cost side of the ledger, some people bear greater burdens than others in paying for policies, but those who carry the greatest financial burdens of a program may not be its primary beneficiaries.

A fruitful place to look at the distribution of benefits is tax policy. "Tax expenditures" occur when individuals or corporations reduce their overall income (on which taxes are levied) through the use of legal exceptions to the standard definitions of adjusted gross income. These exceptions are numerous and are known in popular parlance as tax "loopholes." They include special exclusions, exemptions, and deductions, which reduce taxable income (for example, charitable contributions, mortgage interest payments, and certain income from municipal bonds and corporate stocks); preferential rates, which reduce taxes by applying lower rates to part or all of a taxpayer's income (for example, the special 50 percent maximum tax on personal service income); special credits, which are subtracted from the actual taxes due (for example, the investment tax credit); and deferrals of tax, which generally allow deductions in a current year if they are properly attributable to a future year (for example, accelerated depreciation). The Congressional Budget Office estimated that tax expenditures would exceed $114 billion for 1977 (equal to about one-fourth of conventionally measured federal expenditures.[35]

Not everyone benefits equally from tax expenditures. People with higher incomes receive the bulk of the deductions. As Table 6.1 shows, the richest 1.2 percent of U.S. income earners (those with $50,000 or more of taxable income) received 23.1 percent of the deductions in fiscal 1974. The richest 14.6 percent (earning more than $20,000 of taxable income) received 53 percent of the deductions. A substantial portion of the deductions taken by those in the lowest income brackets went to the elderly, leaving the nonelderly taxpayers earning under $20,000 a year with a small share of the benefits.

Well-off and relatively well-off taxpayers derive the bulk of the benefits from tax expenditures because they have the resources and access to expertise necessary to invest in sources of income (generally economic activity the government wishes to encourage) that receive tax deductions, to make charitable contributions, etc. In addition, people in the highest income bracket benefit the most from a decrease in income because the decrease reduces their tax rate; they would pay a higher rate on their deducted income than less well-off taxpayers.

Even if people in different income brackets use the same deduction, the wealthier person benefits more. For example, one of the most commonly used federal tax expenditures is the deduction of mortgage interest on owner-occupied homes. Yet in fiscal 1974 over half the total deductions (total = $4.9 billion) from this provision went to the less than 15 percent of those with gross adjusted incomes of $20,000 or

Table 6.1 Estimated Distribution of Tax Expenditures to Individuals by Adjusted Gross Income (Fiscal Year 1974)

Adjusted gross income class ($ thousands)	Number of taxable returns ($ thousands)	Percentage of taxable returns By income class	By segment	Total tax expenditures by income class ($ millions)	Percentage distribution By income class	By segment
0–3	4,057	6.1 ⎫		1,085	1.9 ⎫	
3–5	7,579	11.3 ⎬	46.9	1,738	3.0 ⎬	16.6
5–7	8,273	12.4 ⎬		2,357	4.1 ⎬	
7–10	11,428	17.1 ⎭		4,403	7.6 ⎭	
10–15	15,952	23.8 ⎫	38.5	8,875	15.3 ⎫	30.6
15–20	9,856	14.7 ⎬		8,881	15.3 ⎬	
20–50	9,006	13.4	13.4	17,414	29.9	29.9
50–100	655	1.0 ⎫	1.2	6,116	10.5 ⎫	23.1
100 and over	160	0.2 ⎬		7,306	12.6 ⎬	
Total	66,966	100.0	100.0	58,175	100.2	100.2

Figures may not add up to exactly 100% because of rounding error.
Source: U.S. Treasury Department.

more. This is because more wealthy people own homes than those less well-off, and they own more expensive homes—with larger interest payments.

There are several provisions in the federal tax code that grant direct benefits primarily to taxpayers whose incomes place them in the lower 50 percent of all income earners. Those provisions focus on the elderly, the blind or disabled, veterans, students, and the recipients of public assistance. Their main beneficiaries are those whose incomes are temporarily low (i.e., breadwinners at the beginning or end of their income-producing careers).

Not only do different incomes classes benefit differently from tax expenditures, but taxpayers with similar incomes are not all entitled to take the same deductions. A person's tax bill depends to a great extent on how he or she receives his or her income (i.e., does it come from a source given special treatment in the tax code).

Tax expenditures also benefit certain groups and organizations, including educational and other nonprofit organizations (contributions to which can be deducted from the donor's income), local governments (which can sell their bonds below market rates of interest because there is no tax on their interest), savings banks and home builders and their suppliers (deduction of mortgage interest makes it easier for people to buy homes), and corporations (who receive one-fourth of the total deductions).

It is not clear whether the indirect benefits lower-income citizens receive from the activities supported by tax expenditures are commensurate with the direct benefits received by wealthy taxpayers and organizations. We know little about who the indirect beneficiaries are and how much they benefit. What we do know is that direct and indirect beneficiaries of tax expenditures are not the same people, and that neither group is evenly dispersed within the population.

All taxes place a burden on taxpayers, and tax expenditures are not the only aspect of taxation policies that affect people differently. The findings of a major study on tax burdens are very interesting in this regard. Using 1966 data the authors of the study carried out separate analyses of the distribution of taxes based on a number of different assumptions. They counted all income, including transfer payments and capital gains, as taxable "income," and developed a concept of "taxes" that included both taxes paid directly and taxes paid indirectly (through higher prices for goods and services). The authors concluded that the tax system as a whole was proportional or slightly progressive. In other words, each income class (but *not* each taxpayer within the class) paid taxes at roughly the same rate. Federal taxes were mildly progressive throughout income groups (except at the very bottom), and state and local taxes were mildly regressive except at the very top (with some variation from place to place). These findings, the authors suggest, are as valid now as they were in 1966 because the changes in taxation policy since then have roughly offset each other.[36]

The fact that the tax system has very little effect on the distribution of income (because most taxpayers pay at a similar rate) does not mean there is agreement that the real burden of taxation is equitable. Those who favor progressive taxation argue that tax burdens are equal only if the well-off pay at a higher rate. To take a simple example, if two taxpayers, one earning $10,000 per year and the second $20,000 per year, each pay income taxes at a rate of 10 percent, the latter pays twice as much as the former ($2,000 compared to $1,000). Nevertheless, the richer person is left with $18,000 while his or her counterpart retains only $9,000. Thus, the argument is made that the person with less income bears a heavier tax burden because $1,000 is more significant to him or her than $2,000 is to the wealthier taxpayer. Therefore, even what appears to be a straightforward empirical question of tax burdens is open to differing interpretations, which policymakers must resolve before they tackle the even more difficult question of what constitutes an "appropriate" burden.

Inflation (which frequently results from basic federal spending policies) also imposes unequal financial burdens. People with fixed incomes (like pensioners) are hard hit because their income does not rise with prices. The poor suffer disproportionately because they have to spend virtually all their income and are thus fully affected by increases in prices. Even the taxes of the poor rise more rapidly than those of other income groups as a result of inflation. A study for the congressional Joint Committee on Internal Revenue and Taxation found that inflation-induced federal income tax increases in 1974 were 45 percent for taxpayers whose gross adjusted incomes were less than $3,000 and 16.6 percent for those with incomes of less than $5,000 a year. The average increase for all groups was only 6 percent.[37] Public employees are also frequently hit harder than others by inflation. Because government spending is often one cause of inflation, cries for holding the line on public spending by denying raises to public employees are common in periods of inflation, and decisionmakers frequently heed those cries.

An instructive example of the inequitable distribution of benefits and burdens is one of our past energy policies. In the late 1950s, the oil companies lobbied the government to limit imports of gas and oil. The results would be increases in the price of domestically produced gas and oil and a strong incentive to continue explorations for sources of energy in the United States, which in turn would help protect our national security. The policy adopted to accomplish all this, needless to say, increased the profits of the oil companies and drove up the prices consumers paid for oil and gas (by approximately $5–7 billion per year according to one qualified estimate).[38]

There are two important decisional aspects of the above policy that affected the distribution of benefits and burdens. First, the government could choose between two common means of limiting imports: (1) setting quotas on the amount of a good that can be imported, or (2) placing a tariff on a good to make importation less economical than domestic production. Both means accomplish the same goal. The difference is that different people benefit from each one. The United States chose to adopt the quota system. The beneficiaries were the stockholders of the oil companies, because the companies could import oil cheaply and then sell it at the artificially high domestic retail price. If the government had imposed tariffs instead of quotas, the United States Treasury would have received the money instead of the oil companies. This option would have benefitted most taxpayers more than the quota system.

The second distributional choice policymakers faced in formulating the policy outlined above affected the distribution of benefits to the oil companies. Government officials decided to base the percentage of the total imports allocated to each company on the percentage of total imports each company had imported in the mid-1950s. The biggest companies therefore received the largest benefits. The lesson from this point is that we cannot merely lump all beneficiaries together and presume that they share benefits equally.

Like energy programs, policies supporting public systems of higher education do not distribute their benefits equally. A study of the California higher education system revealed that more children of the middle and upper classes go to college than children of less well-off families, and they go to the state colleges that are more expensive to maintain (major universities as opposed to junior colleges, to take polar examples). An examination of these facts in terms of the taxes paid by different income classes (and especially the taxes paid in support of higher education) makes it clear that public higher education does not have the redistributive impact many citizens would like it to have.[39]

Yet other examples of the unequal distribution of benefits within target groups are found in agricultural policy. Almost all farm programs provide their greatest benefits to farmers with the largest farms. As a result, benefits have become highly concentrated and are getting more so because about one-half of all farmers produce almost all of our agricultural output. Water resource development projects in the West are designed to make formerly arid land arable. However, the United States has an excess of agricultural capacity so that agricultural production in the West affects production in other areas, and public funds used to bolster western agriculture are diverted from other regional programs.

This redistribution means that the public policy benefits received by western farmers are lost to farmers in the other regions.[40]

Almost every policy benefits (and burdens) some people more than others. Besides the examples discussed in this section, we have noted earlier rent control and the limits on the interest rates banks may charge and pay to illustrate this point. In addition, urban renewal programs have subsidized high-income groups and burdened the poor by eliminating cheap housing and replacing it with housing only the relatively well-off can afford. Some mass transit systems have been paid for primarily by the poor but utilized primarily by the wealthy.[41] Farm programs like parity pricing and acreage diversion have raised the price of food for consumers and benefitted farmers. Public assistance has transferred resources from middle and upper income taxpayers to certain groups of poor citizens who qualify for various programs. The military draft selected a disproportionately high number of poor, black, and rural young men for service in our armed forces to the benefit of their middle-class, white, and urban counterparts.[42] The minimum wage, although designed to aid those at the lowest income levels, makes it more difficult for the unskilled to find work by giving employers an incentive to mechanize simple tasks; at the same time, it benefits more highly paid workers by reducing the competition for their jobs and the pressure for lowering salaries.[43] A substantial portion of the benefits of social welfare programs has gone to teachers, physicians, and social workers, rather than students, patients, and poor people. Flood relief generally goes to those who choose to live on flood plains but is paid for by those choosing to live elsewhere.

Despite the importance of the distribution of benefits and costs, there is inadequate information on their allocation. It is particularly difficult to assess the distribution of burdens if program costs are transferred into public debt. Who will bear the burden of taxes in future years will depend on political and economic conditions that current analysts can only roughly estimate.

SUMMARY

A policymaker following the rational model of decisionmaking must assess the consequences of policy alternatives. Yet it is no easier to accomplish this task than the previous stages of the model. The consequences of new policies are difficult to predict, and there are numerous difficulties in relying upon policy experiments. Moreover, analytical problems as well as political opposition make it difficult to assess even ongoing policies and incremental changes. Unintended consequences further frustrate the rational process as they are unexpected and therefore elude advance planning.

Additional difficulties arise in attempts to evaluate the consequences of policies in terms of efficiency. Benefits and costs are very difficult to measure and are open to manipulation for political purposes. Finally, the distribution of costs and benefits involves important considerations of equity because some people benefit more than others from policies. Yet calculations of equity are no freer than other aspects of rational decisionmaking from sharp disputes between competing political perspectives and competing techniques of analysis.

NOTES

1. For example, see "House Delays Action on Energy, Strip Mining," *Congressional Quarterly Weekly Report,* May 24, 1975, p. 1063; "Strip Mining Veto," *Congressional Quarterly Weekly Report,* June 7, 1975, p. 1176.

2. "College Aid Grants Unspent," *Washington Post,* April 24, 1975, Section A, p. 29.

3. "Student Aid Fund Depleted," *Congressional Quarterly Weekly Report,* February 14, 1976, p. 327.

4. This discussion has benefitted from Alice M. Rivlin, *Systematic Thinking for Social Action* (Washington, D.C.: Brookings Institution, 1971), pp. 70–78.

5. *Ibid.*, p. 49n; Norman C. Thomas, *Education in National Politics* (New York: David McKay, 1975), pp. 41–43.

6. Mike Royko, "Few Seem to Care if Teachers Cheat," *New Orleans Times-Picayune*, January 9, 1977, Section 3, p. 11.

7. U.S. Congress, Senate, Committee on the Budget, *Growth of Government Spending for Income Assistance: A Matter of Choice*, Committee Print (Washington, D.C.: Government Printing Office, 1975).

8. See Edward M. Gramlich and Patricia P. Koshel, *Educational Performance Contracting* (Washington, D.C.: Brookings Institution, 1975). For evaluations of other educational experiments, see Alice M. Rivlin and P. Michael Timpane (eds.), *Planned Variation in Education: Should We Give Up or Try Harder?* (Washington, D.C.: Brookings Institution, 1975).

9. See Joseph A. Pechman and P. Michael Timpane (eds.), *Work Incentives and Income Guarantees: The New Jersey Negative Income Tax Experiment* (Washington, D.C.: Brookings Institution, 1975); and "Symposium on the Graduated Work Incentive Experiment," Parts I and II, *Journal of Human Resources* 9, Nos. 2 and 4 (1974).

10. Rivlin, *Systematic Thinking for Social Action*, p. 84.

11. John G. Grumm, "The Analysis of Policy Impact," in *Policies and Policymaking*, Vol. 6 of *The Handbook of Political Science*, ed. by Fred I. Greenstein and Nelson W. Polsby (Reading, Mass.: Addison-Wesley, 1975), p. 456.

12. On the ethics of social experimentation, see Alice M. Rivlin and P. Michael Timpane, *Ethical and Legal Issues of Social Experimentation* (Washington, D.C.: Brookings Institution, 1975).

13. See Daniel P. Moynihan, *The Politics of a Guaranteed Income* (New York: Vintage, 1973), p. 423 for an example of this last point.

14. Rivlin, *Systematic Thinking for Social Action*, pp. 115–116.

15. *Ibid.*, pp. 35–36.

16. Melvin M. Webber, "The BART Experience—What Have We Learned?" *Public Interest*, Fall 1976, p. 106.

17. For another example of the unintended consequences of an environmental policy see "E.P.A. Is Curbing Sewer Main Subsidies," *New York Times*, October 15, 1974, pp. 1 and 16.

18. "Unnecessary Surgery," *Congressional Quarterly Weekly Report*, July 26, 1975, p. 1620.

19. David Stockman, "The Social Pork Barrel," *Public Interest*, Spring 1975, p. 14.

20. Bruce C. Vladeck, "Why Non-Profits Go Broke," *Public Interest*, Winter 1976, p. 92.

21. Nationally televised interview of Richard Nixon, May 19, 1977.

22. Dallin H. Oaks, "Studying the Exclusionary Rule in Search and Seizure," *University of Chicago Law Review* 58 (Summer 1970).

23. Westinghouse Learning Corporation-Ohio University, *The Impact of Head Start: An Evaluation of the Effects of Head Start on Children's Cognitive Development*, July 12, 1969. See also Walter Williams and John W. Evans, "The Politics of Evaluation: The Case of Head Start," *Annals* 385 (September 1969).

24. Quoted in Moynihan, *Guaranteed Income*, p. 240. See also the comments of former Price Commissioner C. Jackson Grayson in Theodore C. Sorensen, *Watchmen in the Night* (Cambridge, Mass.: MIT Press, 1975), p. 32.

25. Rivlin, *Systematic Thinking for Social Action*, pp. 80 and 84.

26. Moynihan, *Guaranteed Income*, pp. 144 and 549–550.

27. E.S. Quade, *Analysis for Public Decisions* (New York: American Elsevier, 1975), p. 113.

28. Frederick O'R. Hayes, "The Uses for Policy Analysis in the United States Senate," in *Policymaking Role of Leadership in the Senate*, Committee Print, Commission on the Operation of the Senate (Washington, D.C.: Government Printing Office, 1976), pp. 63–64.

29. "Ford Plans Restructuring of Social Programs," *Congressional Quarterly Weekly Report*, July 26, 1975, p. 1615.

30. "Congressional Budget: Toughest Test Ahead," *Congressional Quarterly Weekly Report*, September 6, 1975, p. 1925.

31. State legislatures are even weaker than Congress in their analytical capabilities and policy interests. One North Carolina committee chairman recently resorted to offering door prizes to obtain a quorum, and it is not unusual for Illinois legislators to vote blindly on dozens of bills at once. See "Prize Idea," *Newsweek*, July 7, 1975, p. 21; and "Rush to Judgment," *Time*, June 16, 1975, p. 8.

32. Steve H. Hanke and Richard A. Walker, "Benefit-Cost Analysis Reconsidered: An Evaluation of the Mid-State Project," in *Water Resource Research* 10, No. 5 (1974), pp. 898–908.

33. *Ibid.*

34. For discussions of the use of cost-benefit analysis in Congress see Robert H. Haveman, *The Economic Performance of Public Investments* (Baltimore: Johns Hopkins University Press, 1972); and John Ferejohn, *Pork Barrel Politics* (Stanford, Calif.: Stanford University Press, 1974).

35. Edmond LeBreton, "114 Billion in Tax Breaks," *New Orleans Times-Picayune*, April 9, 1977, Section 1, p. 1. For a thorough treatment of many aspects of tax expenditures see Stanley Surrey, *Pathways to Tax Reform* (Cambridge, Mass.: Harvard University Press, 1971).

36. Joseph A. Pechman and Benjamin A. Okner, *Who Bears the Tax Burden?* (Washington, D.C.: Brookings Institution, 1974).

37. "Tax Burden Heavier Despite Reduction," *Congressional Quarterly Weekly Report*, April 12, 1975, p. 744.

38. This discussion relies on Douglas C. North and Roger Leroy Miller, *The Economics of Public Issues* (New York: Harper & Row, 1971), Chapter 15.

39. See W. Lee Hanson and Burton A. Weisbord, *Benefits, Costs, and Finance of Public Higher Education* (Chicago: Markham, 1969); Joseph A. Pechman, "The Distributional Effects of Public Higher Education in California," *Journal of Human Resources* 5 (Summer 1970); and Robert W. Hartman, "A Comment on the Pechman-Hansen-Weisbrod Controversy," *Journal of Human Resources* 5 (Fall 1970).

40. James T. Bonen, "The Absence of Knowledge of Distributional Impacts: An Obstacle to Effective Policy Analysis and Decisions," in *Public Expenditures and Policy Analysis*, ed. by Robert H. Haveman and Julius Margolis (Chicago: Markham, 1970).

41. Webber, "The BART Experience," p. 93.

42. James W. Davis, Jr. and Kenneth M. Dolbeare, *Little Groups of Neighbors: The Selective Service System* (Chicago: Markham, 1968), pp. 125–147.

43. See, for example, William R. Keech, "Electoral Politics and the Meaning of Partisanship in Federal Minimum Wage Policy," (paper presented at the Annual Meeting of the American Political Science Association in San Francisco, September 4, 1975), pp. 2–8.

CONSTRAINTS ON DECISIONS

In Parts I and II we considered two different approaches to policymaking: the populist model, according to which decisionmakers assess and resolve the problems encountered in making policy by following the public's wishes; and the rational model, according to which decisionmakers select optimal policies by identifying problems, clarifying goals, and collecting and assessing relevant alternatives for meeting those goals. In Part III we shift our focus to the larger context in which policymakers work. To pursue our examination of the problems and predicaments of policymakers, we discuss two types of constraints on policy decisions: constraints imposed by the nature of the economy (Chapter 7) and constraints originating in the character of government and politics (Chapter 8). Both limit the number of viable alternatives and thereby circumscribe a decisionmaker's range of discretion.

Economic
Constraints on
Decisionmaking

7

Policymakers are not free to move directly from estimating the consequences of policy alternatives to selecting the policies with the most favorable consequences. They are constrained in their decisions by forces in their environment. Some forces prevent options from being chosen while others help determine which policies have priority.

The economy is one factor that helps regulate what is possible or desirable. Policymakers in Ethiopia face a different economic setting, that is, different demands for programs as well as different resources to pay for them, than do policymakers in Washington. Likewise, state officials in Mississippi operate in a much different context than their counterparts in California. To be sure, it is not only the differences in economic environment that distinguish these various policymakers and the policies they produce, but their economic environments do explain many of the differences among them.

When political writers describe the various economic forces that shape public policy, they often refer to the *level of economic development*. This is a cumulative concept that summarizes a set of economic components plus certain social variables that reflect economic conditions. Poor countries and regions suffer not only from a shortage of hard cash usable in the world market, but also from other problems that both reveal and reinforce their shortage of cash. The concept of economic development encompasses:

1. The quantity and quality of *natural resources* such as agricultural land, fuel, and other minerals.
2. The human, physical, and financial *capital*, as measured by the skills of the population; industrial, transportation and power-generating facilities; and financial assets.
3. The quality of *industry and agriculture*. (Developed economies produce a high value of products in relation to the value of the labor required for production.)
4. The capacity of such *financial institutions* as the tax system, banks, and stock exchanges to generate the funds needed for investments.
5. The character of *foreign trade*. (A developed economy exports mainly processed and manufactured goods whereas an underdeveloped economy exports mainly raw materials.)
6. The capacity of *educational and health institutions* to serve the population in a way that facilitates the productivity of workers.
7. The nature of the *distribution of economic rewards*. (More highly developed economies have a relatively even distribution of incomes and opportunities among the various regional and social divisions of the population.)[1]

The various components of economic development are prominent concerns of policymakers. They are an important part of the environment of policymaking, influencing the demands and resources received by policymakers. They are also the targets of much policymaking as policymakers seek to improve the economy in either the short or the long run. Because the economy is the basis of many policies, maintaining its health is a high priority for policymakers.

ECONOMIC DEVELOPMENT AS
THE TARGET OF POLICYMAKING

As a target of policymaking, economic development is a constant preoccupation of governments in both poor countries and more highly developed nations like the United States. In the poor states of the United States and among the spokesmen of low-income populations economic development is a matter of high priority. This is also true in the national capital when levels of unemployment reach the heights witnessed in the 1974–1976 period and when high rates of inflation threaten the purchasing power of all citizens and the capacity of government officials to make accurate financial projections.

Monetary Policy

One policymaking organ for which economic development is a principal concern is a country's central bank. In the United States the Federal Reserve Board has the responsibility of controlling the supply of money in the economy and thereby regulating the rate at which individual firms and governments are likely to invest in new or expanded activities. The Federal Reserve Board establishes the reserve requirements of federally chartered banks (the amount of money they must keep in reserve and not lend), sets the "discount rates" at which banks may borrow from the central bank, and buys and sells government bonds. The amount of money available, the rate of interest that banks charge their borrowers, the degree of inflation, and the availability of jobs flow directly or indirectly from the Federal Reserve Board's leverage on the money supply.

Both inflation and interest rates influence economic growth. Investors are more interested in new projects if they can borrow at low rates and if inflation will not eat into their profits. Also, when interest rates are low, consumers are more likely to borrow for homes, automobiles, and appliances, and manufacturers are more likely to borrow to expand their production capacities. Yet there is no simple equation between low interest rates and economic growth. A moderate rate of inflation may actually fuel economic growth as investors seek to profit from expanding opportunities before future inflation drives the costs of expansion too high.

Fiscal Policies

In addition to influencing the economy through "monetary policies," governments activate "fiscal policies" through their own borrowing and spending. If a government borrows in order to spend more than it receives in taxes, it increases the supply of money available to the private sector. This in turn expands the economy.

Government borrowing may also exert a negative influence on economic development. A government's own pursuit of funds competes with that of the private sector. This competition can drive up the interest rates paid by banks and the purchasers of corporate and government bonds, making both public and private borrowing more costly. Government borrowing also increases the cost of public policies as a result of interest paid over the years. Yet policymakers may decide this cost is worth the gain of increased spending in the present, particularly if some of the spending is for projects that spur economic development.

Chronic inflation and the continual economic growth that is promoted by government borrowing keep down the real cost of borrowing. The dollar amount of the United States government debt continues to grow, but with the overall growth in the economy, the debt's proportion of the Gross National Product has shrunk—from 59 percent in 1960 to 39 percent in 1978.

Another element of fiscal policy is taxation. The government can use tax policies to encourage economic development by offering tax credits to businesses that invest in new manufacturing equipment or search for oil, gas, or coal.

(The reader may recognize that a "tax incentive" is also a "loophole," depending on the perspective from which it is viewed.) With substantial taxes levied on individuals and firms, the government can increase the attractiveness of investments that stimulate economic growth by giving tax concessions to those willing to invest.

Regulatory Policies

A government can also encourage economic growth by the regulation of financial institutions. To make the stock market and savings banks attractive to the public, and thereby facilitate the accumulation of funds for private investments, the U.S. government sponsors extensive programs to assure a fair disclosure of information about the stocks being sold and about the kinds of transactions permitted to banks and stock exchanges. The federal government also offers insurance on certain forms of investment (e.g., the federal insurance that now covers savings deposits of up to $40,000).

Controls on imports and promotion of export also serve to encourage and direct economic growth. Tariffs or quotas on imports protect domestic industries from foreign competition. Some countries go beyond tariffs and subsidize certain industries to produce "import substitutes" for the local market or manufacture goods for sale abroad. Subsidies can take the form of tax credits for engaging in a certain type of production or government-arranged loans at lower than commercial rates of interest. These regulatory policies can be useful to the entire economy if they create more jobs or save foreign reserves which can then be applied to more essential purchases. Or such policies may simply work to the benefit of a private manufacturer who is allowed to charge high prices in the domestic market without the threat of outside competition or who is given low-cost loans for purposes not essential to the larger economy.

The devaluation of currency is a more dramatic way of encouraging exports and discouraging imports. Devaluation reduces the prices of locally produced goods to foreigners by making one unit of a country's currency worth less in terms of foreign currencies. It also increases the price of foreign goods to residents of the country which devalues. When the United States devalued the dollar in 1971, it increased the prices of Japanese cameras and automobiles available in the United States, but reduced the price of American goods offered for sale abroad.

Spending to Maintain the Economic Infrastructure

Transportation arteries, electric power, and systems of communication are vital instruments of economic development. When a country has an abundance of electric power and its cities are well-connected through systems of roads, railroads, canals, and airways plus effective mail and telephone networks, the entire geographical area is available as a source of supplies and sites for production and a market for the outputs of all citizens. Components of the infrastructure receive favorable treatment in the tax laws and regulatory policies of many countries or benefit from direct subsidies; in some countries certain elements are even owned outright by the government. The American pattern has been to subsidize and protect rather than to own. The federal government heavily subsidized the construction of transcontinental railroads in the nineteenth century, and the interstate highway system, airports and airlines, the merchant marine, and atomic energy in the twentieth century. Today the U.S. also has publicly owned electric generating plants and transmission lines, and recently the government supported an effort to "save" northeastern railroads through the creation of federally subsidized corporations.

Agriculture is also a component of the infrastructure essential for economic development. A stable supply of efficiently produced food is necessary to feed a population while freeing labor for other sectors. For these (and other) reasons, the federal government has spent billions of dollars on price supports for agricultural commodities, regulated production, and granted farmers special loans and crop insurance (to stabilize their economic environment). Washington (along with state governments) has also provided farmers with a wide range of technical advice, electrification, and land—free or at a nominal cost. Agricultural policy aids economic development in yet another way: surplus produce is sold overseas to offset purchases of oil and other goods.

The Multifaceted Nature of Policies for Economic Development

Many policies pursue economic development concurrently with other goals. Officials approve subsidies for leisure-time activities (hunting, fishing, camping, swimming, and hiking) partly because such aid helps stimulate economic development in the regions to be visited by those seeking recreation. Decisionmakers justify a host of social programs partly on the basis of their role in increasing the purchasing power or productivity of the citizenry. Policies in support of education, manpower training, employment security, family assistance, pensions, health facilities and programs, and research in the natural sciences, technology, and the social sciences all have economic development as one of their goals. For example, policymakers hope that basic research will pay off through the introduction of new products, techniques, and schemes of organization in agriculture and industry that will increase productivity and release personnel for other economic activities.

"Economic development" includes economic balance and distribution as well as the sheer magnitude of economic resources, productivity, and growth rates. Many economists and policymakers believe that a "developed" economy should offer rewards to a broad spectrum of the population, especially to those who have low incomes and are (or can become) politically organized so as to threaten the status quo. Thus, programs defended as promoting economic development include provisions to spread economic opportunities and social services to groups and geographic regions that are currently getting less than an equal share of the economy's rewards. In the United States there are affirmative action programs to increase the educational and job opportunities of women, blacks, American Indians, and Spanish-American people; plus regional commissions charged with spurring economic growth in Appalachia, the Upper Great Lakes, New England, the Ozarks, a coastal belt in the Southeast, and the "four corner" region of Colorado, New Mexico, Arizona, and Utah.

ECONOMIC DEVELOPMENT
AS AN INFLUENCE ON POLICY

The relationship between public policy and economic development illustrates the reciprocity of the policy process. At the same time that policymakers seek to influence the rate or character of economic development in their environment, their own actions feel the influence of the economy that surrounds them. Policymakers respond to both the resources and the demands of their economies.

Resources Provided to Policymakers
by Economic Development

The degree of economic development in a jurisdiction affects public policy by shaping the magnitude and character of the resources available to officials. The more developed an economy, the more easily its governments should be able to assemble the revenues to pay for their activities. Studies of different nations, states, and cities find that officials in wealthier jurisdictions spend more than other officials for education, health benefits, housing, pensions, and subsistence payments to the poor.[2] Yet even in the wealthiest jurisdictions limited funds continually restrict the selection of policy.[3]

Well-developed economies also make available more of the highly trained professional and technical personnel needed to staff administrative agencies. This supply of trained personnel results partly from earlier investments (both public and private) in schools and universities, as well as from cultural factors that make the pursuit of education and an administrative career attractive to talented individuals. One problem faced by developing countries is a lack of skilled native administrators to staff their bureaucracies. In the United States there is a high proportion of northerners on the faculties of many southern universities. This is one example of our own shortage of native professionals in an underdeveloped region.

In addition to well-trained personnel, the bases of knowledge of a society have an impact on public policymaking. Effective public health programs or food and drug regulation require a strong base of medical knowledge. Likewise, sophisticated social or natural science theories underlie successful economic, environmental, and energy policies. A well-developed economy is more likely to have larger and more complex bases of knowledge than a less developed economy. Government programs aimed at encouraging activities in the private sector reflect officials' cognizance of their society's bases of knowledge. The U.S. federal government's efforts to encourage exploration for petroleum assume not only adequate capital in the private sector, but also enough skilled engineers, geologists, and workmen, enough pipelines, oil rigs, off-shore platforms, and the technology suitable for the task. These are all part of the "infrastructure" of the economy.

Demands Related to Economic Development

The social character of an economy also shapes the demands made on policymakers. Citizens having more education, sophisticated occupational skills, and elaborate personal tastes tend to demand recreational facilities to enjoy in their greater leisure, access to higher education, and investments in sophisticated research and development. The people of lesser-developed economies, and the lower-income citizens in wealthier settings, are more likely concerned with jobs, housing, and public health facilities.

The advanced urbanization and industrialization of a well-developed economy also generate demands on policymakers. Programs of sewage treatment, mass transit, and urban planning promise to relieve some of the problems associated with the congestion and sprawl of large cities. However, not all programs satisfy the needs of everyone. The industrialization attendant on most economic development requires urbanites to acquire a broad range of skills. This requisite diversity of economic roles generates different economic interests whose demands for public policies often conflict. Losers in the private sector of the economy frequently turn to government in an attempt to expand the scope of the conflict and alter decisions reached by private groups.

Labor unions, for example, demand programs to mediate their disputes with management; assure minimum wages, employee health and safety protections, and the payment of pensions to the aged and disabled; and protect the right to collective bargaining. Management wants its own protections including regulations of strikes and picketing. Each side in the enduring labor-management struggle supports governmental regulations to prevent the exercise of undue political influence by the other; such regulations may take the form of prohibitions against certain kinds of fund raising or against overt union or corporate involvement in election campaigns. At the same time, labor and management may cooperate in urging government programs to both expand opportunities for investments and jobs through research and development on new products, and provide protections against foreign competition (providing domestic manufacturers do not own an interest in foreign plants, which makes "foreign" competition less obnoxious to them).

Related to industrialization is the interdependence of developed economies. Activities in one sector of an economy affect those in other sectors. The strength of one sector may generate demands for policies such as anti-trust laws, windfall-profit taxes, wage and price controls, and environmental protection. Similarly, the weakness of a sector may stimulate demands for remedial legislation such as programs for unemployment insurance and public employment.

In a federal system of government like that operating in

the United States, different levels of government make demands on each other that reflect their own economic settings. State and local governments with economic problems press the national government for help, and localities make similar demands on their states. Generally, states with low per capita incomes receive the largest amounts of federal aid. In 1973–1974 state and local governments in the five poorest states (Alabama, Louisiana, Mississippi, New Mexico, and South Carolina) received $209 per capita in federal aid while those of other states received $197 per capita. The poor states spend more of the income resources of the state on statewide programs than do wealthy states. The insufficient resources of the local governments in poor states force the state governments to carry a large share of the burden for public services. The poorest states also tend to make the greatest tax efforts (tax revenues as a percentage of personal income) to pay for these services.

Economic Development and Public Policies in the American States

The fifty states within the United States provide numerous examples of policies that vary with the economic conditions. The per capita income in Connecticut is approximately 175 percent that in Mississippi. Utah has twice as large a percentage of adults with a high school education as South Carolina. California's population is over sixty times as large as Alaska's and New Jersey's is 1,000 times as dense. Such obvious, quantifiable diversity provides an ideal basis for examining the correlation between differences in economic development and different policies.

A comparison of state scores on measures of various aspects of economic development (such as per capita income, average years of education, and urbanization) with public spending (of both state and local governments) in each state reveals the following relationships: states that score higher on the economic measures spend more per capita for education, public health programs, correctional institutions and programs, and police protection than states that are less developed economically.[4]

This correlation is not as strong for per capita welfare expenditures.[5] Federal funds finance a considerable share of the welfare programs for the aged, the blind, dependent children, the disabled, and the unemployed. They account for half the money spent on public welfare, and the federal percentage of each state's welfare expenditures declines as the state's per capita income increases. Thus, money from the federal government frees state and local governments from total dependence on their own resources in providing welfare benefits to their citizens.

Nevertheless, welfare policies remain highly dependent on the resources provided by the higher-level jurisdiction. If we count federal grants-in-aid as part of a state's economic resources, the relationship between advanced economic development and high welfare expenditures is quite strong. The correlation between greater development and larger expenditures for highways and education is also strengthened by the fact that the federal government supports large grant-in-aid programs for these services too.[6]

Viewed from a different perspective, the impact of economic development on welfare policies is clear. The levels of benefits provided by programs like unemployment compensation, old age assistance, aid for dependent children, and general assistance are higher in the more economically developed states. This is particularly true for general assistance which receives no aid from the federal government and is therefore entirely dependent upon state and local resources.

The reason the economic development of a state strongly influences the size of the welfare benefits received by each welfare recipient but is less strongly related to the total amount (per capita) spent on welfare is that poorer states provide assistance to more recipients per population than do the richer states participating in many of the federally supported programs. Therefore, the amount available for each recipient is less in the less-developed states. Thus, our data on welfare expenditures reflect both the economic needs of jurisdictions and the resources available to meet those needs.

The correlation between economic development and per capita spending on highways differs from the relationship described for welfare. Road networks are usually more extensive and state expenditures on them greater (relative to population) in low income and rural states. This may reflect both the need for roads to connect scattered cities and towns, and the efforts of lesser-developed states to invest in their transportation infrastructure to promote economic growth.

Our analysis of the relation between economic development and policy has relied on aggregate measures of economic development, such as the "average" personal income in a state. However, such averages can hide markedly different *distributions* of incomes. In states where there is a large middle class the distribution may be fairly even, but in states where a few persons have high incomes and many people have low incomes, computation of the average income masks an inequitable distribution of earnings. In the United States large discrepancies in income occur where the majority of the population is poor, rural, lacking in education, and largely black.[7] The states of Utah and Georgia have nearly equal average incomes, but different kinds of distributions. Whereas the more equally well-to-do residents of Utah have demanded among the highest standards of education in the country, the state and local governments of Georgia face demands for more equal opportunities in jobs and housing as well as in education. Thus, different income distributions help create different public pressures for policies.

Contrary to what we might expect, however, the magnitude of a population's resources is more important than distribution (as measured by the distribution of income) in determining taxing and spending policies.[8] There is a plausible explanation for this finding. In areas where there is an unequal distribution of income, citizens are less politically active and there is less effective party competition than in regions where there is a more even distribution of wealth. Moreover, citizens at the bottom of the income ladder tend to be the least active in politics. Thus, those with the greatest needs have the least chance of fulfilling them.

Professor Thomas Dye has compared an index of the comprehensiveness of civil rights policies in each state to measures of average income and income distribution. He found that the more economically developed states had more comprehensive civil rights legislation. Moreover, the average incomes were more closely related to civil rights policies than measures of income distribution or Negro-White differences in employment rates, pay, education, and access to white collar jobs.[9] This correlation between overall economic development and support for civil rights may reflect the higher levels of education, and perhaps tolerance, that generally accompany higher levels of income. In addition, those most discriminated against are least effective in bringing political pressure to bear on policymakers, particularly if they are poor; blacks in the more developed states are more likely to have greater political resources, such as skilled leaders, strong organizations, funds, and access to communications.

It is important to distinguish between policy measurements that gauge average levels of services or taxes and those that gauge the distribution of services or taxes from one population group to another. A great deal more political conflict occurs over the question of who pays and who benefits from a policy, than over the adoption or scope of the policy. For much of the period between 1933 and 1965 policy disputes in many of the states revolved around questions of tax burdens. Proponents of the income tax quarreled with advocates of the sales tax about the merits and potential for progressive and regressive distribution of the costs of each tax.[10] (At this point it is impossible to chart the winners and losers in those disputes because 36 states (as of 1975) have adopted both income and sales taxes.)

Recent disputes over national energy policy have also focused on the distribution of costs. The issue is not whether the government should intervene in the "free" market—that happened long ago—but how each regulation will benefit and burden various segments of the population. A high tax on fuel, designed to discourage consumption, for instance, would burden most those citizens with low incomes who must spend a considerable portion of their incomes on heating oil, gas, and gasoline. Rationing would impose its economic burdens more equitably, but the costs and problems of enforcement have so far discouraged its use.

Several authors have examined how the economy affects the distribution of state and local taxation and spending. To analyze the balance between burdens and benefits, they investigated the relation between the publicly provided goods and services a given class of people receive and the taxes they pay. Their findings show that here also economic development is an important factor in determining the distribution of taxation and spending. Economically developed states, which have more resources per capita, are more willing to redistribute those resources from the relatively well-off to the relatively less well-off than are states in which most people live on marginal incomes.[11]

Noneconomic Factors That Affect the Influence of the Economy on Public Policy

It is not possible to develop a simple equation to express the relationship between the economy and public policy. Several noneconomic factors help determine just how the economy influences policy.

Historical setting affects the impact of the economy on policy. In the United States, it appears that economic constraints on public policy diminish when an economy exceeds a certain level of development. Richard Hofferbert has found that the similarity between the economic development of the 50 states has increased steadily. As the populace of each state has become wealthier, better educated, and more urbanized, the economic differences between states has decreased. Moreover, the variations between most state taxation and spending policies have also decreased.[12]

Federal aid has helped reduce the policy differences between states. Washington has provided even the least economically developed states with the resource base for many policies. Also, many developed states do not increase support for policies indefinitely. After they have attained "acceptable" levels of support for major services, they do not pursue further gains but turn their attention to other areas.[13]

The *level of government* within the United States is another factor that affects the weight of economic influence on policymaking. The national government is the least constrained by economic influence, because of its ability to both tax the resources of wealthy areas throughout the country and draw upon the broadest range of available talent and expertise. State economies are more homogeneous and allow state governments fewer opportunities to balance revenue shortfalls from poor locales with revenues from wealthy areas. Local governments, forced to rely upon a limited geographical area for resources, are the most restricted by their immediate economies.

Different levels of government also have different options for raising revenues. The federal government relies primarily upon personal and corporate income taxes. Because of their progressive nature, both provide revenues that increase even faster than the growth of the economy. As the entire society moves generally forward in augmenting its income because of economic growth or inflation, its members pay higher percentages of their incomes to the national government because they move into higher tax brackets.

Local governments generally have only one major source of revenue, the property tax. Being regressive, it is not as responsive as the income tax to economic growth and inflation. State taxes, primarily on income and sales, more nearly resemble the federal income tax in their potential for producing additional revenues in response to economic growth and inflation.

There are some further constraints on state and local revenues. First, many state constitutions limit the types and rates of taxes state and especially local officials may levy; Congress is relatively unhindered in this way. Second, states and smaller localities compete for industry, partly on the basis of taxes. Local and state officials are therefore reluctant to increase existing tax rates or institute new taxes.[14]

The federal government has yet other advantages in overcoming the constraints of the economic environment on its policymaking. Washington operates numerous programs to regulate economic growth, wages and prices, and, indirectly, its own tax receipts. Moreover, simply by passing a law it can borrow more freely and thus engage in deficit spending. Conversely, state constitutions severely limit the borrowing of state and local officials. Some state and local jurisdictions have poor records of fiscal management and thus find it difficult to raise capital at other than high interest rates. The 1978 federal debt of nearly $800 billion is over three times as large as the combined debt of state and local governments.

Finally, different levels of government receive demands from different economic interests. The more developed and interdependent the economy and social structure of the United States become, the more demands there are for federal regulation. For example, only the federal government can provide uniform standards in the areas of banking, securities, environmental protection, energy, labor unions, wages and prices, natural resources, anti-trust, and other aspects of interstate commerce.

SUMMARY

Various aspects of the economy influence public policy by serving either as a target of policies or as a source of the demands and resources that shape policy. Many policies are directly or indirectly aimed at increasing economic development. The importance of economic resources in supporting the whole range of policies encourages decisionmakers to give high priority to economic policies.

The economy provides the funds, personnel, and infrastructure necessary to carry out programs ranging from public welfare to the space shuttle. The level of a jurisdiction's development helps determine the demands as well as the resources policymakers encounter. Wealthy, educated populations living in urbanized, industrialized regions tend to demand different policies than poorer populations in less well-off rural areas. Noneconomic factors such as historical setting and level of government also have an impact on the relation betweeen economic development and policy.

Detailing a number of the prominent findings that appear in studies of the linkage between economies and policies in the United States, this chapter stresses that the economy is one factor in the environment of policymakers that adds to their predicament. Officials cannot ignore economic constraints, just as they cannot ignore the problems inherent in public pressures or in policies that appear to be rationally derived.

NOTES

1. See Irma Adelman and Cynthia Taft Morris, *Society, Politics, and Economic Development* (Baltimore: Johns Hopkins University Press, 1967), Chapter 2.

2. For example, see Thomas R. Dye, *Politics, Economics and the Public: Policy Outcomes in the American States* (Chicago: Rand McNally, 1966); Adelman and Morris, *Society, Politics, and Economic Development*; Frederick Pryor, *Public Expenditures in Capitalist and Communist Nations* (Homewood, Ill.: Irwin, 1968); Friedrich Edding and Dieter Bertecher, *International Developments in Education Expenditures, 1950–65* (Paris: UNESCO, 1969); Thomas R. Dye, "Governmental Structure, Urban Environment, and Educational Policy," *Midwest Journal of Political Science* (August 1967); and Robert L. Lineberry and Edmund P. Fowler, "Reformism and Public Policies in American Cities," *American Political Science Review* 61 (September 1967).

3. For just two of countless examples see Daniel P. Moynihan, *The Politics of a Guaranteed Income* (New York: Vintage, 1973), p. 143; and Norman C. Thomas, *Education in National Politics* (New York: David McKay, 1975), p. 227.

4. Thomas R. Dye, *Understanding Public Policy*, 2nd ed. (Englewood Cliffs, N.J.: Prentice-Hall, 1975), Chapter 12;

Ira Sharkansky and Richard A. Hofferbert, "Dimensions of State Politics, Economics, and Public Policy," *American Political Science Review* 63 (September 1969). See also James W. Dyson and Douglas St. Angelo, "A Methodological Problem in the Socio-Economic Interpretation of State Spending," *Policy Studies Journal* 2 (Winter 1973).

5. Dye, *Ibid*.

6. *Ibid*.

7. Thomas R. Dye, "Income Inequality and American State Politics," *American Political Science Review* 63 (March 1969).

8. *Ibid*.

9. Thomas R. Dye, "Inequality and Civil Rights Policy in the States," *Journal of Politics* 31 (November 1969).

10. A "progressive" tax is a tax in which the tax rates increase as the tax base (the amount subject to taxation) increases. A "regressive" tax is one in which the tax rates remain uniform or decrease as the tax base increases.

11. Brian R. Fry and Richard F. Winters, "The Politics of Redistribution," *American Political Science Review* 64 (June 1970); John L. Sullivan, "A Note on Redistributive Politics," *American Political Science Review* 66 (December 1972); Bernard H. Booms and James R. Halldorson, "The Politics of Redistribution: A Reformulation," *American Political Science Review* 67 (September 1973).

12. Richard I. Hofferbert, "Ecological Development and Policy Change in the American States," *Midwest Journal of Political Science* 10 (November 1966).

13. *Ibid*. This finding is consistent with the results of another study by Hofferbert. Comparing educationa¹ spending in Switzerland and the United States, he found that cantonal traits of economic development are more important influences on cantonal spending than state economic traits are on spending in the United States. He maintains that this stronger cantonal correlation results from Switzerland's rela-

tively lower level of economic development. See Richard I. Hofferbert, "Social Change, Intergovernmental Relations, and Education Finance in the Swiss and American Federations," in *Perspectives on Public Policy-Making,* ed. by William B. Gwyn and George C. Edwards III (New Orleans: Tulane Studies in Political Science, 1975).

14. This occurs despite the fact that tax levels are of only marginal importance in attracting or keeping business and industry. See Clara Penniman, "The Politics of Taxation," in *Politics in the American States,* 3rd ed., ed. by Herbert Jacob and Kenneth N. Vines (Boston: Little, Brown, 1976), p. 448.

Political
Constraints on
Decisionmaking

8

Like the economic development of a jurisdiction, political factors also circumscribe the choices of policymakers. Some alternatives are politically infeasible, some have been pre-empted by previous decisions of policymakers, and some are not viable because they seek to solve complex problems through a comprehensive approach which is impeded by governmental fragmentation.

POLITICAL FEASIBILITY

Policymakers consider an option politically feasible if it meets a minimum of political requirements. Yet political feasibility varies from one setting to another and often defies any straightforward definition. Economic considerations (Will a proposal cost "too much"?) and moral issues (Can a community like ours really consider a proposal like that?), as well as judgments about public opinion and the sensitivities of individual politicians all affect the viability of a policy option. Our discussion of economic resources and public opinion covered many aspects of political feasibility. In this section we focus on some special factors which help to determine the political feasibility of alternatives.

Political Culture

A policymaker must be sensitive to the prevailing public views of the important benefits and significant costs of proposed policies. Such views originate largely in the citizenry's political culture (i.e., its values and beliefs). The jailing or execution of political opponents, a feasible alternative in some countries, is not a serious option in the United States where an emphasis on civil liberties limits the types of policies officials can select. Americans consider deprivations of civil liberty to be extremely costly.

Political culture also affects the electorate's evaluation of the government's role in the economy. Few Britons today disapprove of government ownership of industry per se (although they may bitterly dispute government ownership of a particular industry). This is equally true for the citizens of many other countries, both "developed" and "developing." But few Americans approve of government ownership.[1] A policymaker in the United States can consider the option of nationalization only under the most extreme circumstances and even then at great risks to his or her career.

Related to the issue of who controls industry is the government's role in the provision of public services. The role of government in the American economy is less direct than governmental economic regulation in industrialized countries like Sweden, Canada, Britain, France, and West Germany.[2] In the United States, most services are provided by the private, not the public, sector. (Education and social security are the exceptions.) The United States has no government-owned airlines, coal companies, or telephone companies; no national health insurance for the general population; and little government-built housing. Rather, policymakers have attempted to encourage and regulate the provision of those services through subsidies, tax incentives, and the creation of special commissions empowered to supervise and make rules.

The following facts and hypotheses help to explain the exception of public education. Traditionally, it has not competed with private institutions; it helped "Americanize" immigrants; it has often served as a substitute for social action; and it reconciles, at least superficially, the values of equality (equal education) and liberty (lack of government intervention in the economy: more social welfare legislation might be required if there were not free access to education). Even in the field of public education, however, American values have imposed serious constraints on government support. Federal support for precollegiate education via large-scale financial aid was held up for many years by those who considered this an inappropriate area for government action—despite widespread public agreement about the need for greater funding of preschool, primary, and secondary educational programs.

Within the United States, the affect of political culture on the assessment of policy varies from region to region and state to state. The state of Oregon cut power consumption, banned all electrical outdoor and display advertising, cut the speed limit to 55 m.p.h. before Congress did, cleansed the Willamette River despite union and industrial opposition, placed an extra tax on pop-top cans and nonreturnable bottles (although it is a leader in aluminum smelting), trimmed its budget for the promotion of tourism (although tourism is its third largest industry), banned developers from its beaches, and decriminalized the possession of small amounts of marijuana. Why was this state able to take such rapid, effective action on several of the most intractable problems that Americans face (energy, pollution, control of growth, and drugs) while other states were not? The answer, of course, is very complicated, but it appears that it involves more than leadership, pressure groups, or legislators. The people of Oregon seem to value the benefits of the above policies more highly than do people in other states.

Each policy arena may be characterized by its own political culture, which emerges from the historic resolution of specific issues as well as from the basic cultural and political values of society. This miniculture includes a consensus on goals, means, and the types of political relationships through which policymaking should be achieved. The substance of the consensus is altered by new events. Thus, federal policy on higher education is constrained by a belief in the primacy of the states in that arena, division of responsibility, nondiscrimination in funding between public and private universities, an instrumental (i.e., job-oriented) view of public higher education, and the secondary status of support for higher education in relation to funding for elementary and secondary education.[3]

Bargaining and Compromise

In the midst of the separation of powers that characterizes American politics, policymaking requires common action. Decisionmakers can rarely act alone, especially on important issues. An alternative that cannot be supported by other decisionmakers is of little value no matter how much sense its benefits and costs make. This means that bargaining and compromise are an inherent part of policymaking. Sometimes there is explicit compromise; other times there is implicit bargaining, including the anticipation of opposition and the design of proposals to meet expected objections.

The Model Cities program was originally envisioned as an experiment to rejuvenate one city. However, President Johnson believed that only a big and bold program could get through Congress. Members of Congress would not vote for a program that benefitted only one city—most likely someone else's city—and that black leaders would criticize as tokenism. Moreover, Johnson did not want to choose between urban Democratic powerholders like Chicago's Richard Daley and Detroit's Jerome Cavanaugh. The result was a thinly spread program offering funds to some 150 communities.[4]

The passage of President Nixon's general revenue sharing proposal in 1972 is another example of the "something for everyone" route to political feasibility. Supporters of the proposal devised several formulae by which to distribute the funds, based on a variety of criteria including need (giving most to the poorer states), tax effort (benefitting most those states making the greatest efforts to raise their own revenues), and size of population. The final decision was a compromise which allowed states to choose from among two complex formulae the one that offered them the most benefits.

Sometimes policymakers alter one policy to gain support for another. In 1970 President Nixon agreed to increase federal spending on naval shipbuilding in order to obtain House Armed Services Committee Chairman Mendel Rivers' support for the Safeguard ABM system.[5]

Political feasibility influences the timing as well as the substance of legislation. President Kennedy needed the support of House Ways and Means Committee Chairman Wilbur Mills for the enactment of Medicare. But President Kennedy also needed Mills' support for trade and tax legislation, which meant he could not apply great pressure on Mills for Medicare. Kennedy also avoided pushing for Medicare in the early years of his term because he did not want the members of the Ways and Means Committee to record negative votes that would make it harder for them to change positions in the future. The President therefore attempted to compromise with Mills and his committee, but to no avail. What really tipped the balance in favor of Medicare was the 1964 election which replaced many conservative Republicans with liberal Democrats and altered the composition of the Ways and Means Committee. Mills became an advocate of Medicare to retain control of "his" group.[6]

Sometimes political feasibility means speed. Elected officials constantly face election campaigns which force them to press for quick results from the programs they support. According to Paul McCraken, former Chairman of the Council of Economic Advisers,

> the political calendar does not mesh well with the time required for economic processes to work themselves out. This makes for disinterest in programs with a pay-off beyond one or two years. And it creates a great temptation to embrace

programs that in the short run might be popular even if they are inimical to the longer-run economic vitality of the country. The failure to go for tax increases in 1966 and wage and price controls in 1971 would be major illustrations of this short-run horizon.[7]

Political feasibility is important in altering existing policies as well as in passing new ones. When the Nixon administration took office in 1969 it felt that the model cities program was "terrible," but it supported the continuance of the program because of the difficulty of ending it. Similarly, the President's proposals for welfare reform had to be built on top of the existing system of social services because it was not possible to dismantle that system.[8]

In general, it is easier to compromise on specifics, such as the size of an appropriation, than on questions of principle. The landmark Elementary and Secondary Education act of 1965, which provided the first substantial federal aid to elementary and secondary education, was passed only after legislators had circumvented several matters of principal. The issue of using federal money to advance the racial integration of public schools was settled by the 1964 Civil Rights Act which prohibited federal grants to institutions that practiced racial discrimination. Federal aid to parochial schools was another question of principle, which legislators bypassed by officially designating federal grants as aid to children and not to schools; this play of semantics allowed federal money to be used for items such as books and equipment in parochial schools. Opposition to general federal aid to education was surmounted by providing only categorical aid, that is, aid for specific purposes.[9] Thus, legislators opposed to school integration, aid to parochial schools, and federal intervention in local educational programs could still vote for the 1965 bill.

Bargaining and compromise, with an eye to feasible policy decisions, also take place in the appellate courts. All courts above the trial level are multimember tribunals whose official decisions require agreement among a majority of participating justices. Sometimes a court judges it must reach a unanimous decision to gain public compliance in a controversial case. A prominent example is the *Brown* decision in which the United States Supreme Court declared that public school segregation maintained by law was unconstitutional.[10]

As Charles Schultze, former Director of the Bureau of the Budget and current Chairman of the Council of Economic Advisors, has pointed out, sometimes paradoxical situations result from the limits set by political feasibility. In the areas of agriculture, public works, and maritime subsidies, for example, there are good data, market prices are useful in evaluating outputs, and there is a long tradition of policy analysis. But there are great political constraints in choosing alternatives because of pressure from well-organized, homogeneous groups faced with a potential decrease in their income.[11]

THE WEIGHT OF HISTORY ON PUBLIC POLICY

In the calculation of what is politically feasible, established traditions and programs have the edge. Current policy is one more addition to the accretion of many decisions, perhaps of several generations of choices. Contemporary officials seldom write upon a clean slate. Indeed, the very label for *re*formers suggests a background of hardened precedent and political tradition that must be altered in any effort to make policy fit the demands of the present generation.

The Meaning of History

When we speak of "history" as an influence on policy, we refer to the sum of numerous conservative factors that shape the policymaking process. If we only consider current economic conditions, public opinion, and governmental activity, we overlook the import of previous decisions, events and conditions that shaped the inception of various programs, which then acquired a life of their own and survived subsequent changes in the economy, public opinion, and government.

The hand of the past appears in both frivolous and profound components of politics and public policy. Much of the ritual in the policymaking process is deliberately frozen from a previous era, partly to lend a bit of color to the process and partly to preserve the appearance of an unfolding scene that legitimizes the present by linking it with the past. In this category of ritual are the ceremonial uniforms of the guards around Britain's government buildings; the incantations heard at the opening of the United States Supreme Court; the formal modes of address used by members of the United States Congress when speaking on the floor; and the antique desks, spittoons, and blotting sand that remain in the Senate Chamber from the early days of the nineteenth century.

Tangible signs of the past also appear in the substance of public policy. The programs of public assistance offered by the American states have enjoyed both federal aid and federal regulation since 1937. In 1973 such programs as Old Age Assistance, Aid to Families of Dependent Children, Aid to the Blind, and Aid to the Permanently and Totally Disabled received 51 percent of their funds from Washington. However, the programs were designed to allow each state to continue its historic emphasis—dating from the years before federal aid—on generosity or stinginess toward welfare recipients. Massachusetts' program for families of dependent children provided average monthly grants of $335 in 1972, while Mississippi's grants were only $53.

The weight of the past on the present is likewise apparent in the budgets of state governments. Most states that have high per capita expenditures are states that were high spenders in years past. Likewise, low-spending states of today usually spent less than other states in the past. If the difference between present and past is only a few years, the ranking of states by total budget remains virtually unchanged. All states spend more in response to inflation and the increasing demands for service of a larger population. However, their expenditures rise uniformly, with the high- and low-spenders keeping to their established places in their support of public services. Studies of state spending in the first seven decades of the twentieth century have found sizable statistical relationships between state spending in 1903 and state spending in the 1960s! Analyses of the factors that "explain" contemporary state spending reveal that state spending at the beginning of this century may be a more significant factor than some measures of contemporary social, economic, and political variables.[12]

The Framers and Their Constitution

The views of the framers of the United States Constitution and the governmental structures they created in the eighteenth century constitute a crucial source of historical influence on contemporary American policy. *The Federalist Papers,* written to defend the merits of the Constitution when the states were considering its ratification, make clear the framers' view of a diverse society with citizens grouped into political factions according to their occupations, wealth, and beliefs about such things as religion and government.

By erecting governmental structures that would make the assemblage of a dominant majority difficult, the framers sought to block any tyranny resulting from a combination of dominant factions. This concern produced the famous *separation of powers preserved by checks and balances.* As this mode of government is written into the Constitution, it includes separately selected executive, legislative, and judicial branches. Each branch is somewhat independent of the others in the way its members are selected and in their tenure, and each has the capacity to keep the other two from dominating policymaking. As a result, a spirited movement gaining influence in the population cannot easily gain control of the government for the purpose of implementing its will against the interests of a minority. Interpretation and amendment have changed the details of the Constitution in the course of nearly 200 years, but the written document remains a formidable bulwark against the power of a simple majority. The mode of selection of each branch favors a different faction of the population. The selection of the chief executive is assigned to a complex electoral college; and the selection of the judiciary is assigned to the President. The chief executive and members of the judiciary are protected against dismissal except by the extraordinary process of impeachment. The President can check the decisions of the legislature by his veto; each house can halt a policy proposal by refusing to give its consent; and the judiciary, as its power was defined by Chief Justice John Marshall in 1803, can check the other branches by ruling that a policy violates the Constitution. Further checks come from the federal nature of the government, with the nation and the states having only limited capacity to affect policies in the other's realm.

By its designers' intentions, and by its historical record compiled over close to two centuries of effective operation, the American pattern of separation of powers gives an important edge to established policy. Because numerous participants must cooperate to effect any major change in policy, it becomes difficult to make a significant change. Any one institution—chief executive, upper or lower house of the legislature, judiciary—can block a proposal. This means it is more difficult to introduce a major change than to defend current policy against contemporary challengers.

The separation of powers preserved by checks and balances, established for the national government in the Constitution, was adopted with some modifications by the designers of state governments. Actually, power is even more divided in the states than in the national government, with the result that the weight of history is likely to have an even greater impact on state policymaking. Most governors do not enjoy the extensive control over administrative departments that the President can exercise. A large majority of state attorneys general, superintendents of public education, and heads of other major departments are either directly elected by the voters or are named by boards over whom the governor has only limited control. Therefore, governors are less able than the President to count on the administrative cooperation of department heads.

Other features of state constitutions further restrict the current generation of policymakers. There are limits on state indebtedness and restrictions against using the proceeds of certain taxes for anything other than the support of a particular service. Both of these controls circumscribe the financial options of state policymakers and keep them from meeting currently conceived program needs with the same kind and range of alternatives that are available to the United States Congress. Also, state constitutions set the salaries of some officials and define the services various states agencies may provide. To lift these restrictions, citizens must hurdle the difficult procedures of constitutional amendment —in some states, amendment entails two consecutive approvals of the voters at the polls which means several years of constant politicking and publicity.

The appearance of new governmental structures in numerous localities in the last half century suggests a lack of historical encumbrance on current local policymakers. For example, the council-manager form of government is used by over 40 percent of U.S. cities in the 10,000–500,000 population range; this format puts one professional employee of the council in charge of proposing and later implementing the policies of the council. However, the apparent simplicity and efficiency of council-manager local governments applies only to the internal workings. State constitutions still impose external controls on many aspects of local government. The state limits the nature and extent of local taxation and indebtedness, and can give state administrators and legislators control over the salaries of local officials and the services offered by local departments.

One proof of the success of the separation of powers and checks and balances is their longevity. With the influx of diverse groups from eastern and southern Europe, Asia, and Latin America, the population of the United States has increased more than fiftyfold. Moreover, the descendents of former slaves have become a politically active 11 percent of the citizenry. The resultant social, political, and cultural diversity is even greater than that of the eighteenth century which justified the initial development of the separation of powers.

The venerable age of our government impresses the sanctity of tradition on current debates about policy. At one time the United States was described as the young radical among

the nations of the world. As recently as 1918 President
Woodrow Wilson could declare the New World's experiment
in democracy was sending troops to save the Old World.
Now we recognize that the United States has the oldest regime of any major country. When the U.S. Constitution
began its reign there were powerful monarchs in most capi-
tals of Europe; France had not yet embarked on its First
Republic (it is now on its Fifth); Italy and Germany were not
yet assembled out of numerous smaller entities; and most
regions of Africa and Asia had not even begun their colonial
and national experience. The Constitutional regime of the
United States has not faced a serious uprising in over 100
years. Communist and Socialist Parties—which have assumed antiregime stances in other major countries—have
never had more than token followings in the United States.
Lacking an established church or a figure-head monarch,
Americans seem to focus their secular faith on the Constitution; the original document is enshrined in a marble palace
in Washington and lowered each night into a bomb-proof
vault. For the purposes of analyzing policy, however, the
parchment is less important than the structures it created.
Each branch of government remains viable, especially in its
ability to block proposals for changing policy that come from
another branch.

The Conservative Nature of American Political Parties

The durability of the two major political parties in the United States also has a conservative effect on American policymaking. Republicans and Democrats have been opposing one another since 1854, which makes their competition
older than the current regimes of virtually all major nations.
Each major party has a traditional stance on policy, which
blunts demands for radical change. Other conservative party
features are likewise rooted in tradition: since their inception both parties have most often rallied behind leaders who
took pride in a pragmatic quest for electoral victory. The
goal of electability usually precludes the acceptance of new

causes that might appear radical to the electorate and thereby scare off blocks of voters who support traditional party images and policy.

There is something about the *two-party* nature of the prevailing competition that fosters the conservatism of the major parties. Because there are only two parties competing for supporters amidst one of the largest and most diverse national populations in the world, each party tries to attract followers through an amalgam of appeals that blurs ideological distinctiveness. Seeking the votes of a majority of the electorate, each party strives to gain the support of uncommitted middle-of-the-road voters. One result of this bland effort to appear all things to all people is that the main outlines of each party's platform resemble those of its competitor. Another result is that prevailing tendencies among the party leadership inhibit radical departures from past policy.

The blandness, universal appeal, and lack of ideological or programmatic distinctiveness of the major parties affect their choice of candidates as well as their development of platforms. In putting together national and state tickets each party seeks to "balance" its slate. By selecting candidates that represent different wings of the party each group hopes to broaden its appeal. Balancing also colors policy: the programs endorsed by the party slate are a composite of the preferences of numerous factions and are therefore unlikely to differ greatly from the programs advocated by the party's candidates in the past.

Similar forces toward compromise and moderation are at work among each party's delegation in the national and state legislatures. Republican Senators range from Jacob Javits and Edward Brooke to Barry Goldwater; Democrats from James Eastland to George McGovern. The result of this melange is a series of intraparty and interparty compromises that discourage distinctive new departures in policy. Those departures that do appear muster support despite, rather than because of, party politics, surmounting the hurdles of bland electoral campaigns, internally diverse party delegations in the legislature, and the pragmatic pursuit of pluralities from members of both parties in the legislative process.

The lack of strong national party leadership is both a reflection and a reinforcement of the traits that weaken the innovative thrust of the major parties. State and local organizations are the foundation of American parties. Nominees are chosen on the basis of their strength in state and local competitions. Moreover, most of the money for campaigns comes from party organizations based in the states. American parties differ greatly from their British and European counterparts, which depend heavily on national organs that collect the bulk of party funds centrally and distribute them to centrally selected candidates. Many observers believe that centrally organized parties have more distinctive programs than the major American parties. Reformers who would like United States voters to exercise a choice among policies when they cast their ballots have proposed rebuilding the major parties according to centralized foreign models. The lack of success of these reformers heightens our awareness of how solidly rooted the major parties are in the diversity of state and local concerns, and how this decentralization entails their perpetual coalition-building and concomitant policy blandness.

There have been instances in the recent history of each major party when a distinctive faction has gained control of the presidential nomination and offered a candidate with a distinctive stance on policy. In 1964 the Republicans nominated Barry Goldwater, who identified himself as "a choice not an echo." Yet the choice he offered was an extreme statement of Republican traditions harking back to the 1930s. Goldwater's questioning of public power and social security, his aggressively hawkish posture toward the developing situation in Vietnam, and his opposition to using national government authority to promote racial integration led moderate Republicans to abandon his campaign or to signal their active opposition. The result was a record vote for the Democratic candidate, Lyndon B. Johnson.

The Democrats had a similar experience in 1972. George McGovern was the candidate of those Democrats who wanted a clear alternative to Richard Nixon. McGovern stood for an early withdrawal from Vietnam and radical new measures for income security and tax reform. Like Goldwater, he seemed to push moderate Democrats into abstention or active opposition. Democratic candidates for governor, senator, and congressional representative sought to isolate their campaigns from the national ticket. The result was a landslide for Richard Nixon only slightly less impressive than Johnson's in 1964. Indeed, Nixon's 60.7 percent of the vote in 1972 is more impressive in some ways than Johnson's 61.1 percent in 1964. Nixon built his majority on the smaller base of the Republican Party and he won more party crossovers and Independents than Johnson.

The two major parties have a strong hold on American politics. They have ruled supreme, without an effective challenge by a "third" party, for over one hundred years. The factions behind the Goldwater campaign of 1964 and the McGovern campaign of 1972 did not bolt from their host party; they allowed themselves to be reabsorbed into the coalitions prevailing after their defeat. There have been several third party challenges since World War II: by Henry Wallace's left-wing Progressive Party and Strom Thurmond's right-wing States Rights Party, both in 1948; and George Wallace's American Independent Party in 1968. To date, however, none of these parties has stayed together long enough to achieve electoral success.

The American electoral system contributes its share to the maintenance of two parties and the conservatism of American politics. National officials win election in "single-member, simple plurality" contests. Since only one person represents a district, a party's candidate for the House or Senate must win the most votes in a district to gain a seat in Washington. For a minor party, likely to have a small, committed following distributed across numerous districts, the requirement of a plurality becomes a major hurdle. If there were proportionate representation, the minor party would receive credit in a national pool for the numerous votes it obtained, which, because of their distribution, failed to constitute a plurality in any one district. As it stands in the United States, however, a minor party can win no seats in Washington until it is strong enough to win a plurality in at least one district. Minor parties suffer between elections from a lack of prominent officeholders who can maintain a following from one campaign to the next.

We should not assign too much of the explanation for the American party system to the mode of selecting officeholders. The two-party, pragmatic, centrist character of American politics enjoys much support from politicians and politically astute citizens who are comfortable with things as they are. Party leaders who have achieved prestige and influence under the present system cannot be expected to urge major alterations. And most citizens appreciate the capacity of two pragmatic parties to mediate the political conflicts that could erupt in a country as large and as diverse as the United States. A history of political harmony extracts its price in policy blandness and conservatism; but this seems to have been the preference of the constitutional framers and of most of the policymakers who succeeded them.

Policy Predispositions

The weight of history is also manifest in traditional approaches to policy questions. The clash between advocates of growth and proponents of conservation on the state regulatory commissions, for example, reveals that many commissioners are predisposed to the assumptions of an earlier day. Before about 1965 economic growth was a goal without significant challenge, and it was common to allow utilities to charge large industrial users lower rates per kilowatt hour. The reasoning was that distribution costs were less to the large user than to the numerous private dwellings that collectively would consume the same amount of power, and there was a social benefit in permitting lower rates to the customer who would contribute to economic growth by using the power to support production and jobs. Now environmentalists advance a different argument: utility rates should encourage the use of less rather than more power. Because they must convince regulatory authorities to overturn established precedents, however, the advocates of this position must bear the burden of proof—against the opposition of utilities and their big customers, and against the skepticism of regulatory authorities. This means demonstrating that existing rate differentials have undesirable consequences for either the conservation of resources, the equitable distribution of costs, or the promotion of economic development.

Development in the state of Florida illustrates how the struggle between a policy tradition and its challengers can result in the preservation of the tradition, with a cosmetic change in the policy as a concession to reformers. Florida attracted a large population and built an impressive economy on the basis of promoting its climate and boosting state real estate, tourism, and agriculture. Between 1950 and 1972 the state climbed from 35th to 29th place among the states in per capita income and from 20th to 9th place in population. It has lagged behind no other state in its willingness to re-model land and waterways in the interest of development. Recently the state has come under pressure from conservation groups, but its typically Floridian response has been to support the tradition of development. The 1972 Environmental Land and Water Management Act was passed to provide state standards to limit further development. However, "in an effort to ensure that the Act could not be used to strangle development,"[13] the bill held the amount of land under state control to 5 percent of the total. Moreover, implementation would require the active effort of *local* governments, in a way that may scuttle any claim of "statewide" standards. In reference to this program, the Speaker of the Florida House wrote:

> We have ... learned the phrase "growth policy" has several connotations to various people. Of course, to those whose interests are intimately connected with a growing Florida, there was an immediate suspicion that the growth policy was intended to be an anti-growth policy. In the early stages, however, a consensus was reached that Florida cannot arbitrarily halt its growth, both as a matter of practical economics and as a matter of legal and constitutional principle.[13]

Policymaking Procedures

Many government officials overtly perpetuate the influence of history on their decisions—even though they may not think of themselves as conservative. American political culture places great value on consistency of decisions, equal treatment of citizens in similar circumstances, and the rules of precedence. Judges typically consult the records of past cases as a guide to decisions, and depart from a precedent only under compelling circumstances. Within administrative agencies, thick manuals serve a function similar to that served by the judge's tomes of earlier decisions. The manuals direct officers in different branches of government to make the decisions expected of them by policymakers in the central office, and keep to decisions consistent from one era to the next.

Many of the elaborate procedures in government are designed to blunt the threat of policy changes. Requirements for public hearings by legislative committees or administrative agencies, the scheduling of motions by adversaries in judicial proceedings, and the advance publication of proposed statutes and administrative rulings notify interested parties that certain changes are in the offing, and permit opponents to present their own case. Much of the bureaucracy's "red tape," which invites criticism and ridicule for its slowdown of policymaking, consists of procedures whereby certain officials review decisions so as to uphold governmental standards of equity, consistency, and predictability. Of course, *flexibility* and *adaptability* compete with *consistency* and *equity* as standards of good government. When circumstances change more than the willingness of officials to alter their policies, the charges of red tape, undue delay, and outmoded precedents signal the heavy weight of history on policymaking.

Committed Resources

In Chapter 7 we saw that the limited resources within a government's jurisdiction exert an important influence on policymaking. Previous commitment of existing resources also constrains that process.

The list of commitments that limit the discretion of contemporary officeholders is extensive. Citizen clients of public services expect government programs to remain in force; officials of other governments expect intergovernmental agreements to remain in effect; contractors expect that arrangements to supply goods or services to government agencies will continue as stated; and government employees count on the continuation of present jobs and working conditions, including opportunities for seniority, merit raises, and pensions. Think of the uproar on the campus of a large state university if the state legislature were to seriously consider abolishing major programs or closing the whole institution. Unrealistic? Probably. Such an option lies beyond the realm of reason because the awesome possibility of countless students, professors, staff personnel, plus their friends and families descending on the legislature usually keeps such options outside the realm of political feasibility.

A description of the expansive and intertwined character of intergovernmental programs in the United States illustrates how policies chosen in the past coupled with the need to protect other policymakers from unexpected change confine the actions of policymakers at all levels. In 1974, some 26 percent of the national government's domestic budget went to state and local governments. The sums received were about 23 percent of state and local budgets. The states are donors as well as recipients. In 1973 they committed 38 percent of their budgets to localities, a sum which constituted 31 percent of local government revenues. There are some 78,000 governments in the United States, linked together by national and state intergovernmental payments that now amount to about $100 billion. Whenever serious questions arise about the continuation of intergovernmental payments, uncertainties ripple outward to the politicians in charge of the recipient governments; to their civil service employees; to the contractors from whom they purchase goods or services; and to citizens who are the ultimate clients of their programs.

Most state and federal expenditures for existing programs do not even come under direct review in the annual appropriations process. Approximately 75 percent of the federal budget (and more than 90 percent of nondefense programs) is "uncontrollable" in any given year. That is, the vast majority of federal spending is either mandated under existing law or required to liquidate previously contracted obligations.[14] Moreover, most of the increase in the budget over the previous year also goes to uncontrollable expenditures.[15]

A major component of uncontrollable expenditures is payments to individuals: social security, Medicare, Medicaid, civilian and military pensions, public assistance, veterans compensation, and unemployment insurance. Each of these policies (and others like them) entitle individuals to benefits by law as long as they meet stated eligibility requirements. These entitlements are independent of specific appropriations by Congress. Congress has obligated itself to provide whatever funds are required to serve those who qualify. In recent years the entitlement programs have grown more rapidly than other federal civilian commitments and have made nondefense spending increasingly uncontrollable. Congress has frequently cut the "controllable" portion of budget requests and then increased the costs of entitlement programs by relaxing eligibility requirements and raising benefits.

Other major uncontrollable annual expenditures are outlays from prior contracts and obligations (which the government is committed to pay), interest on the national debt, general revenue sharing (a state and community entitlement program), payments for farm price supports (the government formally reimburses the Commodity Credit Corporation for losses), and deficits in the operation of the United States postal service.

Even those expenditures that can be cut without a change in the statutes are not as controllable as they seem. The largest such items are personnel and day-to-day operating costs. The costs of policies like national defense and the National Park Service, which require direct federal administration and large expenses for personnel, are potentially the most controllable. Salaries and fringe benefits for federal employees are obligated for only a few weeks at a time, and appropriations for them undergo yearly review. However, civil service seniority rules constrain decisionmakers from eliminating employees. Because those with the least seniority must go first, cutbacks could mean retention of the least-needed personnel. Recently hired minority employees usually bear the brunt of layoffs; reducing spending in this way may therefore defeat important affirmative action features of personnel policy. Moreover, it is hard to reduce the salaries or eliminate the jobs of competent and responsible employees. Aside from humanitarian concerns, governmental agencies must be able to attract capable persons to public jobs and honor union contracts.

When there is pressure to reduce personnel expenses, one solution is to "freeze" hiring. Persons who leave public employment are not replaced, at least not for the duration of the freeze. The drawback of this response is that it is divorced from other policy considerations. The people who leave may cause gaping holes in the administration of important programs. The advantage of a freeze is its simplicity. It reduces the complexity and political costs of making personnel decisions.

As long as employees have been hired, it makes little sense to cut their supplies or fail to maintain their equipment. Similar logic prevents the ending of partially completed projects. There is little sense, so the argument goes, in not completing a project and thereby wasting the initial investment. (The counter argument, of course, is that expenditures may simply extend a wasteful project.)

Ongoing statutes fix revenue as well as expenditures and it is often not feasible to introduce substantial statutory changes. This is true not only for the major federal provisions that define tax rates and exemptions, but also for certain statutory oddities that commit some revenues to specific purposes. Visitor fees at Grand Teton National Park, for example, automatically go for the educational expenses of the dependents of park employees; the Department of the Interior receives one-third of the revenues collected from federal grazing lands and uses them for range improvements; 30 percent of custom receipts automatically go to agricultural programs; revenues from gasoline taxes finance transportation policies.[16] Similarly, about one-third of state revenues are earmarked.[17] The proceeds from Oklahoma's sales tax are earmarked for the Welfare Department, making the state's welfare payments higher than its per capita wealth would indicate, and Alabama has designated portions of six state taxes for old age pensions. Finally,

> the Colorado Fish and Game Commission ... enjoys much support among that portion of the populace interested in hunting, fishing, and conservation. The commission derives a lucrative income from various fees, earmarked by law for its activities. Over the years, governors and legislators have come to view the commission's budget as simply outside their purview because of the widespread and vocal support the commission can generate whenever a suggestion is made that its funds might be in excess of its needs.[18]

Tax expenditures—those special features in the tax code exempting certain activities from taxation—are, in effect, both authorizations and appropriations of money for activities the government wishes to encourage and support. There is no established procedure for reviewing these tax expenditures in a regular manner. In fiscal 1977, about $114 billion of federal revenues (about one-fourth of the conventional budget) were not available for other policies.

GOVERNMENTAL FRAGMENTATION

The framers of the Constitution designed a divided government as a protection of liberty. The separation of powers between the major branches and the further divisions of Congress and administrative agencies into specialized units continue to have some appeal to the members and supporters of individual units. However, fragmentation constrains policymakers in their selection of alternatives.

Fragmentation of Administrative Responsibility

President Nixon sought some relief from administrative fragmentation, which he described minutely in his 1971 message on governmental reorganization.[19] The excerpt is lengthy, but the analysis is sound and warrants consideration.*

> As we reflect on organizational problems in the federal government today, one seems to stand out above all others: the fact that the capacity to *do* things—the power to achieve goals and to solve problems—is exceedingly fragmented and broadly scattered throughout the federal establishment. In addressing almost any of the great challenges of our time, the federal government finds itself speaking through a wide variety of offices and bureaus, departments and agencies. Often these units trip over one another as they move to meet a common problem. Sometimes they step on one another's toes. Frequently, they behave like a series of fragmented fiefdoms—unable to focus federal resources or energies in a way which produces any concentrated impact.
>
> Consider these facts: Nine different federal departments and twenty independent agencies are now involved in education matters. Seven departments and eight independent agencies are involved in health. In many major cities, there are at least twenty or thirty separate manpower programs, funded by a variety of federal offices. Three departments help develop our water resources and four agencies in two departments are involved in the management of public lands. Federal recreation areas are administered by six different agencies in three departments of the government. Seven agencies provide assistance for water and sewer systems. Six departments of the government collect similar economic information—often from the same sources—and at least seven departments are concerned with international trade.
>
> Income support programs, including those which administer food stamps, welfare payments, retirement benefits and other forms of assistance, are scattered among three departments and a number of other agencies. The Department of Agriculture, the Department of Health, Education, and Welfare, and the Office of Economic Opportunity all handle food and nutrition matters. Child care programs, migrant programs, manpower programs, and consumer programs often suffer from similarly divided attention.

---

*Although we quote each paragraph verbatim, we have rearranged the order of the paragraphs to enhance the readability of the passage within our discussion of governmental fragmentation.

Such a division of responsibility can also create a great deal of overlap. The Agriculture Department, for instance, finds that its interest in agricultural labor is shared by the Labor Department, its regard for agricultural enterprise is shared by the Small Business Administration, and its concern for providing sufficient transportation for farm products is shared by the Department of Transportation. The Commerce, Labor and Agriculture Departments duplicate one another in collecting economic statistics, yet they use computers and statistical techniques which are often incompatible.

It is important that we move boldly to consolidate the major activities of the government. The programmatic jumble has already reached the point where it is virtually impossible to obtain an accurate count of just how many federal grant programs exist. Some estimates go as high as fifteen hundred.

The diffusion of responsibility makes it extremely difficult to launch a coordinated attack on complex problems. It is as if the various units of an attacking army were operating under a variety of highly independent commands. When one part of the answer to a problem lies in one department and other parts lie in other departments, it is often impossible to bring the various parts together in a unified campaign to achieve a common goal.

Various parts of the *interdependent* environment are still under the purview of highly *independent* federal offices. As a result, federal land policies, water programs, mineral policies, forestry practices, recreation activities and energy programs cannot be easily coordinated, even though the manner in which each is carried out has a great influence on all the others.

Again and again we encounter intragovernmental conflicts in the environmental area. One department's watershed project, for instance, threatens to slow the flow of water to another department's reclamation project downstream. One agency wants to develop an electric power project on a certain river while other agencies are working to keep the same area wild. Different departments follow different policies for timber production and conservation, for grazing, for fire prevention and for recreational activities on the federal lands they control, though the lands are often contiguous.

Even our basic analysis of public needs often suffers from a piecemeal approach. Problems are defined so that they will fit within established jurisdictions and bureaucratic conventions. And the results of government action are typically measured by the degree of activity within each program rather than by the overall impact of related activities on the outside world.

Divided responsibility can also mean that some problems slip between the cracks and disappear from the government's view. Everybody's business becomes nobody's business and embarrassing gaps appear which no agency attempts to fill. At other times, various federal authorities act as rivals, competing with one another for the same piece of "turf."

Sometimes one agency will actually duplicate the work of another; for instance, the same locality may receive two or more grants for the same project. On other occasions, federal offices will actually find themselves working at cross-purposes with one another; one agency will try to preserve a swamp, for example, while another is seeking to drain it. In an effort to minimize such problems, government officials must spend enormous amounts of time and energy negotiating with one another that should be directed toward meeting people's needs. And even when they are able to work out their differences, officials often reach compromise solutions which merely represent the lowest common denominator of their original positions. Bold and original ideas are thus sacrificed in the quest for intragovernmental harmony.

In addition to grappling with executive fragmentation, the President must come to grips with the difficulty of controlling his own administration's relations with Congress. Because the House and Senate appropriate the money for programs and can demand that the President execute the policies it passes, Congress is able to hinder the President's attempts at coherent policymaking. Theodore Sorensen, one of President Kennedy's closest aides, has complained along with countless other officials of the "sweetheart contracts" between the FBI and Congress, and between Congress and the Bureau of Reclamation, the Passport Office, the Forest Service, the Park Service, and the Army Corps of Engineers.[20] At any time Congress may order programs independent of the comprehensive overview of the President.

Systemic Fragmentation of Responsibility

The federal executive branch is not the only place where the division of responsibility constrains the selection of policy alternatives. In a report issued in late 1974, the Subcommittee on Fiscal Policy of the Joint Economic Committee of Congress described the effect of systemwide fragmentation on welfare policy.

> The habit of approaching problems in isolation has led to fragmented and inconsistent legislation and administration. Income security programs alone are shaped by at least 21 committees of Congress and by 50 state legislatures, by six cabinet departments and three federal agencies, by 54 state and territorial welfare agencies ... by more than 1,500 county welfare departments, by the U.S. Supreme Court and many lesser courts. The result is that official action, whether legislative or administrative, never addresses the welfare problem as a whole. Yet action on one segment of the system inevitably affects other segments.[21]

Causes of Governmental Fragmentation

One reason for the fragmentation discussed by President Nixon is that Congress frequently writes separate and dispersed agencies into law so it can watch over each part of the bureaucracy. For the same reason it favors categorical (rather than general purpose) grants that designate specific authority and money to particular agencies to perform well-defined functions.

Congressional jurisdictional jealousies provide another rationale for fragmentation. When President Ford submitted his omnibus energy program to Congress in 1975, it was divided up and parceled out to four committees in the House and nine in the Senate, all of which desired to have their say on energy policy. In water resource policy, the Interior committees have authority over the Bureau of Reclamation, the Public Works committees over the Corps of Engineers, and the Agricultural committees over the Soil Conservation Service. None of these committees want to give up their authority over "their" agencies. And none of the groups interested in these policies want to lose their special access. Thus, the agencies and programs that deal with a common problem remain divided among three Cabinet departments.[22]

Jurisdictional jealousies among agencies are another cause of governmental fragmentation. Former presidential aide Joseph Califano writes that on scores of proposals for executive reorganization he saw cabinet or agency heads who were gaining jurisdiction in favor and those who were losing it opposed. And when President Johnson tried to coordinate urban programs through an executive order vesting the Secretary of Housing and Urban Development with the power to convene the resources of the other departments and agencies for a coherent response to urban problems, the order was widely ignored. Similarly, bureaucratic bickering at both the national and field levels prevented the opening of most of the proposed "one-stop service centers" which President Johnson wanted to establish to provide a central neighborhood access to all federally available social services. The Labor Department, Office of Equal Opportunity, and Department of Housing and Urban Development all wanted the service centers to bear their names to the exclusion of the others.[23]

Interest groups also support fragmentation. In 1966 President Johnson submitted a bill to move the Maritime Administration from the Department of Commerce to the proposed Department of Transportation. The pre-vote line-up in Congress was close until George Meany, President of the AFL-CIO, telegraphed all members of the House that support for the President on this issue would be considered an antilabor vote. The bill was defeated decisively. Similarly, organized labor successfully opposed Johnson's attempt to combine the Departments of Labor and Commerce.[24]

SUMMARY

Political factors limit the choices available to officials. Some alternatives are not politically feasible because they violate important public values and beliefs, and others require bargaining and compromise. History also has a conservative impact on policymaking: The constitutionally determined structure of government, inherited disputes among politicians, and the traditional procedures of policymaking circumscribe the possibilities for substantially changing the status quo or rejecting the legacy of history. Previous decisions create policy predispositions and commit resources in ways that are difficult to alter. Finally, the fragmented nature of government precludes the comprehensive approach required for the effective resolution of some complex problems.

Yet somehow policies are made. In the following chapter we turn our attention to the factors that facilitate policymaking amidst the constraints.

NOTES

1. Donald J. Devine, *The Political Culture of the United States* (Boston: Little, Brown, 1972), pp. 210–211.

2. Anthony King, "Ideas, Institutions and the Policies of Governments: A Comparative Analysis," *British Journal of Political Science* 3 (July, October 1973).

3. Thomas R. Wolanin and Lawrence Gladieux, "The Political Culture of a Policy Arena: Higher Education," in *What Government Does,* ed. by Matthew Holden, Jr., and Dennis Dresang (Beverly Hills, Calif.: Sage Publications, 1975).

4. Edward C. Banfield, "Making a New Federal Program: Model Cities, 1964–68," in *Policy and Politics in America,* ed. by Allan P. Sindler (Boston: Little, Brown, 1973).

5. Morton H. Halperin, *Bureaucratic Politics and Foreign Policy* (Washington, D.C.: Brookings Institution, 1974), p. 81.

6. Theodore R. Marmor, *The Politics of Medicare* (Chicago: Aldine, 1970), Chapters 3 and 4.

7. Paul W. McCraken, "Reflections on Economic Advising" (paper presented at the Princeton University Conference on Advising the President, Princeton, N.J., October 31, 1975), p. 11.

8. Daniel P. Moynihan, *The Politics of a Guaranteed Income* (New York: Vintage, 1973), pp. 420 and 371.

9. Norman C. Thomas, *Education in National Politics* (New York: David McKay, 1975), p. 38.

10. For example, see S. Sidney Ulmer, "Earl Warren and the *Brown* Decision," *Journal of Politics* 33 (August 1971); Walter F. Murphy, *Elements of Judicial Strategy* (Chicago: University of Chicago Press, 1964); J. Woodford Howard, "On the Fluidity of Judicial Choice," *American Political Science Review* 62 (March 1968); Sheldon Goldman, "Conflict and Consensus in the United States Courts of Appeals," *Wisconsin Law Review*, No. 2 (1968).

11. Charles L. Schultze, *The Politics and Economics of Public Spending* (Washington, D.C.: Brookings Institution, 1968), pp. 88–89.

12. Ira Sharkansky, *Spending in the American States*, (Chicago: Rand McNally, 1968).

13. T. Terrell Sessums, "Legislating a Growth Policy," *State Government: The Journal of State Affairs* 47 (Spring 1974), p. 86.

14. Barry M. Blechman, Edward M. Gramlich, and Robert W. Hartman, *Setting National Priorities: The 1976 Budget* (Washington, D.C.: Brookings Institution, 1975), Chapter 7; and U. S. Office of Management and Budget, *Budget of the United States, Fiscal Year 1968* (Washington, D.C.: Government Printing Office, 1977), p. 420.

15. John R. Gist, "'Increment' and 'Base' in the Congressional Appropriations Process," *American Journal of Political Science* 21 (May 1977).

16. Murray L. Weidenbaum, "Institutional Obstacles to Reallocating Government Expenditures," in *Public Expenditures and Policy Analysis,* ed. by Robert H. Haveman and Julius Margolis (Chicago: Markham, 1970), pp. 243–244.

17. Tax Foundation, Inc., *Earmarked State Taxes* (New York: Tax Foundation, Inc., 1965).

18. Richard I. Hofferbert, *The Study of Public Policy* (Indianapolis, Inc.: Bobbs-Merrill, 1974), p. 52, note 29.

19. Richard M. Nixon, "Government Reorganization Message from the President," in U.S. Congress, Senate, *Congressional Record,* 92nd Cong., 1st session, May 25, 1971, 117:8037–8043.

20. Theodore C. Sorensen, *Watchmen in the Night* (Cambridge, Mass: MIT Press, 1975), p. 43. See also Harry McPherson, *A Political Education* (Boston: Little, Brown, 1972), pp. 224–226.

21. U.S. Congress, Joint Economic Committee, *Income Security for Americans; Recommendations of the Public Welfare Study,* Joint Committee Print (Washington, D.C.: Government Printing Office, 1974).

22. For a recent example of committee jurisdictional jealousies, see "Senate Approves Committee Changes," *Congressional Quarterly Weekly Report,* February 12, 1977, pp. 279–284.

23. Joseph A. Califano, Jr., *A Presidential Nation* (New York: W. W. Norton, 1975), pp. 25 and 31–33.

24. *Ibid.,* pp. 139–140 and 29.

POLICYMAKING IV

Making policy is not a simple process. There are so many choices and no dominant guidelines. Neither public opinion nor rational analysis are effective guides to the decisions that shape policy; and although economic and political constraints narrow the range of possibilities, no one constraint is dominant enough to substantially ease the policymaker's task. If it is sometimes easy to know what *should not* be done, it is seldom clear what *should* be done, or what *can* be done.

In Chapter 9 we show how the procedures of policymaking reflect the problems described earlier, generating policy that is safe, conservative, and routine. Yet not all decisionmaking falls into this mold. There is some demand for radical change, and enough dynamism to support occasional changes in the procedures and results of policymaking. In Chapter 10 we look beyond the formulation of policy to its implementation—the actual delivery of its benefits to those it is designed to serve. Again we find problems. Many of the economic and political factors that complicate the design of policy also complicate the tasks of implementation. The basic components and unavoidable complications of those tasks are the topics of our final installment of the policy predicament.

Decisionmaking

9

The numerous difficulties policymakers face in following public opinion, defining problems, clarifying and ranking goals, generating information and options, and assessing alternatives raise a crucial question: How do policymakers cope with the necessity of making decisions about the complex and uncertain situations they must confront? In general, they cope by trying to simplify each situation so they can make decisions according to prescribed routines. Decisions that are genuinely innovative are rare, and for that reason of special interest to us.

DECISION RULES

Incrementalism

Incrementalism is the term most commonly used to describe public policymaking in the United States.[1] Decisions prescribe change in small increments and the focus of the decisions is on these increments, that is, on the difference between a proposed policy change and the status quo. Policymakers consider a restricted number of alternatives, usually concentrating on options whose known or anticipated consequences differ only incrementally from those of existing policy. Because they do not consider all possible alternatives for achieving a goal, there is less of a need for developing options, and gathering and analyzing information.

Since decisions generate incremental change, policy in a given area is not made once and for all; rather it is made and remade continuously in a chain of incremental steps, as in the annual budgetary review. This has several advantages for policymakers. By taking one small step at a time, they can deal with the familiar. They can understand the probable consequences of a marginal departure from past experience. They can estimate which incremental results follow from which incremental changes in policy. Later decisions modify earlier ones as the consequences of previous steps become the new concerns of policy. Moreover, the consequences of an incremental change in policy are usually fewer and less sizable than those of a major change; thus, they require less understanding of comprehensive relationships.

Decisions for incremental change are relatively easy to make. Policymakers do not expect to solve problems through such decisions; they just try to make improvements in an evolving situation. If they view the results of an incremental policy as bad, they can alter that policy at the next opportunity for evaluating it. They can recognize considerations left out of earlier decisions and incorporate them into later ones. Moreover, as the problems and opinions about an issue change with time, decisionmakers can alter policies in incremental steps to reflect this movement.

By considering incremental alternatives policymakers remain close to what has been proven politically feasible. Parties and candidates compete for votes on the basis of increments of change, not fundamentals. Only abnormal circumstances cause major changes in policy. Therefore, policymakers engage in a series of incremental moves about which they can readily agree, and thereby avoid raising issues of ultimate principle or comprehensive reform.

Reliance on precedent and options restricted to incremental policy change means that many potential conflicts pass unexamined. If policymakers opened up the entire area of a policy for debate each time they wanted to make a change, policymaking would be chaos. Incrementalism allows past commitments to remain in effect so that clients, employees, contractors, and recipients of intergovernmental assistance do not continually face the threat of a possible interruption of existing arrangements. Moreover, those policymakers who compromised and bargained in the past to establish present policy need not go through the entire process again. They can save for other matters the time, energy, and goodwill such repetition would consume.

Incrementalism cannot solve all the decisionmaking problems raised in this book. It does not clarify public opinion, identify problems, rank goals, assure that the best options (even the best incremental options) are raised or fully analyzed, or lessen constraints. What it does do is make the task of decisionmaking manageable. As the examples below illustrate, policymakers have found the advantages of incrementalism compelling.

Budgetary Decisions. In making budgetary decisions, decisionmakers generally follow simple decision rules. They accept the legitimacy of established programs and, except under conditions of great economic constraint, agree to continue previous expenditures. They actually consider only the increments of change proposed for the new budget and the limited range of goals embodied in the departures from established activities. They do not debate grand social goals nor do they reassess the benefits and costs of ongoing programs.[2]

The paperwork required of budgetmakers includes the item-by-item listing of expenditures for the past, present, and future years. This effectively isolates expenditures for continuing programs from the increments of proposed new expenditures and invites reviewers to focus on the latter. The United States Office of Management and Budget goes further and requires agencies to categorize funds into those designed to expand programs and those needed to pay "automatic increases," (i.e., to cover required increases in salaries and rising costs for telephone, mail, utility, and other services). "Automatic increases" receive less scrutiny than increases related to programmatic changes.[3]

The actions of policymakers on proposed increments are also incremental. Decisionmakers rarely approve budgetary increases that were not requested in a previous stage of the budgetary process (which we can simplify here as moving from agency to elected executive to legislature). Moreover, decisionmakers rarely support an increase of more than 5–10 percent in the budgets of agencies or programs.[4]

Judicial Decisions. Incrementalism appears in the decisions of the judiciary as well as in the actions of other branches.[5] Judges are normally presented with only two alternatives (one from each contending party). Moreover, because they deal only with "cases and controversies," they face concrete situations rather than abstract questions. This in turn reduces the number of consequences they have to consider for any given decision. A clear change in policy usually comes over an extended period of time, in incremental steps.

The development of judicial policy on racial integration of public educational institutions illustrates the incremental nature of judicial decisionmaking. The first post-Civil War public school integration case reached the Supreme Court in 1899. In *Cummings v. County Board of Education* the Court upheld the policy of segregation by allowing a Georgia school board to close down Negro high schools and provide no high school education at all for blacks. The next case was not heard until 1927. In *Gong Lum v. Rice* the Court again gave its support to segregation when it ruled that it was legal to segregate a Chinese child from the white schools. In 1938, however, in *Missouri ex rel. Gaines v. Canada* the Supreme Court held that a student had been denied equal protection of the law when Missouri failed to provide a law school for Negroes despite the fact that tuition to schools in other states was available. A similar ruling came 10 years later in *Sipuel v. Board of Regents.* In 1950 the Court made another incremental advance when it held in *Sweatt v. Painter* that

Texas' provision of a separate and *unequal* law school for Negroes denied black law students equal protection of the law. The same year in *McLaurin v. Oklahoma State Regents* the Court held that segregation within the University of Oklahoma graduate school was unconstitutional.

It was not until 1954 that the Court directly faced the broad question of segregation in elementary and secondary education. In *Brown v. Board of Education of Topeka* (covering states) and *Bolling v. Sharpe* (covering the District of Columbia) the Court found that governmentally enforced racial segregation in public schools was unconstitutional. The Court saw this decision as momentous, and, in an example of incremental strategy, put off for a year its decision on how to implement it. The 1955 decision on implementation was that schools should be integrated "with all deliberate speed." This was easier said than done, however, and the Court spent much of the 1950s and 1960s making incremental adjustments to foil efforts to evade the *Brown* decision.

In *Florida ex rel. Hawkins v. Board of Control* (1957) the Court told a recalcitrant University of Florida that integration must occur immediately in higher education; in *Cooper v. Aaron* (1958) the Court ruled that *Brown* could not be nullified by evasive schemes of school boards or the possibility of community opposition or violence; and *Griffin v. County School Board of Prince Edward County* (1964) held that it was unconstitutional to close schools to avoid integration. Four years later the Court, in *Louisiana Financial Assistance Commission v. Poindexter* affirmed a lower court ruling that it was unconstitutional to give state tuition grants to students who attend private segregated schools. The next year in *Green v. School Board of New Kent County* and a companion case the Court ruled that the duty to end segregation in the public schools was not discharged unless the integration plans ("freedom of choice" and "free transfer" in these cases) actually led to a unitary school system. Finally, in *Alexander v. Holmes County Board of Education* (1969) the Court ordered an end to "all deliberate speed" and demanded that integration take place immediately in all remaining segregated school systems.

At that point the court had only required negative actions, to end segregation required by law *(de jure)*. But what about positive actions to overcome school segregation? In *Swann v. Charlotte-Mecklenburg Board of Education* (1971) the Court ruled (1) that school districts with a history of segregation had an obligation to act positively to achieve integration; (2) that courts could order districts to reassign teachers, bus students, alter attendance zones, and use racial quotas to achieve this goal; (3) that in school districts where there was no history of *de jure* segregation the courts could also order positive action to integrate the schools, although they were not constitutionally obligated to do so.

Thus, over a period of nearly three-quarters of a century, the Supreme Court went from supporting segregation in public schools, to forbidding segregation, to requiring affirmative action to achieve integration. In arriving at the present policy, the Court displayed decisional tendencies similar to those seen in the other branches of government. There were no sweeping rulings to wipe out segregation and institute integration at one fell swoop; rather the Court redefined policy through incremental steps, starting at the level of graduate and professional schools and working down towards elementary and secondary education.

In moving toward aggressive support of integration, the Court limited its consideration to policy alternatives that seemed the most feasible politically, trying not to impose a greater burden on society than it could reasonably be expected to bear. Thus, integration was to be tested against the flexible standard of "all deliberate speed" rather than "immediately." The Court also made new policies in light of the consequences of its previous policies, as illustrated in its responses to various attempts at evading the *Brown* decision.

Federal Aid to Education. Although federal aid to education began with the 1785 Land Ordinance, which set aside land for the maintenance of public schools, as late as 1940, there was no substantial federal aid to education. Since 1965, however, federal support for a variety of educational programs has increased sharply. If we begin in 1940, we can trace the incremental growth of federal aid to education over the subsequent quarter century.[6]

The Lanham Act (1940) provided federal funds for the construction, maintenance, and operation of schools in districts that were burdened by an increase in population resulting from the defense effort. Near the end of World War II Congress passed the Serviceman's Readjustment Act (1944) which provided servicemen with funds to further their education (similar laws were passed in 1952 and 1966 to aid veterans of the Korean and Vietnam wars). Both of these pieces of legislation were war-related and temporary, but they nevertheless established a foundation for future aid.

Perhaps the most important early precedent for direct federal support of education was the National Science Foundation Act of 1950, which established the National Science Foundation to promote scientific research; improve the teaching of science, mathematics, and engineering; and correlate, evaluate, exchange, and disseminate scientific information.

In 1950 Congress also passed two bills designed to provide funds for construction and operating expenses to school districts "impacted" by federal dependents who lived on nontaxable federal property. Although this act, like those of the 1940s, was initiated in response to the results of other federal activities, it served as a precedent for categorical aid (in this instance the category was "impacted" school districts) without federal controls.

Congress set another precedent in the 1954 Cooperative Research Act, which authorized the United States Office of Education (USOE) to make contracts and cooperative arrangements with colleges and universities for the joint study of education problems. This established the principle of federally funded educational research under USOE control.

A major policy breakthrough came in the National Defense Education Act of 1958, designed to improve instruction in science, math, and foreign languages. It provided loans to college students, up to 50 percent of which were forgiven if the students taught in the public schools. The bill also provided matching grants to public schools and loans to private schools for the purchase of equipment for teaching science, math, and foreign languages. The law also funded graduate fellowships, state educational programs for guidance, counseling, and testing and for guidance and counselor training; research centers and institutes to train teachers to improve foreign language instruction; expanded vocational education programs to train skilled technicians in science-related occupations; and programs for the development of educational television and other instructional communications media. Although the act did not grant general aid, it did provide substantial categorical assistance to public and private institutions at all levels, enabled students to receive direct aid, and gave the Office of Education responsibility for operating major programs.

No further major developments in federal educational policy took place until 1963. In that year Congress passed the Higher Education Facilities Act, providing grants and loans to public and private colleges and universities for the construction of facilities for teaching science, math, engineering, and foreign languages. 1963 also saw the passage of the Vocational Education Act which expanded existing programs and instituted work-study and residential school programs. The following year the Library Construction and Services Act provided grants for the construction and operation of school libraries.

The quarter century of developments outlined above helped set the stage for the greatest expansion ever of the federal government's role in education. In 1965 Congress passed the Elementary and Secondary Education Act (ESEA), which provided grants to local educational agencies for the education of disadvantaged children; for library resources, texts, and other instructional materials used by students and teachers in public and private schools; and for educational research, supplemental educational centers, and regional educational laboratories. Furthermore, it provided state departments of education with funds to strengthen their capabilities.

Also passed in 1965 was the Higher Education Act (HEA) in which Congress for the first time established federal undergraduate scholarships. The act also initiated new student loan programs; instituted the Teachers Corps; and funded programs to set up university extension courses, help solve community problems, improve college library resources, strengthen "developing institutions," improve undergraduate institutions, and construct classrooms.

Congress amended the ESEA and HEA in 1966 to include programs for the physically and mentally handicapped, and has continued to perfect the two landmark education acts in succeeding years through various incremental amendments and extensions; it has done the same for most of the other educational laws enacted between 1940 and 1965. The major point is that over a 25-year period the U.S. progressed from almost no federal aid for education to federal aid for nearly all segments of American education, for a wide variety of purposes. What began as aid to school districts affected by federal government activity (primarily activity related to national defense) evolved into aid to virtually all public schools. What began as aid to returning veterans became loans and scholarships for college students and support for educationally disadvantaged school children.

The examples of budgeting, school integration, and federal aid to education are not unique illustrations of incremental decisionmaking. Incrementalism is widely used at all levels of government. Other prominent examples include publicly provided medical care,[7] air polluion policy,[8] Supreme Court criminal rights decisions, federal income tax policy, and the escalation of the war in Vietnam.

Despite the widespread use of incrementalism in budgetary decisions, reformers are continually trying to find ways to bring fiscal decisionmaking more in line with the rational model.[9] The method for achieving rational analysis in budgeting most recently in vogue is *zero-base budgeting*. In zero-base budgeting officials attempt to evaluate programs "from the ground up," without accepting the historical base and just evaluating requested increases. In this way they are to spot and weed out wasteful programs, releasing funds for more useful programs or for decreasing or stabilizing taxes.

The evaluation of programs is to be complete, with the consequences of programs projected and rated against each other.

Zero-base budgeting has received special attention recently because of President Carter's enthusiasm for it and his campaign promises to institute it in the federal government. Actually, zero-based budgeting was tried in the U.S. Department of Agriculture in 1962. As we should expect by now, it did not meet its goals. In setting priorities or considering options, departmental officials simply could not ignore the past or political or economic constraints. Moreover, they were usually unable to predict the consequences of major alterations in their policies, develop units of the output of programs, compare the output of programs, or find the time to analyze (or even read) all the data they generated. In the end zero-base budgeting did not influence budgetary decisions, which were ultimately based on many of the usual options: that certain programs are needed and the emphasis should be placed on the new level of funding required to maintain each program.[10]

It is interesting to note that the results of zero-base budgeting under Governor Jimmy Carter of Georgia provide no more grounds for optimism about its contribution to rational decisionmaking than do the data from the Department of Agriculture. Indeed, descriptions of the governor's decisionmaking process before and after the institution of zero-based budgeting are virtually identical.[11] The demands of rational analysis are simply too great despite the sincerest of efforts to achieve it. Thus, we look with great skepticism on the prospects for zero-base budgeting in federal budgetary decisionmaking.

Incrementalism in all its forms is a conservative influence on public policy. Nevertheless, it is true that the decision rule of incrementalism specifies nothing about desired social states; it may even actually enable change to take place by eliminating the requirement that policymakers must have complete knowledge and understanding of a subject before they make decisions. Yet, where established programs enjoy the benefit of assumed continuation and new proposals bear the brunt of current examination, it is most likely that the established programs will continue while new proposals will compete among themselves for the limited new resources available. Thus, in any given year, fewer new policies will be enacted than if resources were totally uncommitted. Moreover, as long as decisions are made incrementally, any change will be relatively slow.

Other Decision Rules

Although incrementalism is the most prominent rule that decisionmakers follow to simplify their tasks, there are other decision rules—or routines—which operate within its confines. The budgetary processes of federal and state governments provide some illustrations.

First, the decisions of each official responsible for a policy follow closely those made at the immediately preceding stage of decisionmaking. Executive officials usually make only incremental changes in the budgetary recommendations of the agencies; and legislators make only incremental changes in the executive's budget. Second, officials almost always reduce the budgetary requests okayed in the previous stage. Third, the greatest relative cuts in budgetary requests are made on those requests which ask for the largest percentage increases. Fourth, budgetary items receiving the greatest increases are those for which the greatest programmatic expansion was sought.[12]

Research on state spending has found that these decisionmaking routines are followed more closely on the agency than on the program level (agencies are responsible for numerous programs). Also, policymakers less closely follow these rules on decisions granting programs requesting funds than on decisions okaying budgetary growth. In other words, those deviations from the above rules that do occur are more likely to contribute to incrementalism than to budgetary expansion.[13]

Members of the judiciary observe a very well-known decision rule. *Stare decisis* is the technical term for the rule of precedent, which judges follow in the vast majority of court cases. In ruling on a case, a court will adhere as closely as possible to the precedents set by it and superior courts in similar cases. The technical canons of statutory interpretation support this adherence to precedent. *Stare decisis* safeguards the values of equity, consistency, and predictability; it assures that different citizens having similar problems before the courts receive equal treatment, and allows citizens, business firms, and other interests to predict what will happen to them in court if they embark on a particular course of action.

The conventions set by earlier decisions are sometimes altered by "precedent-breaking" decisions. These significant departures receive the attention of students, lawyers, and judges who seek to elucidate the new precedents that will guide subsequent court actions. However, the predisposition against breaking precedent usually produces elaborate arguments to distinguish one case from another. Lawyers who want something other than an automatic affirmation of precedent try to distinguish their client's situation from that governed by an earlier case. And when judges accept such arguments, they often take pains to point out that they are not breaking a precedent.

Judges employ other decision rules. They generally defer to legislators on questions of the constitutionality of statutes. Justices on the U.S. Supreme Court also use decision rules for deciding which cases they will consider. Research has shown that the Court is most likely to take a case if the national government is a party to the case and urges review, if some aspect of civil liberties is at stake, and if there is dissension within or between lower courts on the issue.[14]

Legislators have an especially urgent need for decision rules because they must make decisions on such a wide range of policies. Studies of congressional roll-call voting indicate that congressmen rely upon their party leaders, state party delegations, relevant committee leaders of their party, or other colleagues for cues on how to vote.[15] Legislative committees also rely on decision rules (in addition to those used on the budget). The Interior Committee tends to pass member-sponsored constituency-supported bills; the House Post Office and Civil Service Committee supports the maximum of pay increases and improvements in benefits for government employees and opposes rate increases for mail users; and the congressional conference committees commonly follow the practice of "splitting the difference" between bills passed by the House and those passed by the Senate.[16]

Bureaucracies use innumerable decision rules; we will discuss only a couple of representative examples. The Internal Revenue Service uses pre-established criteria (such as the maximum level of charitable contributions for an income level) to judge whether or not there is a cause for closer scrutiny of a tax return. Because of the many constraints on the process of searching for and evaluating alternatives, executive officials "satisfice," that is, they stop their search for policy alternatives upon discovery of an acceptable option.[17]

Similarly, state agencies look to other states in their geographic region (especially bordering states) for policy alternatives. They reason that the problems, needs, resources, and political environments of their neighbors are similar to their own, and therefore, policies adopted by these neighboring states should be appropriate for them. This decision rule of regional consultation, like that of satisficing, eases the burden of developing and assessing a wide range of alternatives.[18]

INNOVATION

Despite all the problems policymakers confront, they do make nonincremental changes in policy. Government is bigger and offers a different mix of services today than in the recent past. Compared to figures for 1960, in the mid-1970s government expenditures amounted to 5 percent more of the gross national product, and government employees accounted for 3 percent more of the national workforce. The national government allocated much less of its budget to defense in 1975 than in 1960, and more to education, health, and income security. Within those fifteen years several activities reached their peak and then shrank or disappeared: the space program, the war in Southeast Asia, the War on Poverty, and the Alliance for Progress. The same period witnessed great changes in the laws dealing with the legal and political status of blacks, other minorities, and women; the legal precedents affecting the treatment of criminal suspects and the portrayal of sex in print, films, and theater; and the provision of medical care to senior citizens.

There are numerous pressures for substantial policy change, most of which have their origins in the sources of new problems (see Chapter 4). However, simply being on the policy agenda is no guarantee that a problem will generate specific proposals or that a proposal will become official policy. In this section we will focus on the major factors that lead to nonincremental policy change.

Indivisible Policies

Some policies require comprehensive and not incremental decisions because the resources and political commitment required for their success are indivisible. These policies have organizational thresholds or "critical mass" points closely associated with their initiation and subsequent development. One example of this type of policy is the U.S. manned space exploration program. Others include urban mass transit, urban redevelopment, and certain military enterprises.

The National Aeronautics and Space Administration (NASA) obtained a rapid, nonincremental increase in funds and personnel between the late 1950s and the mid-1960s.[19] Only a ready expansion of the agency's funds could support the large-scale effort necessary to open up the chance of safely landing men on the moon. The success of the program required large research teams, vast acquisitions of land, extensive new facilities, and enormous purchases of equipment as well as major advances in the development of instruments, devices, theory, and technology. Consolidated administration of suboperations was necessary because of the interdependence of the various parts of the space program. In this type of situation, "thinking small" is a major barrier to innovation—to the imagination, planning, and jurisdictional extensions demanded by the nonincremental nature of the policy.

Unlike incremental policies, nonincremental policies are unstable. They seem to be in either a state of rapid growth or rapid decay. They require strong public commitments to reach their productive threshold and are not able to maintain equilibrium once public support wanes. For example, NASA experienced a major decline in both funds and personnel in the late 1960s and early 1970s as policymakers deemphasized the space program. Some analysts believe that the attendant decrease in high quality personnel, morale, organizational performance, and the availability of private contractors caused the agency to lose some of its effectiveness.

Another difficulty faced by nonincremental policies is that it takes a major commitment of public support to initiate them. Officials sometimes oversell policies to obtain the necessary support. This in turn may rigidify policymaking by locking policymakers into an unyielding "all-or-nothing" commitment which inhibits them from making incremental adjustments to new political coalitions or policy needs.

Shifting Public Opinion

Shifts in public opinion can effect major changes in policy. Federal air pollution policy was developed incrementally until 1970 when there was a broad and intense public outcry in support of strong controls on air pollution.[20] Large policy changes were necessary to please the public, and elected officials competed to produce and receive credit for strong legislation. Executive officials and the mass media supported this legislative activity by increasing their attention to air pollution. As a result, the policymaking environment differed greatly from the norm in which officials have a difficult time building an effective policymaking majority. To meet the demands of the public, policymakers went so far as to engage in what one scholar has termed "speculative augmentation." They gave the Environmental Protection Agency responsibility for establishing and enforcing sets of standards for air pollution, and for reviewing and approving state plans. However, the EPA did not have much of a stable organization, was understaffed, and had little information. Moreover, the technology to control and monitor pollution the way policymakers desired had not yet been developed. In sum, policymakers were so responsive to public opinion that they passed innovative policies before the technical capacity to institute them existed.

Dramatic political changes and party turnover of elected offices often signal major policy changes. In these circumstances there is more than the normal probing into established activities and more permissiveness toward the introduction of expensive new programs. After the 1964 Democratic landslide Lyndon Johnson proposed and Congress passed major new legislation dealing with poverty, federal aid to education, urban redevelopment, employment, civil rights, medical care for the elderly, and many other areas of public policy. During the Johnson presidency nondefense federal expenditures increased by 62 percent, federal aid to states and localities by 72 percent, and federal government civilian employment by 19 percent. President Johnson was aware of the unique opportunity which faced him in 1965, and wasted no time in exploiting it. He pushed for the enactment of vaguely sketched-out programs and accepted as inevitable later problems of refinement, coordination, and weeding out.

Crises

Crises are important causes of significant change in public policy. Because of their dramatic impact on a broad segment of the population, they force policymakers to place policies designed to remedy the problems causing and caused by the crisis on the policy agenda and give them high priority. During crises such as wars and depressions new policies are needed to handle the new demands. Therefore, new programs are passed and large, sudden increases in government spending occur. When the emergencies are over, government spending is reduced, but usually not to the precrisis level. Total government expenditures (i.e., national, state, and local) went from 20 percent of the Gross National Product in 1940 to 52 percent in 1944 to 25 percent in 1950.

In addition to increasing the size of budgets, national crises also tend to centralize governmental expenditures in the federal government, which means that after a crisis the federal government's percentage of total expenditures increases. Thus, the federal share of government spending by federal, state, and local jurisdictions rose from 14 percent in 1932 to 42 percent in 1940 and 58 percent in 1944. It fell back to 38 percent by 1950, but this was still nearly three times as much as it had been before the New Deal.

During the Depression the unemployment rate was 25 percent and the Gross National Product declined by 50 percent. In response to this situation the national government under the New Deal entered numerous fields of domestic policy in a big way. Its memorable programs included social security; welfare programs for the aged, blind, and dependent children; public housing; government jobs for the unemployed; agricultural credits and price supports; rural electrification; child health programs; and the ambitious regional development of the Tennessee Valley. Federal expenditures doubled between 1932 and 1938, aid to state and local governments quadrupled between 1932 and 1934, and the civilian staff of the national government increased about fivefold during the 1930s.[21]

World War II came on top of the Depression. From 1939 onward the federal government changed its emphasis from domestic welfare to defense and international relations. Defense expenditures eventually rose to 83 percent of the national government's budget and 38 percent of the Gross National Product. More than 5 percent of the total population worked overseas in the military. New domestic programs were also implemented to aid the war effort. Broad policies controlled wages and prices, allocated resources for industrial production, and rationed consumer goods.

Just what is and what is not a crisis is not always clear. Whereas everyone could agree that World War II, for example, was a national emergency, there was no such consensus in 1964 when President Johnson announced a War on Poverty amidst the relative prosperity enjoyed by most Americans. Thus, perceptions of crises are important in policy change.

Innovations from the Bureaucracy

Although governmental routines normally enhance stability, there are times when they promote innovation. One study, for example, found that the most important factor influencing state adoption of federal anti-poverty programs was the scope of the state's ongoing welfare policy. The bureaucratic apparatus and attitudes existing in states with major welfare programs made their adoption of federal poverty programs fairly routine.[22]

Some agencies have higher aspirations than others. They actively search for new policies, respond positively to the suggestions of their clientele and industrial firms with new products, and aggressively promote their new alternatives. The employees of these agencies take a professional approach to their job: they are more likely to read professional journals, attend professional meetings, communicate with fellow officials in other jurisdictions, set professional standards for themselves and their organizations, and recruit employees from professional ranks (rather than from partisan political organizations).[23]

New Resources

New resources make it possible to adopt new policies. For example, the Sixteenth Amendment made it possible for the federal government to institute an income tax. This in turn made it possible for the federal government to raise large sums of money. The major federal grants-in-aid programs followed this increase in federal resources. The general growth in the economy in the 1960s allowed growth at all levels of government. The real growth (growth not due to inflation) of the Gross National Product was 69 percent between 1960 and 1970 and the real growth in total government outlays was 51 percent.

Intergovernmental Aid

Intergovernmental relations can stimulate growth and change in governmental programs. The large and still growing national and state aids implemented over the last forty years illustrate this point. The rate of growth of intergovernmental (national to state to local) aids outstripped that of total spending from 1934 to 1975. National government aid grew from 3 to 18 percent of state and local revenues, and state aid from 13 to 32 percent of local revenues. No major field of domestic activity escapes the nets of intergovernmental programs.

Money handed down from above provides its grantors with powerful leverage over recipient governments. By seeing to the enactment of a new program in Washington, a federal agency and its interest group allies encourage the development of programs in 50 states and thousands of localities.[24] Some grants require the states and localities that want the money to innovate specific programs. Even if the statutory requirements are not strict, program administrators may use this leverage to encourage the development of new programs. Yet all federal and state programs offer some discretion to the recipients, and an increasing amount of money comes via programs that explicitly leave important decisions in the hands of recipients. The Community Action Program was designed to spur local political initiative in designing policy. It offered localities money to set up new authorities to tap the creative energy of interests left out of established agencies. Revenue-sharing is more establishmentarian in its trappings, but is also heralded for the freedom it allows the states and localities receiving its more than $6 billion annually.

The magnitude and character of national and state aid generate irresistible pressures to propose new policies quickly to meet the grant deadlines. The variety of local projects that emerges is in keeping with the American penchant for diverse programs fitting local circumstances, but it also creates serious problems of coordinating both within and between jurisdictions.

International Events

Links among international and national economics, politics, and public policy foster policy changes. The 1973 Arab oil embargo on shipments to the United States and subsequent increases in the price of petroleum from all members of the Organization of Petroleum Exporting Countries (OPEC) are two good examples of such change. The Arab countries ordered the embargo in retaliation against American support for Israel during the Yom Kippur war; the price increase came as a result of the oil producers' demonstrated capacity for unity against consuming nations. Both the embargo and the price increase caused concern about the vulnerability of United States' supplies of energy and led to several policy changes.

The immediate response to the fuel shortage were state and national policies to establish priorities among consumers of energy, and restrict the use of energy by suggesting or mandating lowered thermostatic settings on heaters and reduced speed limits on the highway. A spillover benefit of reduced speed limits was a sharp drop in highway fatalities, which, combined with the energy savings, caused Congress to continue that policy beyond the end of the fuel emergency. Longer range policies included changes in price regulations to encourage the search for domestic oil and gas. Regulatory policies designed to assure clean air and other forms of environmental protection formulated during the period of cheap and assured fuel supplies were relaxed to facilitate the early completion of the Alaskan pipeline, the more extensive use of coal supplies, and the speedier completion of nuclear energy projects. There was also an increase in funding for research that focused on the extraction of oil and gas from shale and coal deposits. Finally, the government encouraged the development of oil fields considered more reliable than those of the Middle East: in Mexico, Ecuador, and the North Sea.

The domestic economy was quick to respond to the increases in fuel prices. Occurring in a setting already troubled by inflation and unemployment, the problems of energy prices and supply heightened concern for jobs, welfare, and price controls. Washington's international aid policies also came under review, as many poor countries found themselves hit by higher energy bills and by the rising costs of goods and services imported from the United States and other industrial countries that were themselves experiencing fuel-related inflation.

The 1973 war in the Middle East and the changed realities that resulted from it caused additional reappraisal of foreign and military policies. The increased wealth of countries around the Persian Gulf fed demands for massive arms purchases from the United States. These requests forced the United States to formulate policies about both sales and the training programs required to enforce strict safeguards on the use of American arms. There have also been postwar changes in American policy toward Egypt and Syria, along with commitments to rearm Israel and provide its government with extensive economic assistance.

The Dynamics of Domestic Politics

America's combination of a diverse society, free enterprise economy, freedoms of political organization, loosely structured political parties with numerous factions, and multifaceted government assures that a lot of policy is always in the making. However certain aspects of governmental structure work against the actual enactment of many policy proposals. There is a continuing struggle between a dynamic polity and a government designed to resist innovative proposals. One product of this struggle is what appears to be passing waves of policy fads: enactments that respond to certain aspects of a group's demands, but which fail to satisfy those demands before a countergroup forces the enactment of policies that partially meet its demands. The late 1960s and early 1970s witnessed the claims and partial successes of groups struggling in the courts, legislatures, and executive offices of national and state governments to liberalize the treatment of people suspected or convicted of crime, and to strengthen mechanisms of law and order; to broaden the opportunities of minorities and women for education, credit, jobs, housing, and to combat inflation; to resist oil pipelines and strip mines in the name of conservation, and to create national self-sufficiency in the supply of energy.

The contorted experience of the Equal Rights Amendment (ERA) illustrates the waves and counterwaves that appear in American policymaking. Originally passed by the House and Senate by margins of 354 to 23 and 84 to 8 in 1971, the amendment won the approval of 34 state legislatures by 1975. The amendment's supporters included women and men sensitive to the problems of women in competing for jobs and advancement, obtaining credit, and dealing with a host of large and small issues signaling an unwanted special status. Support also came from those concerned about the bias of courts against men in cases of divorce and child custody. Before supporters of the amendment could win the required approval of 38 state legislatures (three-fourths of the total), countermovements appeared. Their appeals combined defense of a romanticized fair sex, moral assertions about dire consequences for the structure of American family life, and claims that the ERA might signal the end of separate rest rooms as well as mandate the conscription of females into the military. The amendment's opponents obtained a majority in several state legislatures to defeat resolutions ratifying ERA, and a majority in three for the questionable procedure of reversing earlier ratifications. By mid-1977, it appeared that ERA had failed to ride the crest of its wave. Some of the public had grown suspicious of its claims, and more perhaps had grown weary of the topic.

Leaders

We have discussed a number of factors that facilitate policy change. But their existence is often not sufficient to bring about change. To exploit a potential for change, leaders with powers of persuasion, intimate knowledge of the legislative process, and public support must frequently probe, jockey, and negotiate to find the politically feasible policy alternative. The history of policy reforms features strong personalities like Franklin D. Roosevelt and Lyndon B. Johnson at the national level, plus Robert La Follette and Huey Long in the states of Wisconsin and Louisiana. While there is much shallow hero worship in the rhetoric of political campaigns, it is sometimes possible to attribute dramatic policy changes to the initiatives of hard-driving leaders.

Multiple Causes of Policy Change

Sometimes it takes a combination of conditions before chance occurs. Certainly the assassination of President Kennedy, the increasing militance of black leaders, and the specter of urban disorder facilitated President Johnson's portrayal to Congress of a domestic crisis requiring extensive social programs. And the availability of proposals of professionals within the government, the large Democratic majorities in Congress, and Johnson's own legislative skills all contributed to the passage of the path-breaking Great Society Legislation.

Limits on Sustained Innovation

Even when there is innovation, it is likely to face severe problems. Much of the time innovation takes place in spurts. Resources do not expand consistently, and even the most aggressive agency eventually runs out of ideas. Rapidly expanding bureaucratic units need a chance to consolidate, hire or train personnel with the appropriate skills, and make the necessary organizational adjustments to their new pro-

grams. Moreover, the political problems of continued innovation increase geometrically as each new policy alienates
interest groups and members of the executive and legislative
branches.

SUMMARY

Despite all the constraints on their actions, policymakers are
productive. They produce enough policy in the United
States to consume some 40 percent of Gross National Product and employ 16 percent of the workforce. Most often they
employ routine procedures to formulate policy, often variations of incrementalism. Yet the dynamics of economics and
politics in an open and creative society do not allow complete
routinization. Sharp breaks in precedent do occur, sometimes because of changes in public opinion, crises, or the
creative skills and financial resources built into the ma-
chinery of government. Often it is difficult to identify the
precise cause of an innovation, as when numerous factors
come together to prompt or support a change in policy. The
issue then becomes the survival of the innovation. A new
program does not come into a benign environment, but en-
counters opponents who both seek to cut its resources and
demand accommodations in the process of its implementation.

NOTES

1. For an early and excellent discussion of incrementalism
see David Braybrooke and Charles E. Lindblom, *A Strategy of
Decision* (New York: Free Press, 1963).

2. See, for example, Otto A. Davis, M.A.H. Dempster, and
Aaron Wildavsky, "A Theory of the Budgetary Process,"
American Political Science Review 60 (September 1966); and
Thomas J. Anton, *The Politics of State Expenditure in Illinois*
(Urbana: University of Illinois Press, 1966).

3. John Wanat, "Bases of Budgetary Incrementalism," *American Political Science Review* 68 (September 1974).

4. Richard F. Fenno, Jr., *The Power of the Purse: Appropriations Politics in Congress* (Boston: Little, Brown, 1966), Chapters 8 and 11; Anton, *Politics of State Expenditures;* Douglas M. Fox, "Congress and U.S. Military Service Budgets in the Post-War Period: A Research Note," *Midwest Journal of Political Science* 15 (May 1971); Robert D. Thomas and Roger B. Handberg, "Congressional Budgeting for Eight Agencies, 1947–1972," *American Journal of Political Science* 18 (February 1974).

5. For a seminal discussion of this point see Martin M. Shapiro, "Stability and Change in Judicial Decision-Making: Incrementalism or Stare Decisis?," *Law in Transition Quarterly* 2 (Summer 1965).

6. This discussion relies on Norman C. Thomas, *Education in National Politics* (New York: David McKay, 1975), Chapter 2; see also Chapter 4 and pp. 175, 183, 188, and 233.

7. See Robert and Rosemary Stevens, *Welfare Medicine in America: A Case Study of Medicaid* (New York: Free Press, 1974).

8. See Charles O. Jones, *Clean Air: The Policies and Politics of Pollution Control* (Pittsburgh: University of Pittsburgh Press, 1975).

9. Planning-Programming-Budgeting (PPB), a system of decisionmaking which was very similar to the rational model of decisionmaking discussed in this book, was introduced throughout the federal government by President Johnson in 1965. Despite its concern for management and efficiency, however, the Nixon administration ended PPB in 1971 as unworkable. For a good illustration of PPB in action see Jeanne Nienaber and Aaron Wildavsky, *The Budgeting and Evaluation of Federal Recreation Programs: Or Money Doesn't Grow on Trees* (New York: Basic Books, 1973), Chapters 4 and 5. For a good critique of PPB see Aaron Wildavsky, *Budget-*

ing: A Comparative Theory of Budgetary Processes (Boston: Little, Brown, 1975), Chapter 18.

10. Wildavsky, *Budgeting*, pp. 280–294.

11. See Wildavsky, *Budgeting*, pp. 294–296 and sources cited therein. For a similar conclusion about zero-base budgeting in New Mexico see John D. LaFaver, "Zero-Base Budgeting in New Mexico," *State Government* 47 (Spring 1974).

12. Ira Sharkansky, "Agency Requests, Gubernatorial Support and Budget Success in State Legislatures," *American Political Science Review* 62 (December 1968); Ira Sharkansky and Augustus B. Turnbull III, "Budget-Making in Georgia and Wisconsin," *Midwest Journal of Political Science* 13 (November 1969); Fenno, *Power of the Purse,* Chapters 8 and 11; Davis, Dempster, and Wildavsky, "A Theory of the Budgetary Process."

13. George C. Edwards III and Ira Sharkansky, "Executive and Legislative Budgeting: Decision Routines for Agency Totals and Individual Programs in Two States," in *Perspectives on Public Policy-Making*, ed. by William B. Gwyn and George C. Edwards III (New Orleans: Tulane Studies in Political Science, 1975).

14. Joseph Tanehaus, Marvin Schick, Matthew Muraskin, and Daniel Rosen, "The Supreme Court's *Certiorari* Jurisdiction: Cue Theory," in *Judicial Decision-Making*, ed. by Glendon Schubert (New York: Free Press, 1963).

15. See, for example, Donald R. Matthews and James A. Stimson, *Yeas and Nays: Normal Decision-Making in the U.S. House of Representatives* (New York: John Wiley and Sons, 1975); and John W. Kingdon, *Congressmen's Voting Decisions* (New York: Harper & Row, 1973).

16. Richard F. Fenno, Jr., *Congressmen in Committees* (Boston: Little, Brown, 1973), pp. 58 and 64.

17. James G. March and Herbert A. Simon, *Organizations* (New York: John Wiley and Sons, 1959), p. 169. See also

Kingdon, *Congressmen's Voting*, p. 199 for a discussion of "satisficing" by Congressmen.

18. Ira Sharkansky, *Regionalism in American Politics* (Indianapolis: Bobbs-Merrill, 1970), pp. 9–15. See also Jack L. Walker, "The Diffusion of Innovations among the American States," *American Political Science Review* 63 (September 1969).

19. This example relies upon the discussion in Paul R. Schulman, "Nonincremental Policy Making: Notes Toward an Alternative Paradigm," *American Political Science Review* 69 (December 1975).

20. This example relies upon Charles O. Jones, "Speculative Augmentation in Federal Air Pollution Policy-Making," *Journal of Politics* 36 (May 1974).

21. See Barbara Deckard Sinclair, "Party Realignment and the Transformation of the Political Agenda: The House of Representatives, 1925–1938," *American Political Science Review* 71 (September 1977) for a discussion of the new agenda items supported by the New Deal coalition.

22. Andrew T. Cowart, "Anti-Poverty Expenditure in the American States: A Comparative Analysis," *Midwest Journal of Political Science* 13 (May 1969). See also Martha Derthick, *The Influence of Federal Grants: Public Assistance in Massachusetts* (Cambridge, Mass: Harvard University Press, 1970), p. 63.

23. Rufus P. Browning, "Innovative and Non-Innovative Decision Processes in Government Budgeting," in *Policy Analysis in Political Science,* ed. by Ira Sharkansky (Chicago: Markham, 1970).

24. For an example of the policy changes resulting from a federal grant-in-aid program, see Derthick, *The Influence of Federal Grants.*

10 Implementation

In 1961 President Kennedy twice ordered U.S. missiles removed from Turkey, but during the Cuban missile crisis the following year he learned they were still there. President Nixon ordered the CIA to destroy its biological weapons, but five years later two of the most deadly poisons were still in the agency's hands. Federal judge Arthur Garrity ordered South Boston High School to desegregate in 1974, but the next year he placed the entire school in federal receivership and ordered all its administrators transferred because "the desegregation plan was "not by a long shot being implemented. . . ."[1]

These are just a few examples of the sizeable gap that often persists between a policy decision and its implementation. The authors of a leading study of implementation maintain that "[t]he cards in this world are stacked against things happening, as much effort is required to make them move. The remarkable thing is that new programs work at all."[2] What comes after a policy decision is just as important as the decision itself. Indeed, policymakers should use the likelihood of implementation as one criterion for evaluating policy alternatives.

Sometimes officials take positive actions contrary to the decisions of superiors. At the end of President Johnson's term in 1968, Attorney General Ramsey Clark filed several large antitrust suits; Secretary of Interior Stewart Udall ordered vast lands absorbed into the federal system; and Secretary of Labor William Wirtz ordered several manpower programs to be more federalized—all against the wishes of the President.[3]

Implementing a public policy can require a wide variety of actions including issuing directives, enforcing directives, disbursing funds, making loans, awarding grants, making contracts, collecting information, disseminating information, assigning personnel, hiring personnel, and creating organizational units. Rarely are policies self-executing, that is, implemented by their mere statement, such as a policy not to recognize a certain government. Most policies require some positive action.

Even the seemingly straightforward policy of federal revenue sharing involves the following fifteen agencies, offices, and bureaus, and commissions: Office of Revenue Sharing, Bureau of Accounts, Postal Service, Government Printing Office, Bureau of the Census, Bureau of Economic Analysis, Bureau of Indian Affairs, Internal Revenue Service, Environmental Protection Agency, Civil Service Commission, Department of Labor, Department of Justice, the General Accounting Office, the Equal Employment Opportunity Commission, and the Civil Rights Commission. Despite the fact that revenue sharing is essentially a simple check-writing policy, employees other than the check writers must calculate the amount to be received by each of nearly 40,000 governmental units; collect the data that serve as the basis for these calculations; ensure that revenue sharing funds are not used for discriminatory purposes or to pay lower than prevailing wages; ensure that the funds are used in a manner consistent with the Hatch Act (prohibiting certain political activities of federal employees) and the Environmental Protection Act; audit, evaluate and report the uses to which the funds are put; and issue, print, and deliver the checks.[4]

The study of implementation is largely (although not entirely) a study of bureaucracy. It is the bureaucrats who control the personnel, money, materials, and legal powers of government, and it is they who receive most of the implementation directives from executive, legislative, and judicial decisionmakers.

Although elected officials or those appointed by the chief executive nominally rank above the bureaucracy, they cannot assume that their decisions and orders will be carried out. Former Secretary of State Henry Kissinger once remarked: "The outsider believes a presidential order is consistently followed. Nonsense. I have to spend considerable time seeing that it is carried out and in the spirit the President intended. . . ."[5] Bill Moyers, former aide to President Johnson adds that the bureaucracy "has a life of its own. It can be a President's worst enemy unless he can find a means to stamp his own ideas and beliefs on it."[6]

For anyone who thinks that bureaucratic unresponsiveness to the orders of superior officials is solely a national government phenomenon, the following statement by former Arkansas governor (and now U.S. senator) Dale Bumpers should dispel that misconception. "The bureaucracy in government is like a 700 pound marshmallow. You can kick it, scream at it, and cuss it, but it is very reluctant to move."[7]

The frequent failure of implementation to meet the expectations of decisionmakers concerns us not only because it belies the promise of abstract policies but also because it functions as a constraint on the decisions made in the first place. For example, a common consideration of officials responsible for welfare policy is whether welfare recipients who are able to work should be required to do so. In recent years many top officials have come to the conclusion that welfare administrators would not enforce a work requirement provision even in the face of presidential exhortations and congressional demands. Thus, they have developed other alternatives, such as tax incentives, to encourage welfare recipients to work.[8]

Before examining the major factors that influence the implementation of policy and some of the reasons why much implementation fails in whole or in part, we would like to point out that the implementation of policies of one level of government often constitutes the decisionmaking of the level below. For the hundreds of federal grant-in-aid programs, which provide money to individual states for use in a wide variety of programs, the federal government sets certain requirements the states must meet in using the funds; its concern is that the money be used as intended by those who decided upon the policy. State officials, however, generally give only secondary consideration to federal requirements, being mainly concerned with dividing up the funds to meet the needs of the state's population, officials, and bureaucratic units. This means that many of the constraints and problems of decisionmaking apply to implementation as well. With this in mind, we shall discuss the difficulties decisionmakers face in attempting to realize their intentions.

COMMUNICATION

The first requirement for effective implementation is that those responsible for carrying out a decision must know what they are supposed to do. Orders to implement a policy must be delivered to the appropriate personnel, and they must be consistent, clear, and accurate in specifying the aims of the decisionmakers.

Transmission

Communication that a decision has been made, including the specification of orders to carry it out, is not always as straightforward a process as it may seem. Ignorance of decisions and orders may result from the absence of a communications system to accomplish the physical transmission of orders or from the blockage of information somewhere in the system.

The lack of transmission of policy is of particular importance in court decisions. There are no regular channels of communication between courts (including the U.S. Supreme Court) and implementors. Appellate courts normally return a decision to the lower court whose ruling formed the basis of the appeal, and not to all the other courts in its jurisdiction (the nation for the U.S. Supreme Court) who are bound by the decision. Moreover, other judges do not necessarily read the decision once it is published, and some decisions are never published. Nor are decisions studied by most of the bar. Indeed, one author found in his study of a school prayer decision that there was "not a shred of evidence" that legal channels were of significance in the transmission of information.[9]

When the U.S. Supreme Court, or any other court, makes a broad ruling, for instance, requiring police to read suspected criminals their constitutional rights, or voiding prayers in the public schools, it does not follow up by sending out copies of its decision to local police departments or school boards. Nor does it issue any type of additional guidelines for implementing its decisions.

Thus, the transmission of judicial orders is very much a hit-or-miss operation which depends heavily on interested private groups (church groups, NAACP) and professional organizations (school administrators, police chiefs, district attorneys). This open-ended system leaves a great deal of room for ignorance and misinformation.[10] For example, Neal Milner found that there was no hierarchy of communication from courts to police. Even the most professional police departments were unaware of information redefining their responsibilities for implementing decisions.[11]

Press coverage of the courts is not really much help in transmitting decisions. It is very limited and nonexpert. Thus, reporters often distort (or ignore) decisions and their impact and basis.[12] Bus lines in eleven Southern cities complied with a decision as it was misrepresented in reportage declaring that intrastate buses must be desegregated.[13]

The communication lines of the executive branch are more highly developed than those of the judiciary, but they still do not guarantee the successful transmission of decisions and orders. The CIA never told the leader of the brigade sent to invade Cuba at the Bay of Pigs that the President had ordered the soldiers to go to the mountains and fight a guerilla war if the invasion failed. The CIA disregarded the President's orders because it felt they might weaken the brigade's resolve to fight or that the brigade might choose to go to the mountains too quickly.[14]

Clarity

The instructions received by those who are to implement policy are often vague about when and how implementation is to be carried out. Title I of the Elementary and Secondary Education Act of 1965 established a program of grants to state education departments and through them to local school districts which were to use the funds to meet the "special needs of educationally deprived children," and not to supplant already existing resources reserved for the educationally deprived. The law, however, did not clearly define educationally deprived or specify what was acceptable as a program to meet their needs. Even many of the officials responsible for designing and implementing the law thought it was intended to be a *general* aid bill under another name.[15] It is no wonder that many local educational agencies also viewed the funds provided under the title as general aid,[16] and often spent them for purposes which did not aid educationally deprived children.

Title V of the same law was designed to strengthen state departments of education and improve educational programs. But "strengthening" is an ambiguous term and the relationships between educational programs and improved performance is not well understood, as we saw in Chapter 6. Moreover, the law contained no objective criteria by which to judge projects and did not tell state departments how they ought to change.[17] Consequently, little change has taken place.[18]

While vagueness of policy can make changes in policy difficult, it can also result in changes far greater than those anticipated. From 1962 through 1972 federal law provided open-ended grants-in-aid to the states for social services. However, neither the law nor the Department of Health, Education, and Welfare (HEW), which administered the program, clearly defined "services." This imprecision became the basis for an unintended rapid growth in the funds expended for the program. Moreover, the states used most of the money to pay for services they already provided. Thus, the act turned out to be fiscal relief for the states, contrary to the intentions of both Congress and the President.[19]

The vague language of the act did not allow or encourage HEW or its regional offices to take a firm stand against state abuses. It is difficult to enforce administrative controls without legislative underpinnings.[20] The vagueness of the act also made administrators vulnerable to political pressure from state officials for more funds for more uses.[21] Thus, there are times when administrators may desire less discretion to protect themselves from battles with special interests.[22]

Independent regulatory commissions also generally receive obscure assignments. The Interstate Commerce Commission is charged with fixing "just and reasonable" railroad rates whereas the Federal Communications Commission is to license television broadcasters for the "public convenience and necessity," and the Security and Exchange Commission is authorized to make certain rules governing stock exchanges "as it seems necessary in the public interest or for the protection of investors."

There are times, of course, when legislatures provide clear guidelines to administrators. A prime example of this is Social Security in which the eligibility requirements, size of benefits, and other considerations are precisely established. It should be noted that official and public satisfaction with the administration of Social Security is quite high.

Whereas vague decisions can adversely affect implementation, orders that are too specific can also hinder it. Highly specific language in federal programs can make it more difficult for officials in the field to adapt those programs to the particular needs of different states and localities. A myriad of specific regulations can also overwhelm and confuse personnel in the field, and may make them reluctant to act for fear of breaking the rules. Moreover, strict guidelines may induce lower-level officials to become more concerned with meeting the specific requirements than with achieving the basic goals of the program. Conversely, implementors sometimes simply ignore rigid legislative decisions, as the Economic Development Administration did when it assigned an expediter to the field to circumvent its own restrictions on making loans, and formulated new (unsystematic) criteria in Washington *after* it saw the applications for loans.[23]

Courts also often provide and receive vague instructions. The typical U.S. Supreme Court decision, for example, ends with instructions to a lower court to reconsider its original decision in light of the more general decision of the Court. Even the decision itself may be vague. The classic example is the 1955 *Brown vs. Board of Education* ruling in which the Court declared that integration of the public schools should take place with "all deliberate speed." Furthermore, appellate judges write in a technical legal language that is hard for the lay person to understand. Therefore, someone has to interpret court decisions to the implementors (such as school boards and policemen), and this increases the chances of misunderstanding the courts' intentions.

There are several reasons for the vagueness of most implementation orders. Perhaps the most important is the sheer complexity of policymaking. Neither chief executives, legislators, nor judges have the time or expertise to develop and apply all the requisite details for implementing policy. They have to leave most (and sometimes all) of the details to subordinates. Joseph Califano has written that when he was President Johnson's chief domestic aide he was unable to meet, consult, or guide more than one-third of the non-cabinet agency and commission heads. Johnson saw even fewer.[24] This in turn provides subordinates (whether bureaucrats, regulatory commissioners and their staffs, or judges) with considerable discretion in interpreting their superiors' decisions and orders. Personnel at each inferior rung moving down the bureaucratic ladder must expand and develop the specifics of the orders they receive from above. In many ways, then, implementation is the opposite of the process whereby information and options move up a hierarchy (see Chapter 5).

Subordinates do not always use their discretion to further the goals of the original decisionmakers. Bureaucrats often use it to further the same personal, organizational, and national interests that we discussed in Chapter 5.[25] Interest groups take advantage of the discretion granted subordinates to push for their own demands in bureaucratic agencies and regulatory commissions. Finally, lower courts manipulate this discretion to evade the decisions of appellate courts; in fact, the winner in the highest court in the land has frequently been the loser in the same case tried subsequently in a lower court.[26] Many blacks who were just entering kindergarten when the Supreme Court declared *de jure* segregation in the public schools unconstitutional in 1954 never attended an integrated school; even though they may have graduated more than a decade after the ruling, their schools remained segregated because some lower court judges found ways to avoid ordering desegregation.

Another cause of vagueness in implemental directives is the difficulty decisionmakers have in reaching a consensus on goals (see Chapter 4). Imprecise orders allow policymakers to maintain a decisional coalition. Earlier we discussed the fact that for a decade the federal government provided states funds for social services without defining what "services" meant. The states used the money for many purposes never intended by the President and Congress, and the program expanded way beyond the expectations of the federal government. The vagueness of the law was in part due to conflict within HEW between the Bureau of Family Services and other agencies, especially the Children's Bureau and the Office of Vocational Rehabilitation, over what constituted "services." Rather than alienate an agency, HEW chose to leave the term vaguely defined. In addition, members of Congress had conflicting intentions. The notion of funding services (rather than grants directly to individuals) appealed to conservatives as a method of saving money and decreasing dependency while it appealed to liberals as a way to help the poor and set up good programs.[27]

A problem related to the general nature of many implemental instructions is that subordinate officials may not comprehend what they are to do because they were not present when the policy decision was made and are therefore not fully aware of the policy's goals. The phrase, "maximum feasible participation," for example, appears in the Economic Opportunity Act of 1964. Daniel Moynihan has written that those who drafted the law originally intended the phrase to mean only that citizens excluded from the political process were to receive benefits from the law. But this was never clearly stated and the people running local Community Action Programs interpreted the phrase to mean involving the poor in running the programs and in political activism. This misunderstanding was compounded by the fact that few persons in the Administration or Congress knew what the architects of the policy intended the phrase to mean.[28]

Consistency

Implementation orders may be inconsistent as well as vague because there is seldom just one order. For example, the Economic Development Administration was given instructions to help jobless persons in areas of high unemployment by attracting or expanding industries. At the same time it was not to subsidize (through loans) competitors for existing businesses.[29] Similarly in 1962 defense officials were told to remove missiles from Turkey *and* to preserve and strengthen NATO; their orders implied they were not to irritate Turkey who wanted the missiles there.[30]

Appellate courts also hand down contradictory decisions. This is most likely to occur either when a court issues an opinion seemingly contrary to precedent (a traditional problem for lower court judges is whether to follow precedent or what appears to be the different trend of recent decisions), or when the judges of a court are unable to reach agreement on a majority decision and a dissent or dissents obscure the majority opinion. In 1972 the Supreme Court held in *Fur-*

man vs. Georgia that capital punishment constituted cruel and unusual punishment, at least as imposed and constituted in the cases before it at the time. The decision was split 5–4 and each of the 9 justices wrote a separate opinion. This did not provide sufficient guidance for the states and many soon enacted new capital punishment laws, some of which were once again voided in a subsequent case in 1976. (Of course, dissents can clarify an issue if they delineate what the majority opinion does and does not hold.)

Sometimes the inconsistency and vagueness of orders increases as directives multiply throughout different branches and levels of government. The implementation of the Comprehensive Employment and Training Act (CETA) is a case in point. The members of Congress most knowledgeable and concerned about CETA, and their staffs, have given the Department of Labor conflicting guidelines. The Department's own standards have become more and more inconsistent as they have been communicated to both its regional offices and local project sponsors. Finally, the communications from the regional to the local offices have been no better than those issued from the departmental headquarters in Washington, with different sources sometimes providing different directions and interpretations.[31]

One reason that decisions are often inconsistent is that they are influenced by interested parties—on both sides of an issue. A number of interest groups formed specifically to represent local CETA programs and urge a passive federal role in local manpower projects. Exerting pressure on the Department of Labor in support of these ad hoc groups were local government interest groups including the U.S. Conference of Mayors, the National League of Cities, the National Association of Counties, and the National Governors' Conference. In favor of a stronger role for the Department of Labor were liberals in Congress, the AFL-CIO, governmental employee unions, the Urban League, the Opportunities Industrialization Centers, and other community-based organizations.[32] Any attempts to please all these groups could only lead to inconsistency.

RESOURCES

No matter how clear the implementation orders are, if the personnel responsible for carrying out policies lack the resources to do an effective job, policymakers will be disappointed in the results. A state official with responsibility for air pollution control once remarked: "The implementation plan was a good idea. Setting these ambient air quality standards was a good idea and setting up program objectives to meet them was a good idea. . . . But what happens as we go along depends on what sort of resources we get as we move into the implementation phase of the plan."[33]

Staff

Probably the most critical resource in implementing policy is staff. A frequent problem is the lack of staff adequate to the task in both numbers and training. Limited manpower prevented the Environmental Protection Agency from classifying 50,000 pesticides on the schedule set by Congress, and the Agency was able to assign only 17 employees to monitor the testing and certification of hundreds of different models produced by automobile companies (domestic and foreign).[34] Findings of insufficient staff come from studies of agencies as diverse as the Federal Energy Office (at one time assigning only one auditor to monitor Exxon's compliance with price regulations),[35] the U.S. Office of Education (with the responsibility for enforcing federal guidelines in over 25,000 school districts),[36] the Agriculture Marketing Service (which had to increase its staff of federal grain inspectors in the face of massive grain scandals at U.S. ports in the mid-1970s); the Food and Drug Administration (which has only 1,000 inspectors to monitor 50,000 U.S. food processing plants and 2,500 drug companies);[37] and the U.S. Immigration and Naturalization Service (which can only allocate a few hundred officials at any one time to prevent illegal immigration along 6,000 miles of U.S. open-land border). And when flesh-eating piranhas were distributed to some home fish tanks, citizens learned that the Florida Game and Fresh Water Commission has only 5 people inspecting 30 million tropical fish each year.[38] Moreover, staff to aid courts in the implementation of their decisions is virtually nonexistent.

It is not only the size of staffs, but also their training which is crucial in carrying out policy. The lack of skilled personnel has greatly hindered implementation in the past. For example, most of the field staffers hired to implement the Comprehensive Education and Training Act had no manpower training experience; few were manpower experts; and most had not worked with local governmental officials or structures before. Thus, they could provide little useful technical assistance to those running local training programs.[39]

Staffing problems are especially acute in new programs and in programs designed to regulate widely dispersed or highly technical activities. There is rarely a staff ready to begin the implementation of a policy. It must be assembled. Frequently, the funds provided for staff fall far short of providing the number and type of personnel adequate for the task. Moreover, even with unlimited funds it is not always possible to find properly skilled personnel. When the national government became active in regulating energy prices and allocations in the early 1970s, there were few people outside the energy industry who had the background to understand the industry. Thus, employees of the Federal Energy Office relied upon "on-the-job training."

Information

Not only must a sufficiently large staff have adequate training, the staff must also have access to information about the issue at hand. Information is particularly critical for policies dealing with technical questions such as air pollution abatement. However, in controlling air pollution or in developing new weapons systems, implementors are asked to meet goals that neither they nor anyone else know how to accomplish. It is one thing to mandate the cleansing of the nation's air and yet another to figure out how to do it. This problem is much less for the more routine functions of dispersing funds, purchasing goods, building public works, and training troops.

Before an agency such as the Environmental Protection Agency (EPA) can order a costly change in an industry or its products, it ought to be able to predict the effects of the change. Otherwise there could be great expenditures (and perhaps economic collapse of the industry or some of its components) with no gain. Despite the need for information, relevant data is frequently lacking. A study of the development of air pollution policy in the Pittsburgh area (including federal, state, and county efforts) concluded that there is little systematic inquiry into effects; what is known is not communicated; few resources are allocated to research; and debate by decisionmakers is generally uninformed.[40] The difficulties of predicting consequences are no less evident in implementation than in decisionmaking (see Chapter 6).

To implement a policy, staff also need information on the compliance of relevant organizations or individuals with government standards. But accurate data on compliance is no more available than information relevant to developing new guidelines. In mid-1975 EPA Administrator Russell Train presented a progress report on the control of air pollution. He could only estimate compliance with his agency's standards because there was a lag of over a year in gathering the required data.[41] Moreover, much of the information needed to monitor compliance with policies comes from those who are supposed to comply.

Authority

Another resource important to implementors is authority, including the power to go to court to seek enforcement of an anti-discrimination law; to issue subpoenas for tax records; to issue orders to other officials; to withdraw funds from projects that are not being conducted according to the law; and to provide administrative funds, staff loans, and techni-

cal advice and assistance to lower-level governments to help
them implement a policy decided by a superior jurisdiction.
Each of these powers increases the arsenal of resources
that implementors have at their disposal to ensure that policies are carried out as intended. Each increases the chances
that those whose behavior is to change (whether private individuals or governmental agencies) will comply with the
law.

The authority to withdraw funds from a program has its
drawbacks. Such an action may embarrass all involved and
alienate members of Congress as well as the ultimate implementors of the policy whose active support is necessary
for effective implementation. Moreover, ending a project
can hurt most those the program was designed to aid—
whether they be schoolchildren, the elderly, or the poor.
Thus, it is more common for a superior governmental jurisdiction to request the return of funds found in an official
audit to have been misallocated than to withdraw funds from
an established project.

But any form of withholding appropriations is unusual.
In our decentralized political system local interests are able
to apply effective pressure on national or state administrators. In 1965 the U.S. Office of Education ordered that
funds under the Elementary and Secondary Education Act
be withheld from Chicago because it had failed to integrate
its schools sufficiently. Almost immediately Mayor Daley con-
tacted President Johnson and the decision to withhold funds
was reversed. The Office of Education lacked the political
resources to actually exercise its authority. This is clear not
only from the case cited above but also from the timidity
with which the Office of Education has implemented the act
since then. When implementors do not receive the support
of their superiors, they are open to pressure from local
interests and officials.[42] In 1973 the District of Columbia
Court of Appeals, in an unusual case, ordered HEW to enforce the 1964 Civil Rights Act, but even this had little effect
because of President Nixon's opposition.

The general lack of effective authority over other levels of government leads federal officials to perceive (accurately) that they must garner local support if they are to successfully administer their programs. Therefore, they often take a "service" rather than a "regulatory" approach toward local officials. A study of public housing programs in Chicago found that the Department of Housing and Urban Development (HUD) was not enforcing the antidiscrimination provisions contained in the law and in court orders. Rather it set as its basic standard of compliance a resolution of compliance by the Chicago Housing Authority (CHA). Even more curious were HUD's activities regarding specific violations. It forced the CHA to adopt a rule to assign public housing on a first-come-first-served basis, but it allowed the CHA to continue to operate contrary to that rule. Similarly, HUD made the CHA remove a rule giving neighborhood residents priority in assigning housing but also allowed the Authority to continue to operate as if the rule still existed. Thus, the federal agency exacted compliance with formal details of federal law but allowed the local agency to have its way in major policy matters.[43]

Although federal officials lack effective authority over state and local officials this lack of control is nothing compared to their lack of authority over private individuals, groups, and businesses—upon whom the successful implementation of policies often depends. The Federal Housing Administration (FHA) was established to guarantee home mortgages and thereby aid prospective homeowners in gaining mortgages with smaller down payments and longer repayment periods. Because the FHA required the aid of bankers (who make the loans) to accomplish its goal, it tailored its loan guarantees to meet their needs. Until 1967 it required that a person's income and prospective home be "economically sound." This helped the banks avoid risks, but it did little for those in greatest need of aid in purchasing homes: very few loans were made to the poor.[44]

The courts also depend on private individuals and groups to guide the actions of public officials in implementing judicial decisions. Through their possession of resources such as money, prestige, and the mass media, local elites can shape public opinion and affect the tone and atmosphere of a community. The behavior and attitudes of local leaders in regard to compliance with school desegregation decisions, for example, influenced the actions of school boards in their communities.[45] Courts also depend on private parties to submit new cases that enable the judiciary to follow up on their decisions.

DISPOSITION OF IMPLEMENTORS

Not only must implementors know what to do and have the capability to do it, they must also desire to carry out a policy if implementation is to proceed effectively. The disposition of implementors is significant because, as we have seen, those who implement policies are in many ways independent of their nominal superiors who made the policy decisions. This independence is magnified many times by the fact that many national and state policies are ultimately implemented by local officials in charge of grants-in-aid, revenue-sharing programs, or carrying out court orders.

Independence means discretion. The way in which implementors exercise their discretion depends upon how they see the policy in question and how they project its effect on the general interest, and their personal and organizational interests. Their judgments can foil the intentions of decisionmakers in at least three ways. First, through the selective perception of instructions, an implementor is able to ignore at least some of the directives he or she receives, particularly if they are not congruent with his or her own policy predispositions. Second, people have a difficult time executing orders with which they do not agree. Therefore, there is inevitably slippage between policy decisions and performance. Finally, because implementors are likely to feel that they know best about a policy area (as we saw in Chapter 5), there is a strong likelihood of purposive opposition to some policies.

Bureaucratic Politics

Sometimes opposition to a policy emerges in the form of interagency feuding over responsibility for an activity.[46] In 1975 a presidential task force on drug abuse complained that interagency rivalry and lack of cooperation between the Bureau of Customs and the Drug Enforcement Agency were hampering efforts at decreasing the flow of narcotics and dangerous drugs into the u.S.[47]

At other times there is *intra*-agency bargaining over funds provided from other governmental units. Jerome Murphy reports that state educational officials gave federal funds provided under Title V of the Elementary and Secondary Education Act to the programs with the strongest advocates (or "squeeky wheels") rather than to priority programs selected after a thorough review. Moreover, once programs received funds, concern for the health of the organizations implementing them caused officials to carry them beyond the point where their benefits outweighed their costs, and many of the programs became permanent.[48]

The case of the Economic Development Agency (EDA) in Oakland also illustrates how the different perspectives of bureaucratic units affect implementation. Even though there was just one federal agency overseeing the policy, and widespread agreement on the program's goals and the basic means of creating jobs through public works grants, the program was not successfully implemented. It was incompatible with some of the other commitments of both national and local agencies. For example, the Department of Health, Education, and Welfare saw EDA's attempts to train people for the airline industry as competing for scarce funds with its own skills centers. Other agencies whose goals were compatible nevertheless preferred to see EDA function in nonurban areas, or lacked a sense of urgency about the project, or had simultaneous commitments to other projects which took their time and attention. Thus, they were not eager to aid in implementing the program. Finally, there were differences of opinion on which people and organizational units should run the program.[49]

Incentives

In their study of compliance with the Supreme Court's
school prayer decisions Kenneth Dolbeare and Phillip
Hammond conclude that the officials responsible for implementing that policy at all levels of government relied on
personal cost-benefit equations to motivate their actions,
seeking to achieve those goals they valued most while sacri-
ficing others. Because furthering the Court's policies on
school prayers served no official's self-interest, none acted to
implement them.[50] The fact that officials act in their own
interests (see Chapter 5) means that incentives can influence
their actions. Increasing the benefits (or costs) of a particular
option may make implementors more (or less) likely to
choose that alternative as they alter their behavior to advance their personal, organizational, or substantive policy
interests.

Robert Levine argues that the U.S.-State Employment
Services constantly pressures the U.S. Department of Labor
to move away from serving the poor or problem citizens in
search of jobs and return to the old mode of satisfying its
employer clientele by providing "attractive" people to fill
openings. But the Office of Economic Opportunity (OEO)
and its local Community Action agencies applied coun-
tervailing pressure to keep the emphasis on creating opportunities for the poor, putting employment offices in the ghettos, and developing new kinds of programs.[51] The OEO and
its local agencies were able to use their political power to
increase the costs to the Employment Services of not helping
the poor by threatening the services' organizational well-
being.

Rewards are more difficult to use than penalties. Part of
the reason for this is that there are very few rewards available.[52] Courts can use several negative sanctions (e.g., cita-
tion for contempt; fines; suppression of illegally obtained
evidence; and the nullification of regulations, statutes, and
even elections), but they have no rewards to offer. (They
may, however, decrease the costs of complying with their
decisions by serving as scapegoats for those who oppose

them. Those complying can blame their actions on the courts).[53] Administrators are rarely able to reward organizational performance, and can generally only reward personal performance by promotions—which is necessarily infrequent. In many important bureaucracies seniority, not performance, is the basis of promotion, and raises are usually given "across the board," with everyone receiving a similar percentage increase in salary. Moreover, even when these rewards are available as incentives for individuals to implement policy, they are often in the hands of officials who themselves oppose a policy, or their effects may be mitigated by peer group pressures.

An additional problem in the use of rewards to encourage implementation is that it is difficult to develop criteria of success because of vague and diverse goals, poor measures of output, and obscure implementation directives for many policies. There is also the danger that bureaucrats will attempt to "beat the system" by emphasizing most whatever is being measured by their superiors. If job placement is the criterion of success in a manpower training program, program employees may try to place as many trainees as possible in jobs, regardless of their suitability or the wages, stability, and possibility for advancement of the job. If the evaluation of performance is based on the potential for increasing the future earnings of trainees, program personnel may concentrate on the young (with more earning years ahead of them) and the most skilled (who can be trained to achieve the highest levels of skill). Thus, the criteria for rewards must measure a combination of goals and be related to the difficulty of the task.[54] Unfortunately, this is not easy to do.

"Goal displacement" (i.e., emphasizing goals other than those originally intended) sometimes takes place inadvertently. In 1976 a Senate study concluded that federal drug officials spend too much time arresting street pushers and compiling numbers of arrests, and not enough time going after the major dealers in illicit narcotics. The explanation officials offered was that the agents of the federal Drug Enforcement Agency perceived their chances for career advancement in terms of arrests made. Therefore, they deemphasized more significant conspiracy cases which could immobilize major traffickers and syndicates.[55]

As we noted earlier, it is not only public officials who implement policies, but also private citizens and organizations. In the private sector positive economic incentives (i.e., profits) have a powerful influence on behavior. Governments make use of this type of incentive when they offer a tax break to businesses or individuals who invest in the production of certain goods or services. Most often, however, governments rely on negative sanctions (such as fines) or provide resources to individuals and organizations regardless of the finished product. Some authors have suggested that governments should use positive incentives to foster private activity consistent with public goals. Thus, they would pay business, not to train people for jobs, but for the finished product of that training; put a tax on pollution and/or provide tax reductions for limiting it rather than setting standards and enforcing them with negative sanctions; and pay part of the cost to business of minority workers actually hired rather than providing cheap capital to business in areas of high unemployment in the hopes of creating jobs.[56]

Bypassing Channels

Sometimes a decisionmaker can choose between officials to ensure the proper implementation of his decision. For example, the President can ask either the State Department or a special envoy to carry out his diplomatic policy. Or a new agency can be established to carry out a policy as high-level officials intended. The Office of Economic Opportunity (OEO) was formed and placed in the Office of the President for just that reason. President Johnson was intensely interested in the War on Poverty and did not want it subverted by an old-line agency with personnel less committed to change. For the same reasons, President Kennedy had the Peace Corps and Disarmament Agency placed in the White House.[57] Other approaches include bypassing governmental units altogether, as was often done in setting up OEO's

Community Action Programs and local job training centers under the Comprehensive Employment and Training Act, and creating new state and local agencies, such as those for urban renewal and public housing, and then attempting to shape their values and conceptions consistent with the intentions of federal policymakers.[58]

Despite these possibilities, decisionmakers usually have no choice in assigning implementation to a given agency; existing departmental jurisdictions usually determine which agency will handle a given program. And appellate courts have virtually no discretion as they instruct the lower court from which a case is appealed and through it the parties or class of parties directly involved in the case.

SOPs

As we saw in Chapter 5, SOPs (standard operating procedures) are routines for dealing with standard situations. They allow large numbers of bureaucrats to deal daily with many "cases" without having to stop and analyze the best way to implement policy in each case. But, as Graham Allison points out, "specific instances, particularly critical instances that typically do not have 'standard' characteristics, are often handled sluggishly or inappropriately."[59]

The frustration bureaucratic mass production can cause executive officials is evidenced in the following quote from President Franklin D. Roosevelt, viewed by many as a master manipulator of the bureaucracy.

> The Treasury is so large and far-flung and ingrained in its practices that I find it is almost impossible to get the action and results I want. . . . But the Treasury is not to be compared with the State Department. You should go through the experience of trying to get any changes in the thinking, policy, and action of the career diplomats and then you'd know what a real problem was. But the Treasury and the State Department put together are nothing as compared with the Na-a-vy. . . . To change anything in the Na-a-vy is like punching a feather bed. You punch it with your right and you

punch it with your left until you are finally exhausted, and
then you find the damn bed just as it was before you started
punching.[60]

President Kennedy, it seems, had a similar experience. "The
State Department," he asserted, "is a bowl of jelly."[61]

SOPs are most likely to hinder the implementation of new
policies. Bureaucratic units find it difficult to alter their orientation toward policy, even if new programs demand it.
Defense analyst Morton Halperin argues that American
troops in Vietnam in the early years of the war fought as if
they were on the plains of Central Europe. He adds that the
State Department, the Agency for International Development, and the United States Information Agency were also
fighting a previous war.[62]

Domestically, a study of the implementation of Title V of
the 1965 Elementary and Secondary School Act uncovered
disappointing results. Each state education agency has its
own SOPs geared to the economy and politics of the state;
the training, experience, and expectations of the agency's
staff; and the structure of the organization, including its system of rewards and punishments, and its political constituencies (the legislature, local school personnel, or the
state teachers associations). Thus, the author cautions, we
should expect the implementation of Title V to adapt to the
existing organizational operations rather than the reverse.[63]

The conclusions of the study support this expectation.
The state education agencies generally have not used the
new federal money to consider alternatives to their SOPs, to
hire new kinds of personnel with new roles (they just hired
"more of same"), or to develop basic new programs (they did
start programs that were "on the shelf" but that could not
receive funding from traditional sources). Any major
changes that have occurred are the result of outside pressure
on an agency.[64]

Sometimes the SOPs of an agency make it less than eager
to accept new programs. The Justice Department was reluctant to assume responsibility for law enforcement assistance
programs because it did not know how to fit grant programs

into its administrative structure, and the Department of Health, Education, and Welfare resisted assuming responsibility for nongrant programs because its administrative structure was built around grant programs.

The reluctance to accept new responsibilities not only stalls the implementation of new programs but can also prevent implementation altogether of part or all of a policy. In the late 1950s the U.S. Public Health Service refused to accept the authority to regulate air quality. It saw itself as an apolitical, highly professional, research-oriented organization that developed health standards to be enforced by state and local officials. It prided itself on its good relations with those officials and felt its own enforcement powers would take away some of their initiative and authority and thus disrupt the traditional close cooperation between federal, and state or local officials.[65] Similarly, the U.S. Office of Education was not as active as it could have been in enforcing the regulations and guidelines governing federal aid to state and local education agencies because many of its employees were accustomed to its traditional passive role in states programs; felt it was inappropriate to tell the states what to do; and viewed themselves as "professionals," not policemen.[66]

The greater the organizational change required for implementing a policy, the less effective that implementation is likely to be.[67] This is another reason why policymakers may try to give responsibility for important new policies to new agencies.

It is possible, however, that the SOPs of an *individual* can aid innovation. John Gardner (later president of Common Cause) came to the post of Secretary of Health, Education, and Welfare in the Johnson administration from the position of president of the Carnegie Foundation. His approach to educational policies as head of HEW was similar to that followed by large philanthropic foundations which give grants for initiating specific innovative programs and not for general purposes or for sustaining ongoing programs.[68]

The influence of SOPs is especially clear during a crisis when nuances become important. The Cuban missile crisis has been closely studied and provides some fascinating illustrations of SOPs in action.

Immediately after President Kennedy and his advisers decided that a blockade of Cuba was the proper response to the Soviet missiles in Cuba, the Navy designed a plan to implement the blockade. But shortly thereafter the President ordered the blockade moved closer to the island. This order however, was not carried out and U.S. naval ships continued to meet Soviet vessels at the original blockade line.[69]

Other aspects of the blockade also deserve attention. President Kennedy was very concerned that the initial U.S. interception of Soviet ships not endanger the U.S.–Soviet balance of power. He sent Secretary of Defense Robert McNamara to see Chief of Naval Operations George Anderson to check on the Navy's rules and procedures for making the first interception. McNamara stressed that the President did not want to follow normal SOPs whereby a ship risked being sunk if it refused to submit to boarding and search. Kennedy did not want to goad Khruschchev into retaliation.[70]

Nevertheless, Admiral Anderson was not very cooperative and at one point in the questioning he picked up the *Manual of Naval Regulations,* waved it in McNamara's face, and shouted, "It's all in here." To which the Secretary replied, "I don't give a damn what John Paul Jones would have done. I want to know what you are going to do now." The conversation ended with the admiral asking the Secretary to return to his offices and let the Navy run the blockade (without outside interference with established procedures).[71]

The SOPs of bureaucratic units not only prevent them from adequately responding to a novel situation, but also cause bureaucratic units to do things superior officials do not want them to do. The Cuban missile crisis provides several dramatic examples of this shortcoming. First, despite President Kennedy's explicit desire that the initial encounter with Soviet ships not involve a Soviet submarine, the Navy, according to established plan, used its "Hunter-Killer" Anti-Submarine Warfare program to locate and stay on top of Soviet submarines that came within 600 miles of the U.S.

mainland. Moreover, the Navy forced several Soviet submarines to surface, following standard "Hunter-Killer" procedures.[72] No one ordered the Anti-Submarine Warfare plan into action, it just "happened" because it was a programmed part of the basic military solution. The fact that those ostensibly in charge of the Navy (the President, Secretary of Defense, etc.) did not order it or did not know of its operation underlines the importance of SOPs and the difficulty of controlling them.

Second, while the Navy was carrying out the submarine operation, the Strategic Air Command sent B-47 bombers loaded with nuclear weapons to forty civilian airports across the country, according to pre-established routine. However, this counteracted Secretary McNamara's "no cities doctrine," designed to encourage the Soviet Union not to attack U.S. population centers. Moreover, several of the airports were in the southeastern United States—within range of the operational ballistic missiles in Cuba.[73]

The other standard operations that took place during the crisis, even though they were contrary to the desires of the President and his advisers (when they learned of them), included lining up U.S. planes in Florida bases in highly concentrated formations, sending a U.S. intelligence ship to carry out its mission close to the Cuban coast, allowing a U-2 to stray over the Soviet Union, and the Air Force's near bombing of a Soviet SAM (surface-to-air missile) site in Cuba on the basis of a *tentative* decision the President and his advisers had made earlier to deal with the contingency of a U-2 being shot down over Cuba by a Soviet SAM.[74]

FOLLOW-UP

In 1970 CIA Director Richard Helms relayed a clear order from President Nixon to Thomas Karamessines, CIA deputy director for plans (the covert action division) that the CIA's stockpile of biological weapons was to be destroyed. Karamessines in turn ordered Sidney Gottlieb, former head of the agency's Technical Services Division, to see that the job was done. Gottlieb subsequently reported that the materials had been destroyed.[75]

Five years later CIA officials discovered two deadly poisons in a secret cache. When asked about this, Gottlieb refused to testify but Nathan Gordon, who was in charge of the CIA's technical services in 1970, stated that he and two colleagues secretly shipped the toxins to a CIA storage facility, separating them from other materials that were to be destroyed without telling Gottlieb.[76]

Gordon said he was aware of the Nixon directive but never received instructions from Gottlieb to destroy the poisons. He added that he did not follow the order because he felt it was not directed at the CIA; that the toxin was costly and difficult to obtain; and that the order did not cover the toxins in question.[77]

Helms, who had initiated the destruction process within the CIA in response to Nixon's order, testified in 1975 that he had undertaken no follow-up check on his own order. When asked who told him the toxins were destroyed, he replied, "I read it in the newspapers."[78]

This example emphasizes the necessity of following up after issuing a directive. Because each of the factors discussed in previous sections of this chapter may hamper implementation, officials must double-check to see that their decisions have been acted upon in the way they desire.

Of course, follow-up is more easily said than done. The following statement of an aide to President Franklin D. Roosevelt shows that busy officials have little time for follow-up.

> Half of a President's suggestions, which theoretically carry the weight of orders, can be safely forgotten by a Cabinet member. And if the President asks about a suggestion a second time, he can be told that it is being investigated. If he asks a third time a wise Cabinet officer will give him at least part of what he suggests. But only occasionally, except about the most important matters, do Presidents ever get around to asking three times.[79]

Some officials, especially presidents, have attempted to increase their ability to follow up on the implementation of their decisions by increasing the size of their personal staffs. Delegating authority to more than a few people, however, creates new problems. Decisionmakers then have to relay implementation orders and receive feedback through many layers of their own staff because they can personally deal effectively with only a limited number of people. An enlarged staff enhances the possibility that communication will be distorted and increases the burden of administration— which the staff is supposed to lighten. Moreover, only a few people can credibly speak for any official, including the President. If too many people have access to the White House switchboard, for instance, and therefore give orders in the President's name, they undermine the credibility of all those claiming to speak for the President.

The staffs of top officials also have to guard against making too many implemental decisions. If they begin acting on every problem, more and more problems will come to them. This will not only overwhelm the peak of the organization and make it top-heavy and slow, but it will also undermine respect for lower officials among their subordinates, members of Congress, and interested groups (all of whom may find the officials too weak to resist any outside pressures). Too much decisionmaking on implementation at the highest levels may also stifle bureaucratic creativity and encourage buck-passing. It can also provide disincentives for capable people to remain in posts where their authority is frequently undercut; lower morale and engender a resentment and hostility that may impede future cooperation; decrease the time bureaucratic officials have for internal management because they must fight to maintain access and support in the White House; and weaken the capability of agencies to streamline or revitalize their management.[80]

The follow-up activities of other officials given the responsibility for overseeing the implementation of policy decisions (including judges and many governors) are severely limited by restrictions on the size of their personal staffs. They have little discretion to obtain aid in their oversight responsibilities and consequently have a particularly difficult time engaging in follow-up activities. Moreover, as previously noted, judges must wait for others to bring cases to them before they can act.

Secrecy also inhibits follow-up. If policies are carried out secretly, there is less monitoring of executive actions by various officials because there are no required reports to Congress (which force officials to examine how their subordinates implement policies). If members of Congress do learn of a secret policy, they will not be able to use this information freely without risking criticism for violating national security. The restrictions of secrecy thus make it easier for Congress to forego its responsibility for oversight and follow-up.[81] Moreover, secret decisions hinder executive coordination as well. President Johnson's fear of leaks regarding decisions on the war in Vietnam led him to restrict his direct communications to a few top officials (the Tuesday lunch group) and to not have a prearranged agenda or minutes which would record decisions and allow for follow-up on them.[82]

Sometimes organizational members fail to report the implemental failures of others out of a sense of identification with their peers or to save a program from budget cuts or bureaucratic battles.[83] Often, however, the information indicating poor implementation is available to top decisionmakers but the top officials choose not to use it. There are several reasons for this. Information coming from the field is frequently circumstantial, inconsistent, ambiguous, unrepresentative, in sum, unreliable. Moreover, it arrives in fragments with no integrated patterns of timing, content, or form. And it does not all arrive at the same place. Thus, top officials are not in a position to see the whole as the sum of a program's numerous parts. Additionally, it is difficult to cull useful follow-up data from the tremendous volume of information received by most offices particularly when more pressing demands, such as those for substantive changes in policy, compete for a decisionmaker's time and attention. It takes dedicated, sensitive leaders to learn of the actions of implementors and correctly interpret the information they receive.[84]

Early in 1973 President Nixon introduced throughout the executive branch a system of follow-up called *management by objectives* (MbO). MbO was not designed to impose objectives on the bureaucracy, carry out performance audits, apply sanctions, offer rewards, make decisions, control actions, or provide causal models of achieving results. Rather, it is a means of circulating information about the goals of bureaucratic units, defining responsibility for meeting those goals, and assessing the progress of those responsible for meeting those objectives.[85]

Despite these modest aims, management by objectives has not done much to increase the adequacy of implementation in the federal government. Neither the White House nor the Office of Management and Budget (OMB) (which has overall responsibility for MbO) has been a client for MbO information. Moreover, departments have seriously adopted MbO when they found it in their interest to do so and not because the President desired it, and they have chosen "safe" objectives to state and monitor, not objectives they would have a difficult time achieving or which would cause disputes.[86]

SUMMARY

Policymaking does not end once a decision is made. The implementation of the decision can have just as great an impact on public policy as the decision itself. No policymaker can assume that decisions will be automatically carried out as envisioned. Top officials must take several steps to assure proper implementation. They must issue policy directives that are clear and consistent; hire adequate staff and provide them with the information and authority necessary to carry out their orders; offer incentives for staff to execute policy as decisionmakers intended; and effectively follow up on the implemental actions of subordinates. None of these steps is easy, but none can be ignored by policymakers who are sensitive to the problems of implementation.

NOTES

1. "Southie Rides Again," *Newsweek,* December 22, 1975, p. 30.

2. Jeffrey L. Pressman and Aaron B. Wildavsky, *Imple-*

mentation (Berkeley: University of California Press, 1973), p. 109.

3. Harry McPherson, *A Political Education* (Boston: Little, Brown, 1972), pp. 450–451. See also Doris Kearns, *Lyndon Johnson and the American Dream* (New York: Harper & Row, 1976), p. 242. For an older example see "Truman's Mideast Policy Undermined," *New Orleans Times-Picayune,* December 29, 1976, Section 1, p. 14.

4. Richard P. Nathan, Allen D. Maxwell, Susannah E. Calkins, and Associates, *Monitoring Revenue Sharing* (Washington, D.C.: Brookings Institution, 1975), pp. 20–23.

5. Quoted in Morton H. Halperin, *Bureaucratic Politics and Foreign Policy* (Washington, D.C.: Brookings Institution, 1974), p. 245.

6. Quoted in Dom Bonafede, "The Federal Bureaucracy: An Inviting Target," *National Journal,* September 13, 1975, p. 1308.

7. Quoted in Neil R. Pierce, "State-Local Report: Structural Reform of Bureaucracy Grows Rapidly," *National Journal,* April 5, 1975, p. 503.

8. Daniel P. Moynihan, *The Politics of a Guaranteed Annual Income* (New York: Vintage, 1973), p. 220.

9. Richard Johnson, *The Dynamics of Compliance* (Evanston, Ill.: Northwestern University Press, 1967), p. 95. See also Samuel Krislov, *The Supreme Court in the Political Process* (New York: Macmillan, 1965) p. 154.

10. See Richard Johnson, *The Dynamics of Compliance,* pp. 85, 87, 91; and Stephen L. Wasby, *The Impact of the United States Supreme Court: Some Perspectives,* (Homewood, Ill.: Dorsey Press, 1970), pp. 90–92.

11. Neal A. Milner, *The Court and Law Enforcement: The Political Impact of Miranda* (Beverly Hills, Calif.: Sage, 1971).

12. Chester A. Newland, "Press Coverage of the United States Supreme Court," *Western Political Quarterly* 17 (March

1964); David L. Grey, *The Supreme Court and the News Media* (Evanston, Ill.: Northwestern University Press, 1968).

13. Stephen L. Wasby, "Public Law, Politics, and the Local Courts," *Journal of Public Law* 14 (Spring 1965), p. 118.

14. Haynes Johnson, *The Bay of Pigs: The Leaders' Story of Brigade 2506* (New York: W. W. Norton, 1964), pp. 68, 69, 86, and 224.

15. Floyd E. Stoner, "Implementation of Federal Education Policy: Defining the Situation in Cities and Small Towns" (paper presented at Annual Meeting of the Midwest Political Science Association in Chicago, May 1–3, 1975), pp. 8–9.

16. Stephen K. Bailey and Edith K. Mosher, *ESEA: The Office of Education Administers a Law* (Syracuse, N.Y.: Syracuse University Press, 1968), p. 103.

17. Jerome T. Murphy, *State Education Agencies and Discretionary Funds* (Lexington, Mass.: D. C. Heath, 1971), pp. 8, 21–22, and 25.

18. For other examples of this ambiguity see Pressman and Wildavsky, *Implementation,* p. 74; Charles O. Jones, *Clean Air: The Policies and Politics of Pollution Control* (Pittsburgh: University of Pittsburgh Press, 1975), pp. 69 and 133–134; Theodore R. Marmor, *The Politics of Medicare* (Chicago: Aldine, 1970), pp. 85–86; Carl E. Van Horn, "Implementing CETA: The Federal Role" (paper presented at the Annual Meeting of the Midwest Political Science Association in Chicago, April 29–May 1, 1976), p. 26.

19. Martha Derthick, *Uncontrollable Spending for Social Services Grants* (Washington, D.C.: Brookings Institution, 1975).

20. Derthick, *Uncontrollable Spending,* p. 107. See also Murphy, *State Education Agencies,* p. 22 and Van Horn, "Implementing CETA," p. 23.

21. Derthick, *Uncontrollable Spending,* p. 13.

22. For more on this point see Gary Orfield, *Congressional*

Power: Congress and Social Change (New York: Harcourt Brace Jovanovich, 1975), p. 168.

23. Pressman and Wildavsky, *Implementation,* pp. 75–78.

24. Joseph A. Califano, Jr., *A Presidential Nation* (New York: W. W. Norton, 1975), p. 23.

25. For example, see Van Horn, "Implementing CETA," p. 26.

26. See Walter F. Murphy, "Lower Court Checks on Supreme Court Power," *American Political Science Review* 53 (December 1959); Jack W. Peltason, *Fifty-Eight Lonely Men: Southern Federal Judges and Desegregation* (New York: Harcourt Brace Jovanovich, 1961); "Evasion of Supreme Court Mandates in Cases Remanded to State Courts Since 1941," *Harvard Law Review* 67 (1954); and Kenneth H. Vines, "Federal District Judges and Race Relations Cases in the South," *Journal of Politics* 26 (May 1964).

27. Derthick, *Uncontrollable Spending,* pp. 9 and 13.

28. Daniel P. Moynihan, *Maximum Feasible Misunderstanding* (New York: Free Press, 1969), p. 87; John C. Donovan, *The Politics of Poverty,* 2nd ed. (Indianapolis: Bobbs-Merrill, 1973), p. 40; and James L. Sundquist, ed., *On Fighting Poverty* (New York: Basic Books, 1969), p. 29.

29. Pressman and Wildavsky, *Implementation,* Chapter 4.

30. Halperin, *Bureaucratic Politics,* pp. 241–242.

31. Van Horn, "Implementing CETA," pp. 22–26.

32. *Ibid.,* p. 22.

33. Jones, *Clean Air,* p. 238.

34. "Pesticide Program Criticized," *Congressional Quarterly Weekly Report,* January 8, 1977, p. 45; Jones, *Clean Air,* p. 268; also see p. 136. See also "Environment: The EPA's New Man," *Newsweek,* February 21, 1977, p. 80.

35. Richard Corrigan, "Energy Report: FEA, Oil Firm

Seeks End to Secret, High-Stakes Case," *National Journal*, December 13, 1975, p. 1707.

36. Bailey and Mosher, *ESEA*, pp. 154–155; Jerome T. Murphy, "The Education Bureaucracies Implement Novel Policy: The Politics of Title I of ESEA, 1965–72," in *Policy and Politics in America: Six Case Studies*, ed. by Allan P. Sindler (Boston: Little, Brown, 1973), p. 173.

37. "Bitter Pills for the FDA," *Newsweek*, July 18, 1977, p. 93.

38. "Pet Store Owners Try to Recall Piranha," *Wisconsin State Journal*, July 17, 1976, Section 1, p. 3. For other examples see Derthick, *Uncontrollable Spending*, pp. 40–41; "Cities Seek Federal Aid to Ease Money Woes," *Congressional Quarterly Weekly Report*, September 27, 1975, p. 2055; Patrick J. McGarvey, *C.I.A.: The Myth and the Madness* (Baltimore: Penguin, 1973), p. 16; and "The Boycott: Premature Panic," *Newsweek*, October 25, 1976, p. 90.

39. Van Horn, "Implementing CETA," pp. 24 and 27.

40. Jones, *Clean Air*, pp. 304 and 306.

41. "Pollution Progress Report," *Congressional Quarterly Weekly Report*, June 7, 1975, p. 1175. On this point also see Derthick, *Uncontrollable Spending*, p. 93.

42. Murphy, *State Education Agencies*, p. 24; Murphy, "The Education Bureaucracies." See also Van Horn, "Implementing CETA," p. 26.

43. Frederick A. Lazin, "The Failure of Federal Enforcement of Civil Rights Regulations in Public Housing, 1963–1971: The Co-optation of a Federal Agency by Its Local Constituency," *Policy Sciences* 4 (September 1973). See also Van Horn, "Implementing CETA," pp. 27–28; and Martha Derthick, *The Influence of Federal Grants: Public Assistance in Massachusetts* (Cambridge, Mass.: Harvard University Press, 1970), pp. 200 and 210.

44. Harold Wolman, *Politics of Federal Housing* (New York: Dodd, Mead, 1971), pp. 26–28.

45. See, for example, Robert L. Crain, *The Politics of School Desegregation* (Chicago: Aldine, 1968); Melvin M. Tumin, *Desegregation: Resistance and Readiness* (Princeton, N.J.: Princeton University Press, 1958); and William K. Muir, Jr., *Prayer in the Public Schools: Law and Attitude Change* (Chicago: University of Chicago Press, 1967).

46. On this point see Theodore C. Sorensen, *Watchmen in the Night* (Cambridge, Mass.: MIT Press, 1975), p. 36.

47. Domestic Council, Drug Abuse Task Force, *White Paper on Drug Abuse,* September 1975.

48. Murphy, *State Education Agencies,* pp. 16, 120–122, and 24.

49. Pressman and Wildavsky, *Implementation,* pp. 99–100.

50. Kenneth M. Dolbeare and Phillip E. Hammond, *The School Prayer Decisions* (Chicago: University of Chicago Press, 1971), pp. 137–138.

51. Robert A. Levine, *The Poor Ye Need Not Always Have With You: Lessons from the War on Poverty* (Cambridge, Mass.: MIT Press, 1970), pp. 232–233, and 235.

52. See Martha Derthick, *New Towns In-Town* (Washington, D.C.: The Urban Institute, 1972) for an example of the inadequacy of the federal government's incentives and its inability to use them to move local authorities.

53. Muir, *Prayer in the Public Schools,* pp. 117–119; Peltason, *Fifty-Eight Lonely Men,* pp. 245–246.

54. Alice M. Rivlin, *Systematic Thinking for Social Action* (Washington, D.C.: Brookings Institution, 1971), p. 128. See also Doris Kearns, *Lyndon Johnson,* pp. 289–290.

55. "U.S. Drug Agency Strategy Faulted," *Wisconsin State Journal,* July 18, 1976, Section 1, p. 7. See also Van Horn, "Implementing CETA," pp. 27–29; Kearns, *Lyndon Johnson,* p. 272; Robert L. Gallucci, *Neither Peace nor Honor* (Baltimore: Johns Hopkins University Press, 1975), pp. 86 and 177; and McGarvey, *C.I.A.,* p. 60.

56. Pressman and Wildavsky, *Implementation,* Chapter 7; Robert A. Levine, *Public Planning: Failure and Redirection* (New York: Basic Books, 1972), pp. 173–174; Allen V. Kneese and Charles L. Schultze, *Pollution, Prices, and Public Policy* (Washington, D.C.: Brookings Institution, 1975).

57. For other examples of the placement of programs with implementation in mind see James E. Anderson, *Public Policy-Making* (New York: Praeger, 1975), pp. 105–106.

58. Derthick, *The Influence of Federal Grants,* pp. 203–204.

59. Graham T. Allison, *Essence of Decision* (Boston: Little, Brown, 1971), p. 89.

60. M. S. Eccles, *Beckoning Frontiers* (New York: Alfred A. Knopf, 1951), p. 336. Quoted in Allison, *Essence of Decision,* p. 86.

61. Arthur M. Schlesinger, Jr., *A Thousand Days* (Boston: Houghton Mifflin, 1965), p. 406.

62. Halperin, *Bureaucratic Politics,* p. 243.

63. Murphy, *State Education Agencies,* pp. 14, 15, 119, 124, 125, and Chapters 3–5. For more on SOPs and attempts at innovation see Herbert H. Hyman, ed., *The Politics of Health Care: Nine Case Studies of Innovative Planning in New York City* (New York: Praeger, 1973), especially p. 195.

64. Murphy, *State Education Agencies,* pp. 7–8 and Chapter 6.

65. Randall B. Ripley, "Congress and Clean Air: The Issue of Enforcement, 1963," in *Congress and Urban Problems,* ed. by Frederic B. Cleaveland (Washington, D.C.: Brookings Institution, 1969), p. 233.

66. Murphy, "The Education Bureaucracies," pp. 173–176; Murphy, *State Education Agencies,* p. 21.

67. On this point see Herbert Kaufman, *The Limits of Organizational Change* (University, Ala.: University of Alabama Press, 1971).

68. Norman C. Thomas, *Education in National Politics* (New York: David McKay, 1975), p. 40.

69. Allison, *Essence of Decision,* p. 130.

70. *Ibid.,* p. 131.

71. *Ibid.,* pp. 131–132.

72. *Ibid.,* p. 138.

73. *Ibid.,* p. 139.

74. *Ibid.,* p. 139–140.

75. "Intelligence Failures, CIA Misdeeds Studied," *Congressional Quarterly Weekly Reports,* September 20, 1975, p. 2025.

76. *Ibid.*

77. *Ibid.*

78. *Ibid.*

79. Jonathan Daniels, *Frontiers on the Potomac* (New York: Macmillan, 1946), pp. 31–32.

80. On these points see Thomas E. Cronin, *The State of the Presidency* (Boston: Little, Brown, 1975), p. 158; Harold Seidman, *Politics, Position and Power: The Dynamics of Federal Organization,* 2nd ed. (New York: Oxford University Press, 1975), pp. 90–91; Robert Wood, "When Government Works," *The Public Interest,* No. 18 (Winter 1970); and Richard P. Nathan, *The Plot that Failed: Nixon and the Administrative Presidency* (New York: John Wiley, 1975), pp. 51–54.

81. See Leon V. Sigal, "Official Secrecy and Informal Communication in Congressional-Bureaucratic Relations," *Political Science Quarterly* 90 (Spring 1975).

82. Chester Cooper, *The Lost Crusade: America in Vietnam* (New York: Dodd, Mead, 1970), p. 414.

83. See, for example, Kearns, *Lyndon Johnson,* p. 290.

84. For the best discussion of this problem, see Herbert

Kaufman, *Administrative Feedback: Monitoring Subordinates' Behavior* (Washington, D.C.: Brookings Institution, 1973).

85. Richard Rose, *Managing Presidential Objectives* (New York: Free Press, 1976).

86. *Ibid.*

Index